ADOLESCENCE

ADOLESCENCE

Talks and Papers
by
DONALD MELTZER
and
MARTHA HARRIS

edited by Meg Harris Williams

THE HARRIS MELTZER TRUST

First published in 2011 by Karnac Books for The Harris Meltzer Trust
Reprinted in 2018 by The Harris Meltzer Trust
60 New Caledonian Wharf
London SE16 7TW

Translation by Consuelo Hackney, Neil Maizels, Vicky Nicholls, Crispina Sanders and Adrian Williams

British Library Cataloguing in Publication Data
A C.I.P. for this book is available from the British Library

ISBN 978 1 912567 51 5

Edited, designed and produced by The Bourne Studios
www.bournestudios.co.uk

Printed in Great Britain
www.harris-meltzer-trust.org.uk

CONTENTS

ACKNOWLEDGEMENTS

A substantial part of this book consists of seminars given by Martha Harris and Donald Meltzer in Novara in 1973-1975 which were first published in Italian in *Quaderni di Psicoterapia Infantile*, volume 1, edited by Carlo Brutti and Francesco Scotti (Rome: Borla, 1975). Material from this volume appears here in Chapters 3, parts of 4, 5, 8, 9 (for the discussion), 10 and 15.

Chapters 11 and 12 document work by Donald Meltzer with the Psychoanalytic Group of Barcelona and were first published in Spanish in *Adolescentes: Donald Meltzer y Martha Harris*, edited by Lucy Jachevasky and Carlos Tabbia (Buenos Aires: Spatia, 1998). The cases were presented by Nouhad Dow and Jesús Sánchez de Vega.

We are grateful to the authors and editors for permission to translate material from both these volumes.

Acknowledgement is also due to the following journals in which certain chapters were first published: the *Journal of Child Psychotherapy* for Chapters 7 (vol. 4[2], 1976) and 9 (vol. 1[3],

1965), both reprinted in Martha Harris' *Collected Papers* (1987); and *Contemporary Psychoanalysis* (vol. 3, 1967) for Chapter 2, also reprinted in Meltzer, *Sexual States of Mind* (1973).

Chapters 1 and 6 comprise extracts from Martha Harris, *Your Teenager* (first published 1969; new edition Harris Meltzer Trust, 2007). Chapter 4 was first published in Martha Harris' *Collected Papers* (1987); Chapter 14 in Meltzer, *The Claustrum* (1992); and Chapter 16 in *Sincerity: Collected Papers of Donald Meltzer*, edited by Alberto Hahn (Karnac, 1994).

We would like to express special thanks to the translators of many of these chapters. Chapters 3, 4, 5, 10 and parts of 9 were translated by Consuelo Hackney; Chapters 11 and 12 by Crispina Sanders; Chapter 8 by Adrian Williams; and Chapter 15 by Neil Maizels and Vicky Nicholls.

Editorial note

Although much of the material in this book has been published before, it seemed useful to collect in one volume these various talks and writings on the key developmental phase of adolescence by Harris and Meltzer, who taught both separately and together over many years. Similar books have existed for some time in Italian and Spanish, but not until now in English, and I am grateful to Romana Negri and Miriam Botbol for encouraging the idea of this collection. Two case presentations by Martha Harris that were previously more formally published appear here in the form of a seminar discussion, which has its own educational interest; and her writings specifically on adolescence are reprinted here rather than in the new edition of her papers (*The Tavistock Model: Papers on Child Development and Psychoanalytic Training by Martha Harris and Esther Bick*, Harris Meltzer Trust 2011).

Meg Harris Williams

Martha Harris (1919-1987) was born in Scotland and read English at University College London, and then Psychology at Oxford. She worked for some years as a schoolteacher, and taught in a Froebel Teacher Training College. She trained as a psychologist at Guy's Hospital, then as a psychoanalyst at the British Institute of Psychoanalysis, where she was a training analyst; her own supervisors were Melanie Klein and Wilfred Bion, and her personal analyst Herbert Rosenfeld. For many years she was responsible for the Child Psychotherapy training in the Department of Children and Families at the Tavistock Clinic. Here she developed a course initiated by Esther Bick in which infant observation played an important role, pursuing the implications of Klein's method of working with children. This training (known as the "Tavi model"), which included the establishment of cross-clinic work-discussion groups, came to attract a very international range of candidates.

Together with her husband, Roland Harris (a teacher), she started a pioneering schools' counselling service based at the Tavistock. With Donald Meltzer, whom she married after Harris died, she taught widely throughout Europe, and also in North and

South America and India. Their travelling and teaching helped to establish the Klein-Bick observational method of psychoanalytic psychotherapy in all the principal Italian cities, and then in other countries (Bick herself taught in Italy, Argentina and Uruguay). Some of their joint supervisory work is documented in Romana Negri, *The Story of Infant Development* (Harris Meltzer Trust, 2007) and in *A Psychoanalytical Model of the Child-in-the-Family-in-the-Community* written in 1976 for multidisciplinary use in schools and therapeutic units and first published in *Sincerity: Collected Papers of Donald Meltzer,* edited by Alberto Hahn (Karnac, 1994).

Martha Harris wrote newspaper articles on child development and the family, and organized a series of books for parents, written by Tavistock therapists. Her most popular book, *Thinking about Infants and Young Children* (1975) has been published in many languages (new edition 2011). Her books on older children include *Your Eleven Year Old, Your Twelve to Fourteen Year Old* and *Your Teenager,* which have since been reprinted in one volume as *Your Teenager* (Harris Meltzer Trust, 2007). She wrote many papers on psychoanalytic training, on clinical work, and on child development, first collected in *Collected Papers of Martha Harris and Esther Bick,* edited by Meg Harris Williams (Clunie Press, 1987); new edition *The Tavistock Model* (Harris Meltzer Trust, 2011).

Donald Meltzer (1923-2004) was born in New York and studied medicine at Yale. After practising as a psychiatrist he moved to England to have analysis with Melanie Klein, and for many years was a training analyst with the British Society, though he later left the Society owing to disagreements about methods of teaching and of selecting candidates. He worked with both adults and children, and was innovative in the treatment of autistic children; his earlier work with children was supervised by Esther Bick, with whom he started a Kleinian study group after Klein's death. Meltzer taught child psychiatry and psychoanalytic history at the Tavistock. His books *The Kleinian Development* (1978) and *Studies in Extended Metapsychology* (1986) pioneered the understanding of the theoretical context and clinical relevance of the work of Wilfred Bion. These and most of his other books have been published in many languages and have become widely influential in teaching psycho-analysis. Others are are: *The Psychoanalytical Process* (Heinemann, 1967), *Sexual States of Mind* (1973), *Explorations in Autism* (1975), *Dream Life* (1983), *The Apprehension of Beauty* (1988; with Meg Harris Williams), and *The Claustrum* (1992). Most of his books were first published by The Roland Harris Educational Trust (Clunie Press), forerunner to The Harris Meltzer Trust which has since reprinted them all. In addition to *Adolescentes* (edited by Lucy Jachevasky and Carlos Tabbia, Spatia, 1998), members of the Psychoanalytic Group of Barcelona have recorded some of Meltzer's later supervisory work in *Psychoanalytic Work with Children and Adults: Meltzer in Barcelona* (Karnac, 2002) and *Supervisions with Donald Meltzer*, with Rosa Castellà, Carlos Tabbia and Lluís Farré (Karnac, 2003). An introductory selection from his writings may be found in *A Meltzer Reader* (Harris Meltzer Trust, 2010).

This rich collection of talks and papers by Martha Harris and Dr Meltzer contains a substantial number originally published in Italy and Spain, but not in English. The talks given by them as they worked as a couple in Novara (1973–75) cover almost seven chapters and, together with the two seminars delivered by Meltzer in Spain, are a powerful tribute to the way in which psychotherapists in these and of course other countries have cherished the memory and sustained the thinking of these truly international figures.

A fascinating aspect of the Novara seminars (particularly in chapters 3 (DM), 4 (MH) and 5 (DM), is that they include the text of the discussions after the presentations. Given that they took place nearly forty years ago the content is remarkably relevant to current understanding of adolescence. Meltzer's description of adolescence is that it provides a point of observation. The adolescent feels part of the community of adolescents which despises adults and children as well as the organization of the world they represent. Adults are envied because they are felt to have taken possession of power, and the world of children despised because of their absence of power. For Meltzer the primary issue in adolescence is not sexuality but confusion, and the feeling of being locked out of knowledge and understanding. The emphasis on sexuality though very present in adolescence is, nonetheless, derivative, 'trying to find an identification with the primitive parents who were joined together in the past in the sense of knowing everything and being able to do anything'. The adolescent therefore is in constant movement, backwards to the child, forwards to being the complete adult, back towards the world of adolescence, outside towards the isolated world of observer, backwards to the world of the family. It is a picture that is still very relevant in the quest to work psychoanalytically with adolescents.

This movement is followed brilliantly in the paper by Martha Harris. The account is of work with a depressed and anorexic adolescent girl. Depression currently features in a number of research projects, and the Paper gives a fascinating view of her ability to communicate with the patient in a thorough yet sympathetic way, using simple, accessible language. For instance, she describes a dream through which the patient came 'into much more contact with her rivalry towards her mother and towards me as analyst, in which she idealised herself as this wonderful sweet patient-child while trying to get between the parents , to make the father complain about the mother, and therefore complain about me'. One can almost sense the combination of tension and yet relief that must have been experienced in the therapy room at such moments!

The Novara seminars give a moving view of a husband and wife team clearly delighting in the closeness between them, both carrying the other's ideas forward, and yet both powerfully present in their own right. The picture is touched by sadness given Martha Harris' early death, but second part is a potent testimony to the genius of Don Meltzer, and includes the previously unpublished "After the hurricane". This book conveys the groundbreaking view of adolescence and the extraordinary insight of Martha Harris and Donald Meltzer.

Jonathan Bradley
Consultant child psychotherapist, Adolescent department, Tavistock Clinic

CHAPTER ONE

On learning to know oneself[1]
(1969)

Martha Harris

The struggle to find an identity is the central task of adolescence. It is a long and slow process during which are laid the final foundations for the personality of the future adult. These foundations, of course, were first begun long ago in the relationship between the baby and its mother and then in that of the infant to both its parents. They have been further developed by later interactions throughout childhood with parents, with brothers and sisters, with friends, school teachers and other important adults. They are affected at every stage not only by the nature of the new acquaintances but also by the child's approach to these and from the expectations arising from the results of his first encounters with the world. These are then transferred to subsequent relationships.

The very first step in knowing people is to be able to identify with them, to feel your way into their minds, into their personalities, to sense their physical reactions and to learn in these ways what it feels like to be them. Little children do this quite literally

---

1 Extracts from Martha Harris, *Your Teenager*, new edition London: Harris Meltzer Trust, 2007 (first published 1969).

when they step into Mummy's shoes and shuffle round the house pretending they are Mummy. The very first way of learning about yourself is also to project yourself, your unknown, unnamed needs and distresses, into your mother and (later) your father. From their greater experience of life and of themselves, and according to their openness to that experience, they may be able to respond to that need, to give you a name for it, a better acquaintance with it and therefore a better grasp of some aspect of yourself (p. 221).

[...]

To quote Mark Twain: "When I was fourteen my father was so stupid I could hardly stand to have him around. At twenty-one I was astonished at how much he had learned in the past seven years!" This expresses very nicely the change that many teenagers undergo in their attitudes to their parents, when they feel sure enough of themselves and their own grownup-ness, and of their capacity to use their own intelligence, to give their parents their due. When we feel that we have something to give, that we are capable of some achievement, we can afford to be more generous and to see in others the virtues that they have.

So if our teenagers are going through an estranged over-critical phase and we feel we cannot do much about it, that our well-meaning overtures are met with scowls and sighs of exasperation, it may be worth while saying to ourselves that this can be a passing phase, and perhaps like Mark Twain they may suddenly discover that we have been developing!… if, indeed, we have been (p. 182).

[...]

It is difficult for parents, and for the older generation in general, to take adolescent portentousness and arrogance about social ills quite seriously. It may remind us of our own adolescent aspirations, and of our failure to realize them, if we have simply abandoned them rather than modified them in the light of increasing experience.

It is not always so easy for parents to adapt to the stage which the teenager has reached, especially as for a while it tends to be a pretty erratic one: the responsible thoughtful young adult of one day can suddenly be the heedless infant of the next. Until he comes downstairs in the morning sometimes you have no idea from which side of the bed he has crawled out!

Just when we are getting used to the idea of being able to regard our teenager more as an equal than as a child, he may behave in such an irresponsible way that we feel let down, exasperated, and all the more so for knowing that he "could do better". It is maybe worth considering that sometimes he may feel let down by himself, and if so, it is not necessary to rub salt into the wound.

When he harbours suspicions that he is unreliable or at times pretentious, he can be very touchy at being treated lightly. Just because he feels passionately about tolerance, justice, freedom, loving his neighbour and so on, he hates to be reminded that these are virtues that so often elude him in practice in his own closer relationships.

Teenage students traditionally tend to be world reformers: acutely aware of the corruption and greed in governments, their ruthlessness for power and lack of concern for the underprivileged. For the would-be reformers it is not always so easy to see among the established elders those who are also aware of these things, or easy to be charitable about the imperfections and the inherent difficulties in mankind which make it such an uphill job to struggle against them. Until we feel more at home with our own inconsistencies, it may be easier to find an enemy in the outside world to express the contradictions of our own nature and to argue against them there.

"I always seem to be in opposition", said one sixteen-year-old boy rather ruefully. "At school I'm standing up for my parents and some of the teachers and their views, and at home I'm always arguing for my own generation."

A clear-cut division between the rights and wrongs in the causes one supports and in those one fights against is a way of gaining some relief from those differences within oneself. The cause which is most vehemently attacked is often one which threatens to remind us of those areas within the self which are most difficult to accept. There is no war more bitter than a civil war, because the enemy is so close and carries so many reminders of one's own nature (pp. 191-93).

[...]

This quest for sincerity and for uniqueness, for an identity that is one's own and no-one else's, leads the teenager to try to struggle free from identifications that he has made earlier in childhood in order to escape his own littleness and inadequacy. The earlier identifications may have been with older brothers and sisters, against whom in consequence rebellion may later be sharpest. They are the people he would have most wanted to be, and whose power he would most have wished to possess.

The more completely he has relied on living through his parents, through brothers and sisters and through authority figures in his childhood, the more difficult it is for him to extricate himself from their identities to find a style of his own. Some teenagers, of course, do not try. They remain conformist, old as it were before their time.

Others break out in a very explosive way, emphasising new conformities of dress and hair which demonstrate to themselves and us the fact that they are, after all, different. This "explosive" reaction was seen in the case of Matthew, who from a predominantly "good" kind of identification with his mother in childhood switched over to being quite possessed by a possessive greedy sexuality that took both him and his family unawares. "Many teenagers", said one of them, "become pregnant to punish their parents".

The teenagers who are able to keep their heads and— despite the turmoil— to really enjoy the unparalleled promise that their sexual and emotional flowering offers them are likely to be those who have identified in childhood with parents whom they have experienced as essentially loving and understanding, whom they have carried within them throughout the years as a protection and a stimulus to learn and develop.

The search for an identity is intimately bound up with the desire to be able to love and to work in one's own way. The teenager seeks to know and to choose the work that he wishes to do and that best expresses his talents, and the partner with whom he can best develop these— the person he finally wants to live with. This means making choices, making a commitment. If you are you, you cannot be anyone else— you are responsible for what you do. Without commitment, only a split and divided life and love is practicable—a double and cross-eyed identity.

It is anxiety about the failure to find commitment that may cause a career to be precipitately embraced, or a "falling in love" that is really a fleeing from uncertainty before true certainty has been earned. The teenager closes off other possibilities and experiences and takes refuge in what seems a planned certainty. This may indeed curtail the adolescent period, but at the expense of settling down prematurely into an apparent maturity. It is known, for example, that the chances of divorce increase with the decrease in the age of marriage.

Later on, maybe not till middle age, there may be depression or resentment about opportunities missed, talents not developed, relationships never explored. Then maybe the fear of being left out, left behind, of being inadequate, which was avoided in adolescence by an over-hasty flight to safety, can no longer be kept at bay.

Thus for some young people the uncertainties of adolescence, with its emotional work and self-questioning, provoke an intolerable anxiety. They go in consequence to extremes to avoid the struggle. They make premature choices, and so fail to pass through a fully worked-out phase to maturity.

What happens to them?

Some carry on in the same old tramlines, perhaps narrowly wedded to an ambition mapped out for them since childhood. They may become the kind of bookish, uncreative student who ages without ever really having been young, without experiencing the delights, the uncertainties and the follies of youth. Such a person hasn't been able to afford the luxury of doubt. Among them is the little girl who realizes her childhood dream by becoming a little-girl bride and mother, without ever maturing to be a woman.

Others seem to find it difficult to get beyond the early adolescent stage of taking refuge in some group of peers: groups of boys go about together meeting groups of girls. As they grow a little older, individuals tend to separate out, to pair with some particular person, and more intimate personal relationships develop. Then the teenagers who are not developing, or who are developing more slowly, can feel a little lost and lonely, for they are not learning how to be more independent.

Panic may drive them to take refuge in a boyfriend or a girl-friend, and maybe eventually to marry so as to conform and be like the others, but without relish for the relationship itself. Young people like this take on the colour of the people with whom they consort. Sometimes they remain amenable to firmness, to being guided in the direction of social usefulness, but almost as easily it would seem they can be led astray towards delinquency, idleness or antisocial behaviour (pp. 222-24).

[...]

Drug addiction is another kind of flight, an increasingly common and dangerous one, from self-discovery and self-responsibility.

We all use some form of drug to sweeten reality and to avoid pain. Forms range from smoking and alcohol to daydreams, flattery and reassurance. The harmfulness of the "drug" depends on the degree to which we rely on it, and on how much it is used as a substitute for self-awareness.

The additional danger with actual chemical drugs is their habit-forming nature—the organic effects that add a bodily craving to the mental craving. It is the social seduction of the drug that usually provides the initial attraction; it speaks to that part of the teenager which is hostile to the parents and to the older generation. One young student said, "I can think of several of my friends who took pot for the first time and then could hardly wait to get home to tell their parents." The object, she implied, was to flaunt independence and to worry them.

An essential feature in the seductiveness of the drug is the conventional assumption among teenagers that it leads to a fuller living, a heightened consciousness—and if you haven't experienced that, then you are simply not with it. This is one way whereby teenagers can establish their own particular in-group where the parents in their turn become the unknowing, helpless infants outside it all (pp. 226-27).

[...]

The teenager who is struggling with himself and winning through to some kind of maturity is learning to contain and to live with his inconsistencies instead of being dominated by them. His improving mental and emotional organization gives him gradually a little more tranquillity, and more impetus to appreciate the world outside. He becomes more able to see people and ideas as something in themselves, less strongly coloured by projections of his own personality. He may learn to argue less fiercely, but more rationally and dispassionately. He is better able to consider the merits of the case he is arguing, when he needs to argue less against himself.

Each teenager proceeds at his own pace and begins in his own time to win more freedom from himself to be objective in his learning and in his relationships. But time to grow is very often the very thing he fears that he does not possess.

It seems paradoxical that those whom the middle-aged envy for being at the beginning of life, the golden time of youth, should so often be obsessed with the passage of time, bedevilled by the thought of death and impatient to grasp at fulfilment lest tomorrow never come. There are a number of factors that account for and intensify this panic about wasting time.

Greater self-consciousness about the nature of his work and capacity leads the teenager to assess his achievements in a more realistic way. He has examinations to face towards the end of his years at school which are in many cases going to determine what kind of work he will be able to obtain, and are seen as the verdict on what he has done throughout his school career. In addition to omnipotent daydreams and also to neurotic undervaluations of one's own powers, there is probably in most of us some unconscious awareness of our own true potential. The teenager begins to have some sense of it, and thus can often be plagued by a guilty feeling of time wasted in his schooldays when he should have been learning how to grow up.

Emotionally, he often feels the acute and vulnerable sensitivity of the small child, and is only too apt to veer from a position of poised sophistication and arrogance to that of an infant on the threshold of adult life. If he has not had a solid enough experience of working at acquiring skills in his middle-school years he feels he has little to fall back upon, and is all the more vulnerable and panicky about being unable to grow up in time.

As all his emotions tend to be more accessible and acutely felt, he is also more aware of his destructive ones. He recognises, moreover, that he can actually do more damage than he was able to do as an infant, however strongly he felt then. The young child is very largely his parents' responsibility, but the teenager becomes more and more his own; and this, although desired, can be a heavy burden.

This fear can, of course, have foundations in reality. It is worth taking a longer look, however, at some of the factors that make some teenagers particularly sensitive to envy, and indeed make them anticipate it. They are always ready to feel that they are being grudged their place in the sun, even when they have little real reason to complain of their treatment.

These grudging teenagers tend to be the ones who in childhood did not manage to face up to and to live with their envy of their parents' greater power and possessions, of their sexual and grown-up social relationship with each other. If inwardly they have not managed to accord their parents some degree of freedom and integrity, they tend to be dogged by a grudging inward image of them, by an inner expectation of being deprived of fulfilment themselves.

We may remember from our adolescent days some nagging superstitious fear of an envious fate which can step in to spoil things when they are going too well— "those whom the gods love, die young". The fact that happiness is not everlasting, that it may be interrupted by misfortune, is an observation that experience forces us to make.

The teenager's sense of the precarious nature of joy, or his feeling that there are parents and a grown-up world which want to do him down, is not of course necessarily based on actual experience of harm done and of restrictions imposed upon him from outside. Rather it is often related to an apprehension of the restrictions endemic in his own nature, which he has not been able to understand and manage as part of himself. Projected outside himself into the external world, these return to plague him, either in specific people and instances or in vague apprehensions.

This fear of the imminence of danger to what he loves and values, or to what he wants to achieve, lends an urgency to "gather rosebuds while ye may", and adds to his sense of time passing rapidly. The realities of the nuclear age give a good reason in the world outside for the fear—which the teenager is already apt to have—that his personal world is liable to disintegrate.

Perhaps in a very simple and stereotyped society the social norms and practices would be so rigid and established that the many adolescent doubts, the troubled searchings for an identity that we have been discussing, would not arise. We can, however, never return to such a society, if indeed it ever existed. We can only try to help our teenagers by expecting honest self-criticism in them, by responding with honesty about ourselves and by offering the opportunity and the stability within the home for the teenager to work safely towards real independence.

This will be based on his finding himself, not on merely rejecting the faults in our adult world; and it is encouraged by our attempting as parents to understand his search, even when that takes a form which may be hurtful to us, and to which we are tempted to respond—like teenagers—with rashness, anger or contempt (pp. 230-32).

CHAPTER TWO

Identification and socialization in adolescence[1]
(1967)

Donald Meltzer

Surely, it will be said—and rightly—the analytic consult-
ing-room, in its heat of infantile intimacy, is not the place
to study the social behaviour of adolescents. But it can,
through clarification of the internal processes—of motivation
and expectation, identification and alienation—throw a special
and unparalleled light upon social processes to aid the sociolo-
gist, educator, psychiatrist, and all those persons of the adult
community whose task it is to preserve the boundaries of the
adolescent world and foster the growth and development of
those still held within its vortex.

Our times reveal more clearly than other historical periods the
truth of the existence of an "adolescent world" as a social structure,
the inhabitants of which are the happy-unhappy multitude caught
betwixt the "unsettling" of their latency period and the "settling"
into adult life, the perimeter of which may not unreasonably be
defined, from the descriptive point of view, as the establishment
of mating and child rearing. From the metapsychological point of

---

1 First published in *Contemporary Psychoanalysis* (1967), vol. 3, pp. 96-103;
reprinted in Meltzer, *Sexual States of Mind* (1973).

view of psychoanalysis, stripped as it is of social and moral evalua-
tion, this passage from latency to adulthood may be described
most forcefully in structural terms, whose social implications this
chapter is intended to suggest.

The developmental pathways which traverse this world of
adolescence lead from splitting in the self to integration, in
relation to objects which, also by integration, are transformed
from a multitude of part-objects to a family of whole objects in
the internal world. Upon this model the external relationships
must be regulated. As long as splitting of self and objects is still
considerable, the experience of self will be highly fluctuating,
depending on the dominance of one or other of the three types of
psychic experience of identity in consciousness (described below).
In a sense one may say that the centre of gravity of the experience of identity shifts—and in the adolescent it shifts wildly and
continually.

This phenomenon, the continual shifting of the centre of
gravity of the sense of identity, produces the characteristic quality
of emotional instability seen in adolescence and since it is based
on the underlying splitting processes, the varying states of mind
are in very little contact with one another. Hence the adolescent's
gross incapacity to fulfil commitments to others, to carry through
resolutions of his own or to comprehend why he cannot be
entrusted with responsibilities of an adult nature. He cannot fully
experience that the person who did not fulfil and the person who
undertook to fulfil the commitment were the same person, namely
himself. He therefore feels a continual grievance of the "brother's
keeper" type.

His solution to this terrible state is a flight into group life where
the various parts of himself can be externalized into the various
members of the "gang". His own role becomes simplified greatly,
though not completely, for status and function in the group is
in flux to a certain extent. This flight-to-the-group phenomenon is equally evident dynamically in the adolescent who is not
apparently a member of any gang, for, by being the "pariah", he
fulfils a role which the gang formation requires: that of the totally
alienated psychotic part of the personality in relation to those who

are integrated in the gang. The isolate in turn projects his own more healthy parts.

I would remind you that this is not a descriptive definition of an age group but a metapsychological description of personality organization typical of this age group; for we may meet "latency" in a fifty-year-old and "adolescence" at nine, structurally. The most important fact to be kept in mind in the following discussion is the transition from excessive and rigid splitting in latency, through the fluidity of adolescence in that matrix of personality where the more orderly and resilient splitting and differentiation of adult personality organization must eventually be fashioned in order for the sense of identity to be established without rigidity.

The experience of identity is complex in structure and various in quality. Its unconscious basis we express by the concept of "identification" on the one hand, and the experience of "self" on the other. It contains both characterological and body-image facets and must be taken, in toto, as a summation of momentary states of mind, an abstraction of highly variable integration – from individual to individual, from moment to moment. The experience of identity also cannot exist in isolation, but only as foreground to the world of objects, internal and external – and to the laws of psychic and external reality.

There are three types of experiences which carry the feeling of identity: the experience of a part of the self; of identification with an object by introjection; and of identification with an object by projection. Each of the three has a very distinctive quality. The experience of a part of the self carries a feeling of limitation akin to littleness, tinged with loneliness. Introjective identification contains an aspirational element, tinged with anxiety and self-doubt. But the state of mind achieved by projective identification is fairly delusional in its quality of completeness and uniqueness. The attendant anxieties, largely claustrophobic and persecutory, are held very separately in the mind from the identity experience.

I wish to come back now to the more central problem: the underlying severe confusion at all levels with which the adolescent is contending. As I have said, with the breakdown of the obsessional, rigid, and exaggerated splitting characteristic of latency structure, an uncertainty characteristic of the pre-oedipal development reappears with regard to the differentiations internal-external, adult-infantile, good-bad, and male-female. In addition, perverse tendencies due to confusion of erogenous zones, compounded with confusion between sexual love and sadism, take the field. This is all "in order", as it were: the group life presents a modulating environment vis-à-vis the adult world and distinct from the child-world, well-equipped to bring this seething flux gradually into a more crystallized state—if the more psychotic type of confusion of identity due to massive projective identification does not play too great a role. To illustrate this I will shortly describe two cases briefly.

But first to clarify the concept. Where the reappearance of masturbation brings with it a strong tendency, driven by infantile oral envy, to abandon the self and seize an object's identity by intrusion into it, the stage is set for a type of confusional anxiety which all adolescents experience to some extent. This confusion centres on their bodies and appears with the first pubic hair, the first breast growth, first ejaculation, and so forth. Whose body is it? In other words, they cannot distinguish with certainty their adolescent state from infantile delusions-of-adulthood induced by masturbation with attendant projective identification into internal objects. This is what lies behind the adolescent's slavish concern about clothes, make-up and hair-style, hardly less in the boys than in the girls.

Where this mechanism is very strongly operative and especially where it is socially "successful", the building up of the "false self" of which Winnicott has spoken takes place.

Case material

Rodney entered analysis at eighteen after the complete academic failure of his first year at university. He was, two years later, able to regain a place and continue his education; but in the analysis scholastic failure had promptly appeared as the least of his difficulties.

His latency period had been built on a severe split in his family adjustment, as he had been a devoted, endlessly helpful and unfailingly polite son among the otherwise rather stormy children. In fact in his own eyes, he was never a child but a father-surrogate in all matters other than sexuality. To compensate, he appropriated as his due an absolute privacy and self-containment which, with the onset of puberty, became converted into a cover of absolute secrecy for a florid delinquent bisexual life, while his family behaviour remained unchanged—now he was a "manly chap" instead of a "manly little chap".

In dividing himself among his gang he retained as his "self" the worst, most envious and cynical bit of himself. Consequently his relation to others tended to be both forceful and corrupting. The best parts of himself tended to remain projected into younger siblings, from whom he maintained a severe, protective distance.

More delusional states of identity occurred relatively infrequently and only under special circumstances—if he were driving his mother's car, or entertaining friends in an outbuilding he had been given as a study. These states could be dangerous indeed, physically and morally, but were soon recognized in the analysis and could be avoided. The establishment of contact with good parts in a therapeutic alliance with the analyst and with internal objects could take place. Progress was steady and rewarding.

Paul, on the other hand, had entered analysis in pre-puberty owing to severe character restriction, with obsessional symptoms, nocturnal rituals, obvious effeminacy—all of which had existed for years but had been worsened by the break-up of the parents' marriage. The first period of analysis with another analyst utilizing play technique had been virtually non-verbal. In those sessions he had been preoccupied with painting and art, producing a few pictures analyzable in content but mainly endless preparations-for-painting consisting of mixing colours, making colour charts— in fact, concretely being daddy's artist-penis preparing the semen for the coming intercourse. As his symptoms had lessened and his school adjustment and work had improved he broke off the analysis, returning to it only three years later, when after passing his O-levels and working his way to being vice-captain of his school, he found himself confronted with A-levels for which he was totally unprepared.

What had happened in the intervening time was that the building up of the school-self of athlete-artist-vice-captain had become totally time-consuming. It had to be compensated for by a gradual retrenchment from all academic subjects requiring thought or exact knowledge, in favour of those which he felt just required talent or were based on vague statistics. He had become unable to study and his time at home and in school was consumed in the business of preparation or the postures of absorption. His paranoia, particularly in relation to laughter, had to be hidden and his own mocking laugh—irreproachably tolerant in timbre—kept a steady stream of projection of feelings of humiliation penetrating into others.

Analytic work to gather together his infantile parts into the transference and to differentiate the delusions-of-adulthood from his true adult personality was the most tedious uphill work. Every separation brought a renewed flight by projective identification: represented in dreams by intruding into gardens, climbing into houses, leaving the main road for a trackless swamp, and so forth. For instance, in a Thursday evening session he had experienced a reawakening of gratitude toward his mother for providing the analysis, along with guilt about the motor scooter he had insisted on having and the hours of analysis he had missed or wasted. It had been his unusually strong reaction to the analysis of a dream which showed clearly that the preponderance of his infantile parts wanted analysis, not masturbation. In the dream the crowd at a school dance was sitting at tables demanding food rather than going into the ballroom to "twist". By Friday, however, he had whipped himself into a state of arrogant contempt for the analysis because the analyst did not realize that Paul had now finally emerged from the chrysalis of "student". His art teacher by contrast had said that his new picture was the first to show a style of his own rather than mimicry of others' styles. Relentlessly then, he would spend the weekend mixing paints.

Paul presented a façade of social integration—the school captain—while Rodney seemed delinquent, corrupted, and isolated from society. But in fact, closer scrutiny shows that Rodney had a gang in which his identity was disseminated and from which it could be retrieved; while Paul had only "friends" who were his enforced colleagues while he was vice-captain and later captain of the school. In fact he was isolated—"well-liked", to use the immortal phrase of Willy Lomas in Arthur Miller's *Death of a Salesman*.

These two cases are intended to show the important role of the group as a social pattern in adolescence, indicating that no matter how delinquent or anti-social it may appear vis-à-vis the adult world, it is a holding position in relation to the splitting processes. By means of the dissemination of parts of the self into members of the group, amelioration of the masturbatory urge is achieved and social processes are set in train which foster the gradual lessening of the splitting, diminution of the omnipotence, and easing of persecutory anxiety through achievement in the real world.

We must however turn back to our analytic experience at the other pole of the adolescent process to comprehend the basis of this dissemination. Experience in carrying latency children into puberty during analysis reveals this in a brilliant way which I will describe by means of a third case:

Juliet had come to analysis at the age of seven for deeply schizoid character difficulties which rendered her doll-like in appearance and demeanour, utterly submissive to excellent but highly idealized parents. This façade was fissured in two areas: explosion of faecal smearing on rare occasions, and a witch-like hegemony over a younger sister and her little friends.

Six years of the most arduous analytic work broke through this, enabling her true femininity, artistic talents, and rich imagination to emerge by the time of her menarche. But her masculinity formed the basis of her social adaptation to peers, as shown by the formation of a gang of five girls, all intelligent, attractive, and athletic, who became the "trouble-makers" of her girls' school. The general pattern of a very revealing dream of that time was subsequently repeated, again and again. She seemed in the dream, to be one of five convict men who were confined in a flimsy structure made of slats at the top of a tall tree. But every night they escaped and prowled about the village, returning unbeknown to their captors before dawn.

This dream could be related to earlier material regarding masturbatory habits in which her fingers, in bed at night, explored the surfaces and orifices of her body, often accompanied by conscious adventuresome phantasies.

Two years later, when her femininity had established itself in the social sphere as well, she attended her first unchaperoned party, where the boys were somewhat older; drinking occurred, and sexual behaviour became rather open. To her surprise she behaved with a coolness and provocativeness which earned her the shouted epithet of "frigid tart" from a boy whose attempt to feel under her skirt she had skilfully repulsed.

That night she dreamed that five convicts were confined to a wooden shed from which they were released by a bad squire on condition that they would steal fruit from the women with fruit stalls in the village and bring the loot to him.

Here one can see that the delinquent organization of the masculine masturbating fingers had been projected into the boys of the party by her "frigid tart" behaviour. The fact that the phantasies acted out were infantile and pregenital (anal and oral) was clearly indicated by the stealing of food, from the bottom, a theme well known from the earlier years of analytic work.

The masturbatory theme, the personification of the fingers, seems in fact to turn up with extraordinary frequency in our analytic work and would lead us to the expectation that the typical "gang" of the adolescent would tend, by unconscious preference, to contain five members, or multiples of this number. In other terminology we might say that the gestalt of the adolescent gang would tend most strongly to "close" at five members.

This brief account presents some of the knowledge gained by recent analytic experience with children carried into puberty and with adolescents carried into adult life. The work was conducted within the framework of theory and technique which is an extension of the developments in psychoanalysis associated with the name of Melanie Klein. It draws very heavily on her delineation of the pregenital Oedipus conflicts, the role of splitting processes in development, and the phenomenology of projective identification as a dynamic mechanism, and may not be readily comprehended without a general understanding of her work. A most lucid description of this will be found in Hanna Segal's book (Segal, 1964).

I have discussed how the return of severe splitting processes, characteristic of infancy and early childhood, which attends the adolescent flux, requires externalization in group life so that the omnipotence and confusional states precipitated by the return of masturbation at puberty may be worked through. The implications for sociological comprehension of the "adolescent world" as a social institution are apparent:

(1) Individual psychotherapeutic work should be directed toward the isolated individual, to promote the socialization of his conflicts.

(2) The "gang" formation of adolescents needs to be contained in its anti-social aspects but not to be intruded upon by adult guidance.

(3) The emergence of individuals from adolescence into adult life is facilitated by measures which lessen the conflict between the sexual aspirations toward mating and other areas of ambition.

CHAPTER THREE

Adolescent psychoanalytical theory[1]
(1973)

Donald Meltzer

Today I will talk about the concept of adolescence in rather an "ideal" way, as though it were something which always happens in a calm and natural way leading towards adult life, mental health, happiness and so forth—trying to understand how this might be possible and whether it ever is. Tomorrow [*Chapter 4*] Mrs Harris will present a case of a girl in analysis in order to highlight the difficulties of adolescent psychopathology. The day after tomorrow [*Chapter 5*] I will talk about the vast field of adolescent psychopathology and the technical problems relating to the treatment of adolescents according to the psychoanalytic method.

First of all I believe it is important to point out that the psychoanalytic method is not particularly efficient for the investigation of adolescence in as much as adolescents live mostly in the external world of adolescents and are not naturally or comfortably in touch with adults. Our understanding of adolescence does not come so

---

[1] A seminar conducted in Novara, 1973, published in *Quaderni di Psicoterapia Infantile* no. 1 (1975), ed. C. Brutti and F. Scotti, pp. 15-32; translated by Consuelo Hackney.

much from treatments of adolescents themselves as from successful and complete analytical treatments of children approaching the age of adolescence, from adult patients and from analyses of children which continue throughout their adolescence or beyond it. So today I will try to describe and discuss three different communities with you: the community of the child within the family unit, the community of the adult world and the community of adolescents which sets itself as a community outside either of these two. I will try to give you a picture of the internal world of the individual and of the way the adolescent moves backwards and forwards within these three communities, during the process of development and evolution of his internal structure.

I will start by describing the adult world into which the adolescent tries to enter, then the world of the child which he is trying to leave and finally the world of adolescence. I shall put myself in the position of the adolescent and try to describe how he perceives these three communities through the "fog" of adolescence, rather than how I perceive them or how psychoanalysis structures them.

Seen from the point of view of the adolescent, the adult world appears above all like a political structure and a class system: adults are experienced as though they had power and control of the world. To adolescents this does not seem as though it is due to knowledge or ability but to the fact of their having ownership of a sort of aristocratic organization which has as its main objective the preservation of power against all intrusions.

So adolescents have the impression that adults are all frauds and hypocrites, possessing something they never had the right to own. From this originates the notion that children are slaves or servants, or else the illusion that the parents are all-knowing and all-powerful. The adolescent feels part of the community of adolescents which places itself between these two classes: the "aristocratic" adults who hold power, the "slaves" who believe in them as though they were gods or live with the illusion that adults know everything. The adolescent thus places himself in a position where he despises both adults and children as well as the organization of the world they represent. I would like to draw attention to the problem of the knowledge of the world and the ability, through this knowledge, to manipulate and maintain order in the world; because the adolescent, while appearing to be mainly preoccupied with sexuality, is in reality mostly concerned with knowledge and understanding. This seems very important to me because generally the adolescent is considered as if he were principally interested in achieving sexual satisfaction, whereas in reality sexuality is considered by the adolescent as the very essence of the authoritarian situation. Having the right to indulge in sexual activity becomes for him the lynchpin of authoritarian control held by the world of adults on all material aspects of the world: money, houses, food and so on.

Now I would like to highlight the problem of knowledge, on the one hand, and that of confusion on the other, and to describe the adolescent putting the emphasis on the problem of confusion. In psychoanalysis we find ourselves facing various types of confusion. The main ones are: confusion between good and evil, confusion between the different parts of the body and the different ways in which these parts can exist in relation to the outside world and other people, the confusion between male and female; and between adult and child. Typical of adolescence for example is the confusion between tongue and penis for a boy, and mouth and vagina for a girl.

Let's now go back to the problem of knowing and understanding, relating this to the world of children: they imagine that knowledge is something concrete which really exists somewhere. The devotion and respect which children have for their parents are closely connected with the conviction that their parents together possess all the knowledge of the world and, in the most primitive phantasies, this knowledge is felt as though contained, quite concretely, in the mother's breasts. These phantasies may be observed in dreams, as in dreams of libraries: in London, for example, the British Museum Library which is particularly large and housed under a vast cupola, often appears in patients' dreams as a library-breast, a breast containing all the knowledge that exists in the world.

The mental quality that the father and mother possess, or that, at a more primitive level, the breast possesses, is omniscience. The "parents together" (primary scene or combined object, in psycho-analytical terminology) are experienced as having the power to do anything, that is to say as omnipotent and omniscient. These two qualities—the omniscience of the breast and the omnipotence of the combined object—are the object of the most intense envy on the part of the child and it is this that he wants to have most from his parents. This seems to arise very early on, when the child becomes able to use language, which represents the parental ownership of omniscience and omnipotence.

So the child does not only develop his capacity to use language but also invests it with concrete and magical powers. I want to speak of the small child's attitude to language and in particular to highlight the role of language in the child's deference to his parents.

When the child begins to go to school during the years that we call the latency period, the concept of learning is concentrated mostly on learning the names of things. When the child learns the name for something he believes he knows everything about that thing: if a small child learns that an object is called an aeroplane, not only does he believe that he can fly one but he believes he can make one and, when he begins to build a small toy aeroplane, this in his mind is a real aeroplane. The child in the latency period who is able to use language in this concrete way and believes he knows everything about something when he knows its name, is exercising his sense of omniscience, but this sense of omniscience is differ-ent from the parent's omniscience, in as much as it is based on a constriction of the imagination. He does not know everything, but believes that everything he knows is all there is to be known. The belief that the parents know everything, associated with the power of language, is shattered with the arrival of puberty.

This way of looking at puberty is one which places the empha-sis not on sensuality but on knowledge and understanding. The great mystery for children is that parents "know how things are done": knowing how to make babies is the essence of their great power. At the time of puberty, the child discovers that his parents do *not* know how to make babies. This could be considered the greatest disillusionment of adolescence, which allows the child to free himself from his awe of his parents as all-knowing divinities. And when the adolescent releases himself from this belief in his parents as people who know everything and who must know everything because they know the great secret of how to make babies, the whole world of confusion bursts through, which had been obscured by the belief in the parent's omniscience. And he also discovers that words do not mean what they say, that they do not contain meaning within themselves, that the same words have different meanings depending upon the mouth that uttered them. So he feels that he has discovered that the whole adult world is a mass of hypocrisy. This has the result of making him doubt everything and naturally the main thing he has to doubt is the fact of being his parent's child in any real sense. He has to choose between the theory that he is his own parent and made himself by himself, in some way, or that his parents are "somewhere else" in the mythical or abstract sense. The choice between being one's own parents (feeling and theorizing that he created himself on his own) and being the son of some abstract parental entity (such as, for example, God or a particular football team), is extremely crucial. This is the identity crisis: it is an area of confusion which subsumes all the other confusions—it is the essential problem of the adolescent world. It is very important to remember that everything that emerges in adolescence already existed before the latency period and that the family myth, when it is strongly rooted in a child, derives from a deficiency during latency and contains infantile phantasies which have not been sufficiently repressed.

In this identity crisis and in the acute loss of family identity that the child experiences at the time of puberty, what is important is the choice between the idea of having made oneself alone and the idea that one's own parents are in some other place, in as much as from this arises the possibility of identifying oneself with the community of adolescents or not. The decision to temporarily accept the identity of a simple adolescent in the community of adolescents, or of being an isolated individual who has created himself alone and has a single mission in the world—a grand mission—represents a crucial decision for the adolescent.

I have now in fact described not three but four different communities: the child within the family, the adult world, the adolescent world and the isolated adolescent. It is important to remember that the individual is constantly moving backwards and forwards between these four positions: backwards towards being a child, forwards to being completely adult, back to being in the world of adolescents, outside to being in an isolated position, backwards to being within the family.

It follows from this that attempting analysis with an adolescent is extremely difficult because he is not really anchored in any one place. Each participation of his within one of these four separate communities implies a state of his mind, or manifests with states of mind that are all very isolated from each other. He therefore finds himself in a position which is full of torment, in which he feels that no-one can help him. And it is precisely because he feels that no-one can help him, and that he must in some way help himself, that the adolescent tends to concentrate his attention on sexuality, trying to find an identification with the primitive parents who were joined together in the past in the sense of knowing everything and being able to do everything. While the adolescent feels he is trying to go forwards and become powerful—a person who knows everything and who can control the world in order to adapt it to himself—he also tries to find his way backwards, towards something that he abandoned for latency at the time of the crisis of the Oedipus complex, at the age of five or six years old. Trying to find his way forwards to becoming an adult in the sense of being powerful and independent, and at the same time in trying to find his way backwards—to an identification with the objects that knew everything and could do everything—he splits himself into two parts and experiences great confusion. He finds his way forward by acting in the outside world: through sexual relationships, passing exams, finding work, earning money, etc. The way in which he finds his way backwards is by dreaming, by being interested in art, literature, dealing with problems to do with the cultural development of the community, in politics considered in the abstract sense—in the ideal, which emerges in adolescence, of the type of world which he would like to help to create. So in the adolescent one finds this extraordinary splitting: on the one hand there is envy, egocentricity, ambition, the ruthlessness that leads him towards independence; on the other there is altruism, concern for others, emotiveness, sensitivity that take him back towards the arts, literature and intimate relationships.

Mrs Harris asks Dr Meltzer to clarify the meaning of the word "backwards", which could be confused with regression.

Dr Meltzer: I'm not changing the word "backwards" because I think that the adolescent feels pushed backwards towards his childhood, into a state of lack of help and tends to experience all the tender sensations, art, altruism, as aspects of himself that threaten to take him backwards to the point of becoming a child again.

One of the paradoxes of adolescence is precisely this: the adolescent thinks that what leads him forward into the adult world is in reality regressive, while what he experiences as the thing which pushes him back, to the point of making him into a child again, is in reality the very thing which makes him an adult. In other words, you could say that the adolescent finds himself in a state of enormous confusion and disappointment regarding the organization of the world which he had experienced in childhood.

As regards the outside world he finds himself having to move between these various positions: going backwards so he becomes a child, going forwards to be an adult, staying in the middle of the adolescent world, or finding himself very isolated—separate and grandiose. His feeling is that in order to grow he must progress ruthlessly and achieve success. What he believes might take him back towards childhood—feelings, emotions, the fascination of childhood itself, of attachment and awareness of the beauty of the world and of his own impotence and weakness—lead him instead towards the adult world; while the ruthlessness, in reality, prevents him from becoming an adult. The crucial point in his decision whether to go forwards or backwards is the problem of mental suffering: should he be ruthless, inflicting suffering on others in order to achieve success, or should he turn backwards and be the one to suffer?

This also creates a problem from the technical point of view. We are generally sent two types of adolescent for treatment: those who suffer and who seem to be afraid, and who probably do not really need our help because they are finding their own way backwards; and isolated adolescents—those who have isolated themselves and do not feel themselves to have any problem but who are cause for concern to others. Very rarely do young people come to us who are advancing relentlessly towards success and who have learned how to inflict suffering on others.

For this reason adolescent patients can be divided into two categories: the first is the category of those who, more or less, come to us alone because they find themselves in a state of great stress and it is wonderful to work with them. The youngsters who are sent to us by their parents or by their schools belong to the second category, as do the delinquents, that is to say those who are sent by the courts etc. It is much more difficult to work with these. The adolescents that we do not generally see are those who belong to that vast third category in the middle—the unproblematically successful who end up as adults living a life which is no more than a repetition of the latency period. These are the bourgeoisie and they become neurotic in their later adult life.

I will open a discussion here on the external adolescent situation before going on to describe the internal structure upon which this confusion and these "attempts" to cope rest.

Discussion

Dr Nissim asked for further description of the third category, that of the ruthlessly successful adolescents and their relationship with the bourgeoisie, and for more details of the other categories also.

Dr Meltzer: Generally we receive two types: the type who is sent to us because the parents or school are worried about them, and the type who comes more or less of his own accord because he is in a state of great stress either due to some physical breakdown or due to anxiety. The third type consists of those who owing to success have managed to avoid breakdowns, anxiety or suffering, instead making others jealous, envious, worthless. This category carries on advancing and seems to become fixed around the age of twenty in a type of "bourgeois latency" organization. Neurosis generally breaks through as they approach thirty or even later.

I would remind you that today is dedicated to general adolescent psychology, and that later I will deal in broad terms with the different types of psychopathology: the psychopathology of the isolated adolescent, the adolescent who is suffering, and the successful adolescent.

Dr Mancia asked for more information on the disappointment felt by the child in his parents when he discovers that they do not know how to make children.

Dr Meltzer: At the time of puberty it is as though the child discovered that his parents only have sexual relations, that not only do they not know how to make babies but that his mother is not even able to change a plug and his father doesn't know how to fix the plumbing; that they are both incompetent; that they can do hardly anything and in particular they are unable to construct a child piece by piece—their sexual relations are in fact not so different from those engaged in by cats and dogs. I will explain later, when I talk about the internal world, what making a baby *means*.

Dr Nissim asked whether adolescents might even come to deny any form of sexual activity by their parents, not only from the point of view of its creativity but denying that they really have sexual relations at all, and she recalled a patient who said that she was not her parents' offspring but had only been brought up by them.

Dr Meltzer: For an adolescent it is very easy to deny the parent's current sexual relationship, it is perhaps harder for him to deny that his parents may have had sexual relations once or twice.

I have been speaking today about adolescence from a perspective which emphasizes the problem of knowledge, of understanding, and therefore of identity. I have described how during latency the child experiences this disappointment in his parents, particularly in relation to his theory that they know everything, can do everything, and how he discovers that they don't know how to do anything and that it is only with difficulty that they can do anything at all. This throws him into a state of almost total confusion and puts paid to the theory that he had during the period of latency, that is to say that he only had to be good and that the adults would show him everything he needed to know.

The child comes to the conclusion that his parents' claim to knowledge is simply in order to maintain a kind of aristocratic tyranny over all the children in the world. In this way he joins and becomes part of the community of adolescents, which is fundamentally a rebellious one whose aim is to take over power. The way in which he tries to do this is by trying to be successful, earning money, achieving power, influence, etc. And naturally the central point of all this concerns the achievement of sexual freedom. Now he has reached the conclusion that sex is a sport, the preferred sport of adults and something which has precious little, or nothing, to do with making babies. He is, however, in a state of extreme confusion with regard to sexuality—as indeed he is in regard to everything.

I would now like to return to the problem of early and later childhood, to talk to you about the nature of this confusion which is momentarily set aside during the period of latency. One of the first, and probably one of the most important changes in psychoanalytical theory, introduced by Melanie Klein into the work of Freud, has been the emphasis on early knowledge. Klein discovered that for the small child knowledge essentially means knowing his mother's body. Her theory is that the child's demand for knowledge is connected with phantasies of penetration into the mother's body, which he believes to be the container and repository of all secrets. But in the child's imagining penetrating his mother's body in order to discover its secrets, there is also the discovery that he could cause serious damage to her body, as a result of his bad intentions. Already very early on in childhood he has experienced the need for a split between good and bad intentions. The good intentions consist in a desire to understand and acquire knowledge, the bad ones in wanting to steal knowledge, signifying power, from his mother. Klein believed that this primary splitting—the primary idealization of the self and the division of the object into good and bad—is the foundation of a normal development. Confusion between good and bad returns in puberty.

Later on comes the discovery that the phantasy of penetrating the mother's body also implies identification of an illusory sort which we call "projective identification". This is the second type of confusion which emerges in adolescents: the confusion between self and object as a result of this identification. It re-emerges in puberty, as soon as the body begins to develop adult characteristics: the pubic area, breasts and the development of the genitals. The most typical form it takes is looking in the mirror and no longer knowing, at that moment, if he is looking at his own body or that of his parent. From this stems the adolescent preoccupation with clothing. It is due to these primitive phantasies of entering into the object, that accompany projective identification, that there emerges a gender confusion. This confusion is expressed in the adolescent's worry about the development of his body and appropriate sexual characteristics.

The gender confusion is aggravated by the entry into bisexuality at the time of adolescence. These two kinds of confusion—between male and female and between good and bad—when combined, cause confusion between good sexuality and perverse sexuality. For example, a boy cannot distinguish clearly between his interest in girls and his perverse homosexual tendencies. When a child enters the latency period, he mostly reverts to the mechanism of denial of psychic reality—rejecting phantasies, the world of dreams and emotions linking to his internal relationships. When this denial of psychic reality crumbles, at the point of puberty, he finds himself facing an enormous confusion between internal and external relationships. During the course of the pre-genital and genital Oedipus complex, the child has to process a number of confusing questions relating to the functions of the various parts of the body in relation to the object. These zonal confusions tend to give rise to particular combinations: the mouth-vagina-anus combination and the nipple-tongue-faeces combination. So the child has to learn to distinguish between having the nipple in his mouth, the penis in the vagina, the faeces in the rectum and the other connected areas.

All these confusions which re-emerge with puberty and accompany the adolescent's disappointment in his parents, tend to make him cynical. This cynicism could be defined as "moral relativity": everything is relative, without meaning, one can do whatever one wants. This tends to be the ethics of the adolescent community, in as much as they find themselves in a rebellious relationship with the adult world, and it implies a type of idealization of confusion, that is to say that confusion is a good thing. The only way to maintain this ethic is through indifference to the potential consequences of one's own actions on others. This generates the concept of success as the ultimate goal. This kind of cynicism and lack of concern can only be maintained by a means of a continuous denial of psychic reality in the specific sense given it by Melanie Klein, and it can be overcome by entering the depressive position. I would remind you that the essence of the depressive position is that the object and the object's wellbeing appear more important than one's own wellbeing. It is extremely difficult for young people to keep up this denial of psychic reality when they begin to care about someone else. It is precisely at this time that affection for another individual begins to manifest itself and so, from denial, the depressive position emerges with regard to the internal object. So when adolescents begin to suffer, it is almost always due to depressive states of some kind, which take the form, in their unconscious phantasies and their dreams, of depressive anxieties about the damage wrought to the object by their search for knowledge.

To emerge from their state of confusion they have to rediscover their desire to understand, which has its childish foundations in the desire to enter into the mother's body, where the truth of all things is originally contained. This reawakens all the childish anxieties relating to greed, envy and jealousy. It especially reawakens envy for the mother who possesses all this knowledge; it reawakens the greed, already experienced in infancy, for food which was provided by the breast; and it revives a very primitive kind of jealousy toward the babies contained within the mother, who are felt to be privileged and to share the mother's knowledge. So the adolescent who has started to experience depressive anxiety in his attempt to emerge from his confusion, finds himself falling ever more deeply into depressive anxiety and, just as he tries to find his way out of the confusion, he finds himself increasingly immersed in it. It is at this point that the depressed adolescent must rediscover the generosity of the object: he has to rediscover that if he expects to be fed, if he expects knowledge to be given him, if he formulates his problem and waits for a reply, all will come to him. He therefore has to rediscover that he cannot use his mind like a car: he can't drive it, he can't force it to do what he wants, he has to rediscover that his mind is essentially something on which he is dependent and not something that he can use in the same way as he uses his sports cars or his girls.

So the adolescent who is able to tolerate being miserable and to suffer depressive anxieties with the sense of helplessness that these engender, will rediscover the object in his inner world, the object upon which he can depend to solve his problems. In other words you could say the adolescent rediscovers that his internal object can clear up his confusion and tell him the truth about things, provided he can put up with the pain of feeling once more dependent like a child. From the acceptance of his own impotence and from the renewed sense of dependence that he had experienced in his relationship with his own mother, the adolescent discovers an internal object with which he can identify in a different way. He discovers introjective identification which consists mostly of admiration and "inspiration". And through this process of inspired identification, he gradually becomes a real adult, whose qualities are fundamentally parental ones.

This form of identification with the parental qualities of strength, generosity, goodness and above all the beauty of the object, contrasts with the projective identification mode which relates to an object obsessed with success and power. So, on the one hand there is introjective identification which is not an immediate but a gradual inspiration; on the other hand there is projective identification of an instant, narcissistic, type, based on a primary identification with the power and success of the object. These identifications are diametrically opposed in terms of both form and content.

I would like to highlight the pain, slowness and impotence which is implicit in this rediscovery of the object. The adolescent is in continuous flux between these different communities, because the process of growing up is so painful that he can only tolerate it for a short time; he escapes from this either by finding refuge in the cynical community of adolescents or by turning back so as to become a child again in his own family, or by fighting to achieve success and status. Putting oneself in the adolescent's shoes, in therapeutic work, one should try to create a place where this process could be carried out as systematically as possible whilst at the same time allow the adolescent enough room for manoeuvre, to allow him to escape when it becomes too much for him.

So with adolescents one can't contemplate a psychoanalytical therapy carried out in the systematic and organized way one would hope to do with an adult, or that one generally succeeds in doing with children.

To conclude: the description I have given of the adolescent has left sexuality almost entirely in the background; I chose to do this because the problem of sexuality will emerge in the presentation of the case study which Mrs Harris will make tomorrow and you will have the opportunity to discuss it then, and also because I believe that almost any discussion on adolescent sexuality tends to become extremely moralistic if there is no prior understanding of the adolescent's confusion and the effort made to escape from it. If one thinks that for the adolescent sexuality consists principally in a search for sexual pleasure, then one puts oneself in a position of approval or disapproval. It is impossible really to understand the pressing need for sex, without an understanding of the stress caused by the confusion which the adolescent tries to solve through sexual activity. In other words, if you think that adolescent sexuality is principally driven by a search to satisfy desire, either you approve of it, saying that it is a good thing, or you disapprove of it considering it a bad thing, but you do not understand the essence of it, because the pressing need derives from the confusion that the adolescent is trying to sort out.

Dr Nissim pointed out the difference between the Kleinian and the Freudian approach, with regard to Dr Meltzer's comments on sexuality.

Dr Meltzer added that in fact, Freud tended to consider sexuality from the point of view of the id rather than that of the ego.

Dr Moretti asked if this going backwards and forwards which was typical of the adolescent period could also happen at other ages.

Dr Meltzer said that by placing the emphasis on the confusion he was trying to explain what it meant for an adolescent to try to live in different communities at the same time and why the adolescent must move "backwards and forwards" during his development: different states of mind would correspond to the different communities. He once again emphasized the concept of the four communities and their relationship with the confusion: 1) in the adolescent community the adolescent idealizes the confusion; 2) trust in the adult community, in the search for success and status, implies denial of that confusion; 3) going back into the family re-establishes the idealization of the parents; 4) isolation has the consequence of intensifying megalomania and omnipotence. In this sense the process of psychic development is different for the adolescent from that occurring during childhood or adulthood.

Dr Giannini asked for further clarification on the concept of knowledge.

Dr Meltzer: The psychological theory of knowledge that I follow is the one which was first formulated by Dr Bion most particularly in *Learning from Experience* (1962). This theory is based on the idea that there exist two types of knowledge: the knowledge of things that comes directly from an authority, and that which derives from experience and which is true knowledge. To achieve the latter a person has to involve himself in the world in a kind of emotional relationship which brings him to a state of confusion and distress; that person must then turn to his internal object and project into it that part of himself which is in a state of distress and confusion. The internal object sorts out the confusion and gives back that projected part, with the confusion resolved. In other words, thinking makes one part of the mind dependent on another which is experienced as object and not as self.

Mrs Harris pointed out that Bion's theory could be linked with Mrs Bick's theory.

Dr Meltzer agreed that it was certainly linked to Mrs Bick's theory, which highlights the role of the mother as the first container of the childish part of the self, when it finds itself in a state of distress: it is the theory of the function of the skin as the first container of infant distress—the beginning of introjective identification.

Mrs Harris added that in order for the internal object to establish itself, the child needed to have an external object, which had to adequately perform these functions as a container.

Dr Meltzer: The container which becomes the internal object is that object with which the ego can identify and that is capable of containing its distress. As regards the theory of knowledge and the problem of sorting out the confusion, the self cannot carry out this function alone, but must turn to the internal object. For this reason we believe that one of the most important contributions that analytical work can make to adolescents is to enable them to discover their dream life and realize its importance, in terms of advancing their development. For example, in analytic work it is very important for the adolescent to learn to wait for his dreams, to wait until something is put together and resolved, so as to be able to understand the dream that contains the solution to the conflict. All of this will be specifically described tomorrow by Mrs Harris.

Mrs Harris: The adolescent reaches the point of saying that he needs help because he can't manage any longer, and realizes that he cannot do everything by himself, but also manages to understand that he has, in the past, experienced something that exists and that he can recover through his dream.

Dr Meltzer: In treating adolescents the problem of acting-out is very important. When the adolescent is fully immersed in confusion he can try to sort it out by waiting for dreams to emerge and continue the analytical work, or else he can distance himself from the analysis when the distress becomes too overwhelming. When this happens you have to let the adolescent distance himself. This is an economic problem. I would also like to emphasize that the adolescent's movement from one community to another, as I described earlier, is not the same thing as acting-out. Acting-out is what Mrs Harris was referring to just now, the not waiting but trying to resolve conflicts by experimentation. In working with adolescents, when dreams run out, when the patient misses some sessions, when the material is still very distant, it often happens that one has to wait. And it should not immediately be assumed that the patient is acting-out. I think this can be understood in relation to the material: if in the presence of the material and waiting for the interpretation the patient distances himself from the analysis, it means that the analytic situation has become so unbearable that he removes himself, he goes away. You will see this tomorrow in the material that Mrs Harris will present [*Chapter 4*]; for this patient who is having analysis and living in London, the situation becomes so unbearable that she leaves, going back to her own family who live in a different city.

CHAPTER FOUR

Emotional problems in adolescence: an adolescent girl[1]

(1973)

Martha Harris

I would like to explore further, using material from a particular adolescent girl, some of the problems of adolescents in general as introduced by my husband yesterday. It may be worthwhile first of all to rehearse briefly some of the general points that he made, and which she seems to illustrate.

First of all there is the adolescent's disappointment about the latency child's fantasy of knowledge as something concrete which he would be able to achieve, to have when he is grown up.

Then there is the fading, in adolescence, of the young person's belief in omniscience and omnipotence, as attributed to his parents and to grown-ups in general; and in particular the omniscience and omnipotence that is attributed to sexual relationships—which almost always contain elements of disappointment for the adolescent when he first embarks on one.

Then there is the task which the adolescent has of getting in touch with the experiences that he has internalized from the past:

---

[1] This paper, given at a seminar in Novara in 1973, was published as "Discussion of an adolescent girl" in Harris' *Collected Papers* (1987), pp. 201-16. Additional parts of the discussion are included here, translated by Consuelo Hackney from *Quaderni di Psicoterapia Infantile* no. 1 (1975), pp. 33-61. The case of Rosamund also appears in Chapter 7 of this volume.

the task of trying to get in touch with what we would call his good internal objects, and to become receptive as to what they have to teach him and the means they have to help him. I think my husband suggested yesterday some of the ways in which the adolescent is able to do this: in analysis in dreams, and in ordinary life through literature, music, the arts.

And then there is the adolescent's problem of dealing with the enormous confusion in his feelings about himself and about his objects, the people in his life; the confusion about what is good and what is bad; and how to know more of what he feels about the distinction between good and bad. This of course in later adolescence becomes very much linked with sexual experiences. In the girl we are going to talk about, a disappointing sexual experience is a very important factor in her uncertainty and confusion about her own feelings: associated with confusion in her idea of what is going on inside—what is her internal world—and what is happening in the world outside.

Then there is the confusion about the adolescent's own identity: in either male or female, what are the masculine and what are the feminine characteristics? There is confusion between adult and infantile. There is confusion about the different zones and parts of the body and their functions—which is the basis for the difficult concepts that I hope will be illustrated in some of the dreams I am going to present, which my husband will discuss, and I would like people here to give their ideas as well.

Then there is the adolescent's problem that comes out very forcefully in this girl, of tolerating the pain of depressive states —the depressive states that are precipitated through awareness of violence, ruthlessness, greed or envy towards loved objects in both the internal and external worlds.

And I think there is in particular something one finds in very intelligent adolescents, as this girl is: namely the damage that is thought to be done to one's loved object through a greed for knowledge or the hunger for knowledge in the service of ambition.

And then there is the point of fluctuation in the adolescent between the four groups: between being the child in the family, being one of the adolescents, being a member of the adult world, or being isolated.

I think that Rosamund, the girl I am going to talk about, illustrates this fluctuation particularly. She came to analysis after a period of seven years in which she was one of the most successful members of a group of adolescents at boarding school, where she was very much liked by the other girls and very much a member of their group but in a sense it was not a very typical adolescent group because it was not particularly rebellious against authority. The girls were intelligent, gifted, good at work, and actually hadn't quite come across the need to have to be rebellious to get what they wanted. From this, her venture into the adult world through a sexual relationship with a man a few years older than herself, during a long holiday, brought about a very severe disappointment which resulted in her cutting herself off and becoming isolated. Then, getting in better touch with some of her feelings resulting from the analytic work and from the consultation she had before this, seemed to bring up some of her infantile childish dependent feelings, and a longing to go back to her family again as a little child.

My patient was eighteen and a half years old when I first saw her. She is a quite exceptionally beautiful girl in a very delicate refined way, both sophisticated and graceful in her manners; she talks very perfectly and very musically. A particular symptom that precipitated her seeking analysis was anorexia. She was indeed very thin; though she was anyway fundamentally a very slim, willowy, graceful girl. The effect this beauty had on me was striking; it did not make me feel inferior as a very beautiful girl might make one feel, because there was something vulnerable and somehow affectionate. She aroused in me the immediate feeling of liking her very much and wanting to help her; and this is the feeling she evokes in people generally. She is also extremely intelligent and responsive, always listening courteously to what one says to her.

She had finished attending a girls' boarding school, and in order to proceed with the analysis she had to postpone starting her university course for a year. She came to me in London from the north of England where her parents were staying at that time. She was initially invited to a consultation by Dr Meltzer and this is partly the reason for my choosing this case study. Dr Meltzer saw her three times and so he will be able to tell us what he knows about her.

Dr Meltzer: She was referred to me by her grandfather who is a psychiatrist for whom I was doing a supervision at the time. She was supposed to be taking university admission exams at that time and she was suffering from anorexia, becoming increasingly weak and increasingly convinced that she would fail. I don't think I have ever had an adolescent who made better use of the three hours of consultation, not only because she drew some relief from her anxiety, but also in respect of the quantity of material about herself and her life. She was evidently expecting everything to be clarified in the course of a few sessions. In fact everything *was* very clear in three sessions—but what was clear was that she needed analysis. On the other hand, the fact of having arranged for analysis so strengthened her that she was able to take her exams, passed with flying colours and was offered her place at university. Then, rather happily I believe, she began her analysis with Mrs Harris.

What I would like to point out about her which struck me particularly was the fact that she did not have the characteristics of a tortured adolescent; she came across like one of those girls they called "debutantes"—that is to say, young women who expect their culture and their family to guide them gently from their childhood state to the adult state without any discomfort or battle. So one of the things that emerged clearly during the consultation and which interested her a great deal, was the discovery of how limited her life had been up till that time, from both the emotional point of view and the intellectual one. She could then understand that, in a sense, the anorexia was the expression of a desire to live, deep inside her, which had been covered up and which had remained concealed since her latency period.

Mrs Harris: As her father is a high ranking officer in the Air Force, Rosamund had lived from birth onwards in a number of different countries and the family was always moving; and that of course was why she was at boarding school. The idea was that she should come to London, find a job and keep herself from her own earnings, while her family would pay for her analysis. She was with me only nine months. For the first seven weeks she stayed with friends and with her godmother. She found herself a job very easily in a fashionable beauty salon in Bond Street. I think she expected almost as easily to be able to find a flat; but that of course was much more difficult than she had anticipated, and after some time looking for one together with another girl, she gave up this idea and ended up in a rather shabby bedsit. There, after the initial elation of being grown-up, managing her own room and so on, she became really very lonely and very miserable at times. And then she took to going home to the north of England, a long journey, nearly every week-end.

Dr Meltzer: I think this is something that often happens. I don't know if it happens so often in Italy, but in England, when young people leave school to go to university they lose their adolescent groups. Generally, they quickly join in and form part of a new group of adolescents; but this girl, having lost her adolescent group and come to London like a girl from the provinces, did not succeed in finding a new group to join. As a result she immediately clung to analysis as to something which would introduce her into the adult world.

Mrs Harris: The parents, as far as I could see, seemed to be still very much in love with each other. The child next to Rosamund in age was a brother, David, who was rather less than two years younger than herself, and then there were two other daughters, six and seven years younger. They are a "county" family as we say in England—well-bred, provincial, country people, but not intellectual in any way. The girls' boarding school she had attended since the age of ten was a "good" school but not very academic. She is a very intelligent girl and her intelligence was as yet pretty well untouched. She attained her university entrance to study fine art, but I had the impression from her that art was associated rather with being a rather beautiful "Elizabeth Arden" girl, than with appreciating the great painters of the past.

I have a very definite picture from her analysis of how she coped with having a younger brother. She very quickly became a sister to her mother, joining her in looking after the baby and later the other children. From the material I got the impression that she was hardly ever a troublesome child, owing to this very close, mutually idealized relationship with her mother, then her father, and later her grandparents. Her boarding school is in the town where her grandfather practises as a doctor; and these grandparents, from the age of ten onwards, became second parents to her. When she first went to boarding school she felt desperately miserable, although she did not remember this until feelings of intense depression came up later on in her analysis. But it seems she managed to shake off this misery by becoming witty, amusing, a good storyteller, and the centre of a group of girls who admired her.

Her first boyfriend at school was the brother of one of her best friends. This was when she was seventeen and a half, and she had intercourse with him on one or two occasions that seem to have left her quite untouched.

Dr Meltzer: It is interesting that her first sexual experience happened in a way that I believe to be characteristic of her. For a time she went out with the brother of her best friend as part of the group. During this period she had some problems with her menstrual cycle and, to treat this, a doctor put her on the contraceptive pill. She seemed to have taken this prescription as a sort of official permission from the adults to embark on a sexual relationship and so she did, for the first time, with almost no emotional reaction.

Mrs Harris: Then in the summer holidays before her last year at school, she went to Germany, where she met a beautiful young actor with whom she had an intense love affair for about one month. She seems to have been extremely happy with him but was absolutely devastated when, about a week before the end of the holidays, he told her that he was engaged and intended to marry his fiancée. Until that moment it had apparently never crossed her mind that they would do other than get married and live happily ever after.

When she went back to school for her last year, she broke off with her former boyfriend entirely. But as she had been used to going out with him every weekend for the past year, she found herself completely at a loose end during the weekends at school. She dealt with this misery by cutting herself off from her former schoolfriends, withdrawing, hardly even chatting with them. She also stopped eating and, as she described it later in analysis, wanted to feel that she could do without food: that she was special, did not need it, and would go on not eating for as long as possible. Her teachers and friends were worried about it; then when she went home for Christmas her family were absolutely devastated by the change in her appearance. This was the point at which she was referred for analysis through the grandfather and had three consultations with Dr Meltzer. She began analysis with me about six months later. She had planned to come twice a week, but I suggested to her that three times would be better (which was all I could offer at the time) and she welcomed this idea.

At the beginning of the analysis she concentrated on talking about her problem with eating, but said she was much better; she had in fact been eating and putting on weight and feeling well for some months. But it was necessary that she constantly think about every morsel that she ate, and supervise extremely strictly all the food she took in. It wasn't a question of not wanting or not liking to eat, but of feeling very greedy, so that when she began to eat she was afraid she was never going to stop. It is as if she were really trying to canalize all her greedy feelings into the actual eating of food, and to supervise and control them in this way. When I said something of this kind to her she at once agreed, and said: "I like to bake cakes, I like to bake cakes and to feed all my family, but even when I bake for all the family I still like to feel that it is mine and, although everybody should eat it, I always feel possessive about it." She went on to say that almost as much as the eating, she liked to study recipes, which she would often read in the bathroom.

Dr Meltzer: I would say that this is rather a fine example of the way in which a hypochondriac element can be hidden in the symptom of refusal of food. If one had only the information that Rosamund monitored her food intake, one would not have known that what she was also monitoring was the "eating" of her internal objects. Her response to Mrs Harris's interpretation indicates that when she prepared a cake she behaved as though she was the mother feeding the members of the family as though they were her children. In this way she demonstrates to us the confusion between the self and the object—the one that was hidden in the symptom that seemed, essentially, only a compulsive symptom.

Mrs Harris: At the time I had not picked this up. Initially I linked her possessiveness towards the cakes that she baked with the way in which she listened with great interest to everything I said, as if she was reading it as a recipe that she was going to be able to feed herself later. This material came just before the first weekend; so I said that I thought she was telling me here—though she might not know it—that she was going to resent very strongly feeling that I was to determine when she could eat this analytic cake. I had said several times that very soon she was going to be annoyed about the coming weekend. She listened with tolerance and interest when I said this, but it didn't touch her. Then I went a little further to say I though her too she was telling me about some baby part of herself that wanted to pretend that she was the mummy, that pretended when feeding from the breast that it was really making the food that came out. Here again she listened with interest and agreed, but I didn't find until after the first weekend that it had gripped her and made a link with her internal object.

Rosamund had gone home to her parents; her brother happened to be at home, and at one point—when David was talking to her mother—she suddenly found herself going into the kitchen on her own, ready to burst into tears. But instead of doing so, she had an inexplicable crisis of rage and wanted to smash all the crockery in the kitchen. From then onwards, we had very great problems every weekend and at any unexpected or unusual break in the analysis. She told me that she was very surprised at such a reaction in herself—she who did not remember being jealous of her younger brother at all, as a child, and had in fact always felt quite motherly towards him, friendly and protective. Clearly the separation situation, lived strongly in the analysis, had stirred in her a violence which till then had been hidden from herself as well as from others: a violence, jealousy and possessiveness in a part of herself with which she was very unfamiliar.

The way in which, from the start, she listened attentively to everything I said, reflected on it, and replied in a very controlled way, was her normal way of having a dialogue. When I spoke about her more childish and violent part, she tried to keep her reply on an intellectual level. But in reality she was an intensely emotional girl and every so often some comment of mine seemed to penetrate beyond her control, so she would dissolve into tears. This would happen mostly when the interpretation suggested how inside she felt she was damaging or denigrating her mother (in particular) but also both parents.

Dr Meltzer: I have an anorexic patient whose anorexia is very close to an anti-intellectual aspect of herself, although she comes from a very intellectual family—her father being a professor at Cambridge and her husband a professor at Oxford, and she herself a university graduate. This anti-intellectual quality in her seems to be connected also with a great inhibition towards work—work of any kind—and with choosing social graces instead as a path to success. And I think that Rosamund too evinces this same quality of expecting that her beauty, her grace, will simply open the whole world to her. Now in today's material, in particular, I think you will see how in Rosamund the desire for knowledge, and oral greediness, are absolutely melted together.

Mrs Harris: I was also thinking of a period in Rosamund's analysis when the anorexia returned in the form of vomiting and being unable to stomach food. It seemed to me as if she were rejecting physical food and at the same time rejecting thinking and feeling about some very unfamiliar, ancient part of herself with which she was being put in touch; and vomiting gradually ceased as she became able to tolerate thinking again, and able to have feelings again.

Dream material

I would now like to describe in some detail the first dream that Rosamund had in her analysis. I had told her at the beginning that it would be helpful if she tried to remember her dreams, but it was nearly three weeks before she managed to do so. This first dream, she said, was about a girl called Virginia, and she prefaced the dream by telling me about Virginia. Virginia had been one of her friends at school over a number of years, who at about fifteen years of age began to become anorexic, and over the course of one whole year became progressively more anorexic and more withdrawn until she was finally removed from the school. Rosamund had felt very guilty about this in some obscure way; she felt that she was the cause of Virginia's anorexia, because it was connected with her own growing up, being attractive and able to have boyfriends; whereas Virginia had remained less attractive, rather childish, in the background. As she herself had grown more beautiful (she didn't quite say that, but she implied it), she moved into a rather more exciting social circle in the school. So Virginia was her abandoned best girl friend.

She then said she had in fact dreamt of Virginia more than three months before this, some time following her last consultation with Dr Meltzer. In that first dream, before starting analysis, she had been telling Virginia that she herself was much better, and thought that Virginia should come with her to see the doctor when Rosamund had tried to take her into the analyst's office. She said then that her present dream about Virginia, from the previous night, was quite different. In this dream, *Virginia was looking very well and plump and happy and seemed to be quite cured, and Rosamund felt very pleased about it.* In fact she did not know what had happened to Virginia; since she had been taken away from school at the age of sixteen she had neither seen nor heard anything about her.

This was the first appearance of Virginia, who from then onwards figured very prominently in the analysis in Rosamund's dreams. At a later date she actually made contact with this girl again. At this period I was not quite sure how to take Virginia; I assumed she represented some part of Rosamund herself. From the first dream, it seemed this part of Rosamund did not want to be cured, did not want to come through the door to see the doctor. I suspected at that time this might be connected with a resentment about Dr Meltzer not continuing with her, because it was after her last session with him that she had this dream. I think in the second dream, where Virginia is plump and smiling and quite cured, she seemed to represent both some part of herself that was confused with the object—a virgin mother, or a virgin breast—and also Rosamund herself as the one doing the curing. I felt there were elements of projective identification with the mother, with the breast, and with the analytic situation, with me.

Some tentative interpretations along those lines seemed to produce the following dream, associated with her being about to move into the bed-sitting room which she had discovered. It occurred at the point when she was feeling very elated at having her first room with her first little gas-cooker in it, and at being able to do her own cooking for the first time. This dream I called the "talking cat" dream. In it, *Rosamund went into her back-garden at home and in it there was a large white cat that said to her: "Hello, Rosamund!"* She seemed to take it quite for granted that cats should talk to her; but her family and friends were around her, and they exclaimed in admiration, saying to Rosamund: "How clever of you! How did you manage to teach it to talk?" She felt a little modest and confused and was trying to say it was nothing really. After relating this dream, she said that the same night she had had another one, that she called "the aeroplane": *She was in an aeroplane flying high up at the top of a very tall building and it was very exciting; she was going up and up and up and going to go over the top; and then she became afraid that it would fall on its tail.* Rosamund said she thought she had many other dreams that same night, because there seemed to be a lot of talking, talking, talking going on; but these were the only two she could remember.

I should say the aeroplane is clearly related to her father, who flew aeroplanes and was in the Air Force. This aeroplane going right up and up represented some identification with father and father's penis. It seemed to be related to the elation about being grown up and moving into the room of her own, as if entering and taking possession of the mother's inside space. It also seemed that this aeroplane was somehow linked and a bit confused with the cat in her back-garden, because the aeroplane was going to fall on its tail. There seems to be some confusion here between the breast and the bottom, anus: the large white cat that is in the back-garden and doing the talking there. The confusion is about possessing a talking cat or a talking breast or a talking penis that is somehow linked with her tail, her bottom. Some sort of infantile mobilization is brought about, idealizing her own back-garden, her own bottom doing the talking. The tail of the plane (anus) and the white cat (father's penis) and her own tongue, are confused with each other and also with the analyst's admired tongue (nipple).

Dr Meltzer: The situation at this moment in the analysis is one in which all the confusions are about to break out; and it is quite typical that they are about to do this at a point when she is also somewhat manically elated owing to moving into her own room. You can see that in the background is the dream about herself and Virginia (the virgin mother) in which she was about to invite the mother to have intercourse with this analyst-daddy and be cured by it the way she has been cured. Now in the analysis, also, there is an intercourse taking place, and Rosamund is about to move into that too—both as the mother represented by the talking cat (really a part-object, the mother's breast) and as father's penis, represented by the aeroplane. That is the manic situation; but behind it is the proliferation of confusions about to break out: she cannot tell whether it is the breast or the bottom she is in; she cannot tell who is doing the talking—the mouth or the anus; she can't tell whether it is herself or her object that is having this intercourse; she can't tell whether it is a good penis or a bad faeces engaged in it, and she can't tell whether it is moving in the direction of happiness or of catastrophe.

Dr Nissim: I wonder whether the dream of Virginia already cured might not be the sign of a need to already be cured and not have to face all this disaster—an escape into health.

Mrs Harris: I believe so, because I believe that she thought she was the one to have cured Virginia: that it is Rosamund who is about to enter into the world of adults, and who is in some way healing herself.

I would say that what one does not see at all in all this is the feeling of loss and of depression. Rosamund was living with her godmother before she moved into the flat, and she was clearly cutting off some feeling of uncertainty about moving out of her family into the flat on her own. What was also being cut out at that moment was anxiety about a forthcoming long weekend in the analysis. It would appear that she was denying the sadness about separation in the same way as she had done when she went to school at the age of ten, when she overcame it by talking and talking, to the admiration of everybody at school. I think this is also linked with liking to bake cakes to feed others, as if she were the mother and they the children.

Another dream she had shortly afterwards was a bit of a corrective to the manic element. This dream was associated with actually going back to her school to the prize-giving, where she was to receive the art prize. In the dream she was going back to school with Virginia (who had in fact left the school two years before) and with Jean to receive a prize. Now Jean was her best friend in the last year or two of school, the sister of the boy with whom she first had intercourse. Jean was an attractive, intelligent girl whom Rosamund in fact admired greatly and who got a very good university place. In the dream, *she goes back to school with Virginia and Jean and all three of them are feeling very excited and important in relation to all the younger girls who are still at school, and felt to be whispering about and admiring the three. When Rosamund's turn came to receive her prize, it seemed to be a man who was giving out the prizes and she was astonished when he stopped to make some special speech about her. He was going to present her with a book of poetry which apparently she had written herself. It was something like Wordsworth's. She became terribly distressed about this and wanted to say this was all a mistake, she hadn't written this at all. Then when she looked inside the book, at the poetry, she realized it did bear some kind of relation to things that she had said: that in fact the poetry was really made around some of her words or statements. So she then accepted the book, thinking perhaps she wasn't a total fraud to accept this prize.*

In this dream one can see the adolescent going back to school, hungry for admiration from all the younger children, wanting them to see how marvellously she has got on in the outside world. She is hungry also to get the special prize given by the man, who seems to represent daddy but is also, judging from her associations, linked to Dr Meltzer who referred her to me. But most importantly, one gets some feeling of the essential truthfulness in Rosamund. When she looks at this Wordsworth-like book it isn't all her words, although the poetry has been made from some of her words. I think there was some recognition here of the value of the words of the analyst, of what is in a sense my "words' worth" in relation to what she said to me: some recognition that poetry of a kind was being written from her material through our co-operation. So this dream is a more truthful version of her "talking cat".

Dr Meltzer: I think you can also see how at this point Rosamund abandoned the manic position whereby she felt herself to be her father and mother having a sexual relationship, but is instead the good girl who is about to receive a prize, the equipment for adult life, and this equipment consists of the book which, I believe, essentially represents the breast which has been filled with the poetry of this Wordsworth-father; in this sense it also represents the child. But she also finds herself at a point when she wants to be admired and also to be given this equipment; but she feels the danger of a great humiliation. The humiliation seems to be that of not deserving it, but behind this there is an even greater humiliation which connects to the dream of the airplane falling back on its tail, and the talking cat in the back garden—that is to say, the very child-like humiliation of realizing that what makes her parents so happy is the fact that she has succeeded in defaecating in a potty. In other words, her parents aren't happy because her faeces are so wonderful, they are only happy because they have been put in the right place.

So you can see that the material is shifting slightly from preoccupations connected with eating to preoccupations which are more connected with the process of defaecation. When she tries to mitigate this humiliation she does so saying: yes, but faeces are used to make milk; my words are used to make poetry, my associations are transformed into interpretations by the analyst.

Mrs Harris: I hadn't thought of this. I must say that I probably agree. I certainly had not said so to her.

Dr Meltzer: I am not saying that I would have told her; this is just my interpretation.

Mrs Harris: But I can imagine that those elements were present, recalling a later dream which I had not intended to describe here... I will try to tell it as I remember it: *she was going back to school and once again for the prize-giving; there were a lot of cream cakes. It was a party with a lot of cream cakes. She had a great desire to eat them. She liked cream cakes and sweets very much but she was very worried because she couldn't remember where the lavatory was and she knew that as soon as she had eaten the cream cakes she would have needed to go and defaecate.* The dream showed her child-like anxiety about getting wet or dirty before reaching the right place for depositing urine and faeces; but at the time of the other dream I didn't make the connection with this problem.

The next dream I wish to cite was again connected with the new bed-sitting room into which she had moved. She arrived in distress one morning, having proudly fixed the plug on a new electric fire and then, apparently, plugged it into a lighting point not a power point, so that it fused all the lights. So she had to go to bed in darkness and had the following dream: *She was with her godmother and her godmother's two children and was waiting to be burnt alive. It seemed quite inevitable that she had to be burnt and both she and her godmother accepted this as an inescapable fact. But she was wondering with a little surprise why her godmother was allowing her two children to witness this, since surely such an event would not be good for children. Then it seemed in the dream that she had been burnt alive, and she was reappearing as a ghost to tell her godmother that it had not been so bad after all, that it hadn't hurt.* She then said to me with a smile: "I suppose that's my old omnipotence again—as if I were indestructible."

I was puzzled by this dream to begin with. I could see that it had something to do with the electric fire. Rosamund then said she thought it had something to do with her anorexia and the wish to do everything by herself; but she couldn't explain or add more. Then she said that in the dream, when she was being burnt, it was not at all clear what was happening, except that she noticed at one point the flesh seemed to fly away from her face. I said that something about the way she described it made it sound like diarrhoea, as if there were again some kind of confusion She immediately fastened on this, connecting it with the enteritis she had had as a baby. She couldn't remember whether it was after she was weaned or after her brother was born, but she had been told that at that point she became very thin. So that seemed to confirm the unconscious connection with her anorexia that she couldn't explain. I thought perhaps there was a link with the electric fire that was too strong for the electrical system, that broke the system because it took too much from it; and this might then link with her passion and greed towards the breast—the warmth of the breast engendering some feeling that her greed broke up the breast, sucking out all the milk current and destroying it. The dream would therefore illustrate an immediate identification with the destroyed breast, the burnt-out breast, in that she herself becomes the one who has to be immediately burnt up.

Dr Meltzer: I would say that this represents another step towards acceptance of what she feels to be the humiliation of a dependent child. First she is the breast, then she has to accept that no, she is not the breast, she is only the bottom that produces the material for the breast. At this point comes the terrible humiliation of realizing that she is the greedy child who empties the breast, damages it and produces in her faeces the consequences of the damage wrought to the breast. Her association poses the problem of whether as a little girl she had experienced either her weaning or the birth of her brother as the inevitable consequence of her being this greedy and destructive child. In this way we have an indication of the fact that, in that period of her life, it was to escape from this terrible humiliation, this crushing experience of being a bad child, that she was led to feel as though she herself was one of the two breasts and her mother the other, in a relationship like that of two sisters.

Mrs Harris: I deduced a little later on in her analysis that this dream came at a period when she was being extremely demanding and infantile towards her mother when she went home to her parents; she seems to have been very offended if mother wasn't always on hand to speak to her alone, instead of in the presence of her brother or father. It is quite characteristic of the analysis of adolescents that the strong infantile feelings evoked in the analytic situation can very often not be felt in relation to the analyst, but are taken and worked out in the home towards the family, as a small child will do.

Dr Meltzer: This seems to me to be a very important element in relation to the problem of acting-out and to the question of whether such behaviour is acting-out. I have the impression—and I believe that Rosamund's material demonstrates this—that these types of behaviour occur when insight begins to develop, and this is developed outside analysis: these should not be considered to be acting out. The reason why I am inclined to think that they are something else is the absence of hostility towards the analyst; the adolescent is still a child and it is absolutely natural for him to go back to his parents to process his feelings.

Mrs Harris: I believe this was the first period in Rosamund's life when she was actively troublesome to her parents: spiteful, possessive, demanding, and in fact a real burden to them. It can be a very difficult problem for the analyst to help the parents of adolescents in analysis in such situations; although in Rosamund's case, the grandfather helped the parents very capably.

Dr Meltzer: At that time her grandfather would come to me once a week for supervision, and half the supervision time was spent giving him support so that he could support the parents.

Mrs Harris: A few weeks later, there was a valuable dream following the Christmas holidays. Rosamund had missed the last couple of sessions before the holiday owing to contracting flu, so she had been taken home by her parents. With this complete justification, she allowed herself to be an infant, put to bed and looked after. Then after the holiday, appeared the first signs of any avowed reluctance to come to analysis. Those two sessions had been missed for a very good reason, as it were; but now, she began to become aware of not wanting to come, of feeling persecuted, very angry with me and wanting to shout at me. These nasty emotions ruffled her lady-like exterior and idea of herself. She was still having dreams at this point, but was more reluctant to tell them. When she did tell them they were long and compli-cated. In the first part of a double dream, *she was given a dog that was supposed to be a corgi, like the Queen's; but somehow she was disappointed with this dog. The dog seemed actually to be Dalmatian; but this was not quite what disappointed her. Then her grandfather took her to the opera and this dog seemed to be the star of the show; it was singing, and her parents, aunt and uncle were all coming to hear it. She was rather late in getting ready for the opera and seemed to be hanging back in the background; her grandfather started to tease her as he used to do when she was ten or eleven and first went to boarding school (when she would answer him back with short clever retorts). In the dream she was also answering back, but with rather more biting and sharp replies than she remembered them to have been in actuality.*

The scene of the dream then changed, and she found herself in Germany with the family, looking at an album of photographs that had been taken of her parents before she was born; but the scenes in the pictures didn't actually look like Germany as she remembered it, but like a garden in Cambridge in the summer-time at a place where she had stayed with her parents when she was seven years old. And when she looked at the photographs she seemed to be back in this idyllic scene in the summer garden at Cambridge. Then she was looking at a photo of her mother who looked indescribably beautiful in a very floating, romantic, idyllic fashion, and Rosamund said as she looked at it: "Where was I when that photograph was taken? I wasn't born." Then she thought: "Of course I'm inside mother; mother was pregnant with me at the time this photograph was taken." Then it seemed in the dream to become the summer garden in Cambridge again, but this very beautiful mother in the photograph was now much more like a particular young aunt who had just married her mother's brother. Rosamund remembered this very romantic couple in the Cambridge garden: being her young aunt who looked like a German fairytale princess with long golden hair and was only eighteen or nineteen years old at the time, and her mother's younger brother—of whom Rosamund was particularly fond, for he was very handsome and she remembered him turning somersaults on the lawns of Cambridge, to the delight of the children and the applause of the grown-ups. She also remembered how he helped her to shake the cherry trees to get the cherries.

This was rather a long dream, which took most of the session to tell. Although it was quite clearly shaking her emotionally, it was not at all clear what the emotion was, apart from nostalgia. Rosamund said the second part of the dream about the garden in Cambridge was really a lovely dream and she wanted it to go on and on and never stop, so she was very disappointed when she awakened. The one thing she felt sad about was that this fairytale princess aunt, whom she had admired and loved so much as a young child, no longer makes her feel the same way, since she feels this aunt does not like her now. She had no evidence to justify this; it might just be a feeling, not a reality. She also said that the reason she wanted the second part of the dream to go on and on, was that it seemed to cancel out the first part about the dog, which was somehow very unpleasant. I asked her what it was about the dog that was so unpleasant; she replied that it was very peculiar looking: it was white with black spots but it also had a long neck and very staring pink eyes that were bleeding. In the dream she very much wanted the dog, but she had the feeling that she was being palmed off with something second-rate. Then she added that she hadn't told me before she is actually very afraid of dogs, dating from the time she tried to make her grandparents' dog Oscar (also a Dalmatian) dance on his hind legs; it had bitten her, though not badly. It was not the actual physical pain that hurt so badly, but the sense of being horribly let down.

Immediately after telling me that, although it didn't seem to follow in any logical way, she said: "I never feel... funny... I never feel resentful or hate my mother; I always feel warm and protective towards her; in the dream I felt warm and protective as I do in reality." It is a long and difficult dream, and very difficult to convey how Rosamund and I worked it over together. Clearly she had wanted a dog-penis-nipple like the Queen (the male consultant), but felt fobbed off with a Dalmatian breast with black-spot or bleeding-eye nipples (the female analyst), who interferes through being the poet-singer-star of the analytic show and does not allow Rosamund to step into projective identification as the princess who marries mother's brother (the daddy). Instead she feels ridiculed by the grandfather-daddy and bites him back, in order to divert her hostility from the mother; the breast, the nipple, the bleeding eyes. This is a new experience in the analysis, because "of course" she has always been "in mother" previously, being mummy's mummy, protective, nurturing, never resentful.

This in fact turned out to be a very important point in the analysis, because this was the last real dream that I had for quite some time. What set in instead from this point was a gradual onset of compulsive vomiting. The anorexia in a sense returned, but in the form of being unable to hold down what she was eating. The compulsive vomiting, linked with the inability to remember dreams and her great difficulty in producing material, clearly declared that the analysis had become something that was extremely unpalatable and difficult for her to swallow.

Dr Meltzer: I would like to draw attention to the cherry tree with the cherries and to the dog with black patches and bloodshot eyes. At this point the beauty of her object had collapsed on her despite her attempt to reach it: so her mother is simply pregnant with her beauty, Rosamund's beauty. It is the beauty of this cherry-breast tree that, in her greed and in collusion with her father or uncle, she shakes, making all the cherries fall so it turns into the dog with bloodshot eyes, into her aunt who does not love her, into the dog that bites her.

I think that at this point her hypochondriacal anorexia is transformed into symptomatic anorexia. The difference in these two types of anorexia is quite well demonstrated: hypochondriacal anorexia consists in starving one's own objects and maintaining an omnipotent control over the sexual relationship through which these are nourished. The identification is with an object which has been deprived of its sexual nourishment: fundamentally the breast deprived of semen. Symptomatic anorexia consists of alternate greedy feeding, and envious and disdainful refusal of food in the form of bulimia, vomiting or diarrhoea; greed in relation to the object results in refusal of food as a consequence of envy.

To transform hypochondriacal anorexia into symptomatic anorexia seems to me to be an important therapeutic objective, because it means overcoming the defense of massive projective identification and the confusion of identity.

Mrs Harris: Regarding hypochondriacal anorexia as identification with an object which has been deprived of sexual nourishment, I think it is useful to mention a dream which Rosamund had a short time before. In the dream she went back to school and began to have fun with the others and had to hide this very fact— that she was having fun. It would therefore be possible to say that in some way she felt threatened, as though she felt threatened by the pleasure of learning and this shook her omnipotent control over objects which were not allowed to have fun.

Dr Meltzer: This is a typical change that can be observed in the transference: the patient who ceases to be so omnipotent and to feel always in intellectual control becomes significantly more child-like, greedy and ungrateful.

Mrs Harris: This vomiting difficulty continued for nearly two months; Rosamund was staying at home because she felt too ill to come out. She was trying very hard to remember dreams, but they would be gone by the morning. At this time she was aware of feeling extremely jealous of her father, possessive of her mother, and of continually wanting to take her mother's part in any little argument that happened between the two parents. She came back after one weekend, having had a dream *about some forscythia, but she couldn't remember whether it had been that this forscythia had burst into bloom, or that all the buds were dead and had not managed to bloom at all.* She then went on to say she had had a much longer, very strange dream which seemed to her very significant. This dream was about *her father, who went to fetch an orphan from the cemetery and was bringing the orphan back from the dead. Her father told her that this orphan went to heaven every nine days on her own, but never with a friend. Rosamund said the orphan was small and plump with a very cross expression and was just like Bernadette Devlin* (the Irish militant who was unmarried and pregnant at that time). It seemed to me that this small, plump Bernadette Devlin-orphan was a somewhat new introduction into analysis of a very rebellious, anti-government, antiparental part of herself that wanted to have a baby without a husband, that was very negativistic and whose idea of heaven—perhaps—was "nine" (nein, "no"). Rosamund had spent quite a bit of her youth in Germany and spoke German. The idea was heaven on her own, very egocentric. It would represent the typical adolescent rebellious part of herself of which she had hitherto been totally unaware, managing to keep it quite split off.

Dr Meltzer: So here we have reached another therapeutic objective: this graceful and ladylike young woman has been transformed into a rebellious adolescent.

Mrs Harris: I think Rosamund did not like my interpretations on that day, pointing out the cross orphan and Bernadette Devlin within herself.

The next day she came saying she had had a dream in the night from which she woke up feeling very satisfied and pleased with herself; then she went back to sleep again and had another dream that chased the first one away. She didn't like the second dream at all, but it was all she could remember. This dream was about my family (the first time she had really dreamt about them): *She seemed to be a friend of my family. I was not there but my husband was, and he was tall and fair, in his late twenties with long curly hair. He had a lovely child with him, also with long, curly and very bubbly hair, a beautiful baby. He said to her that his wife wasn't a good wife at all. Rosamund said she longed to have this child as her own, and my husband told her how wonderful she was with children, to which Rosamund replied very modestly: "Oh no, not at all. It's not me, it's the child; anyone would love this child". And then she said the wife must be a hard person not to adore this lovely cuddly child.* Rosamund awoke feeling very annoyed about this dream, and tried hard to remember the other one she'd had. And before I could say anything about it, she said to me: "I'm feeling there's no point in eating anything, because I only vomit; it's completely hopeless." I think that she was anticipating the sort of interpretation I would make about such a clear dream, and pre-empting me by saying: there's no point in telling me that, I'm only going to spit it out, I'm not going to hear it.

I think that in this dream Rosamund has come into much more contact with her rivalry towards her mother and towards me as analyst, in which she idealized herself as this wonderful sweet patient-child while trying to get between the parents and to make the father complain about the mother and therefore complain about me. This dream was very important in Rosamund's analysis; for although she did not like it, she nevertheless brought it to me and recounted it to me.

CHAPTER FIVE

The psychopathology of adolescence[1]

Donald Meltzer

Adolescence can be viewed from a certain perspective as a place where we have been and which we have passed through during a phase of our lives. We are still trying to understand what happened at the time. We have seen the four "communities" within which the adolescent moves: the adolescent community; the family and the parents; the isolated adolescent; how the adolescent feels about the adult world which he desires to enter; and the continuous movement between these communities. As I have said, the individual usually moves between these four communities and eventually finds the path which proves to be the way out. I will now try to describe the psychopathological characteristics of an adolescent representative of each these four communities, bearing in mind the risk that he or she runs of remaining in a fixed position and not being able to emerge from it.

First I shall consider the adolescent who tries to remain within the family; then the adolescent who tries to make a rapid entry

---

[1] A seminar given in Novara in 1973, published in *Quaderni di Psicoterapia Infantile* no. 1 (1975), edited by C. Brutti and F. Scotti, pp. 62-78; translated by Consuelo Hackney.

into the adult world; then the isolated adolescent; and finally the adolescent within the adolescent community. Of these four types, as I have already said, the ones who come to us for treatment are the isolated individual—whom everyone is concerned about—and the individual in the adolescent community who is suffering and who personally make the request to have treatment. We shall not see the other two types—the adolescent who remains in the family or the one who tries rapidly to enter the adult world—during their adolescence; they do not seek our help for the time being, but we do see them later on and when they come for treatment, we need to "construct" the period of their adolescence.

To begin with I shall attempt to describe the prototype of the adolescent who remains within the family. In extremely tight-knit families, where the child has a stable latency period generally spent with parents who try to provide help, the theory of latency maintains that the only thing the child needs to do is to wait; his parents must introduce him into the adult world, present this world to him and provide him with the necessary equipment to enter adult life. These children are good children who follow the ambitions and aspirations of their parents, complete their schooling, generally embark on careers which have some connection to their family; while their social world is essentially their parents' social world. Their boyfriends or girlfriends are generally linked to their parents' world, in as much as they are friends of their parents. They set up families with a minimum of previous sexual experience and reproduce the family model which had been presented to them by their parents. The sort of home they make is "love in a cottage"; they plan to have one or two children and to raise them in the same way that they themselves were brought up. We see them often later on, because they find they have problems and feel impotent with their own children. These individuals represent one type of psychological development: they basically remain the same throughout their lives, in an extension of the latency period, perpetuating an "unreal" approach to life with some fairytale aspects, typical of the latency period.

The second type of adolescent is, in contrast, characterized by a family environment which, towards the end of the latency period, creates dissatisfaction within the family in relation to the external community. This sense of dissatisfaction is frequently linked to a disappointment of the parent of the same sex. This type of child develops extremely rigid and precise ambitions, often linked to the ambitions which the parent of the same sex was not able to fulfil. On reaching adolescence, it seems that the child is entering a tunnel and that he must get to the end of this tunnel. Without being able to be distracted by the adolescent world outside, he must reach what lies at the end of the tunnel at whatever cost. Obviously the type of ambition to which he aspires may vary considerably, so it is not possible to clearly describe his aims and various possible objectives: it might be fame, money, a certain kind of husband or wife, etc...

Now I will talk about the isolated adolescent. He belongs to a category with a more severe and serious psychopathology. The essential feature of such an individual, if we bear in mind our starting point, is the collapse of a serious idealization of the parents and an inability to reconstruct this idealization, moving towards something more concrete, which may be political involvement, community life, etc. He retreats into a narcissistic organization in which he "constructs" himself, behaving as his own father or mother. These are the types of individuals who develop a calm megalomania, as a result of which they feel they have a mission to accomplish in the world. It is fairly natural for these children— who feel that they are their own parents since they have abandoned their own parents—to regard their experience as unique, personal and different from that of all the others.

Naturally most youngsters emerge from the period of latency and discover the possibility, during adolescence, of forming a community of young people of their own age. This circumstance, which is fairly typical of our own culture, seems to begin from the formation of a group of one sex, of either boys or girls. These groups are very different from the groups of friends during the latency period, since they are held together mainly by intense processes of identification. It becomes fairly natural for pubescent youngsters who have found a group or gang, to talk in terms of "us" instead of "I". The main anxiety during puberty seems to be the confrontation with gangs formed of people of the opposite sex and rivalry with other gangs of the same sex. Initially these gangs may be in a state of revolt against the adult world and have the aim of carrying on the war of the sexes: they are bands of guerrillas who launch small attacks on other groups and bring back trophies of sexual experiences, which represent the part of the partner's body which is considered to have been occupied during the sexual battle. When this happens, during puberty, young people have the desire and phantasy that this way of being can continue for ever: it is the most exciting and significant activity that exists in the world. Then, however, "traitors" begin to appear in the group, namely those who become friends with members of the opposite sex: girls begin to feel sorry for boys whom they have given enormous sexual frustration, while boys begin to feel guilty towards girls they have seduced and cheated, and gradually these "traitors" start to leave the pubertal group and form couples. These couples begin to form a new group which is the real group of the rebel adolescent community.

I think that, from the psychopathological perspective, the most interesting group is the pubertal group, since from the time the adolescent enters the true adolescent group he begins to have depressive experiences, is capable of suffering and therefore of developing well. What happens in the adolescent community is that there is a movement backwards and forwards between the old homosexual group and the new heterosexual group. I believe that the psychopathology is mainly to be found in the homosexual group, which we might also term the psycho-paranoid group, while the heterosexual group is essentially a depressive group and has good chances of development. You will appreciate that I am not referring here to homosexual or heterosexual behaviour, but instead to motivation, because from the descriptive point of view, it is very difficult to say whether a form of behaviour has a heterosexual or homosexual significance. For example in schools and colleges, where there are frequent references to homosexual behaviour, this has for the most part a heterosexual meaning. While, in contrast, in couples who live together there may be heterosexual forms of behaviour which have a homosexual significance.

Now I would like to talk about the pathological implications of the homosexual group and its organization. This pubertal group is of a very primitive type and consists of identifications which intertwine: every member of the group identifies himself by projecting onto other members. This means that the members do not identify themselves so much with the group but rather with each other, with the other persons who make up the group. This identification is created by splitting processes: each person in the group plays a specific role and to succeed in becoming a real human being, it is necessary to assemble all these roles. Naturally these roles may change very often: a person may be aggressive one day and passive the next; another may be mean one day and generous the next, and the roles carry on rotating. So it is a group whose main function is to avoid pain and which operates in a specific way. As soon as the individual experiences a certain degree of pain he "slips away". The group functions in order to avoid all suffering, casting it out into the group of the other sex.

As I have already mentioned, this group tends to disintegrate when, one by one, the members end up joining the heterosexual adolescent group. Usually the last person to abandon the pubertal group is the most homosexual and perverse; when the group is tending towards disintegration, there is always someone who tries to hold it together. This person is the one who runs the greatest risk of remaining stuck within a perverse psychopathology. He tries to detain the others from joining the heterosexual adolescent group. The individuals who are thus prevented also run serious risks of a perverse psychopathology. So there are two types of homosexual psychopathology which end up in this group: the active one and the passive one. The crucial phase in terms of personal develop-ment is the life within the pubertal group. When this group is formed serious things may take place without the parents having any sort of control over them. My impression is that once the transition from the pubertal to the adolescent group has taken place, the risk of a serious disorder or extremely rigid personality structure is, at least partly, avoided. At this point, all the risks that the teenager has run are, at least in part, diminished. Clearly this does not mean that that an individual who joins an adolescent group no longer runs risks; there may be even quite serious risks, but these now derive from the world of adults who do not know how to give adequate life space to the adolescent group. Essentially, the adolescent group is extremely safe and very healthy; the adolescent can have his painful and difficult experiences, but there is no risk of fixation or catastrophe, unless adults impose restrictions which drive the group towards negativism.

I have tried to give you an assessment of the adolescent on the basis of what I hear when they talk to me about these problems during counselling sessions or discussions with university students etc. It is certainly not easy to predict the development of a young person nor to identify the reasons why he might find himself in a given situation; however I have the impression that things evolve in the way I have described. I believe that adolescence must be viewed from a wide-ranging perspective which takes account of the importance of the transition from one community to the other, from the world of childhood to the homosexual pubertal group to the heterosexual adolescent group. It is extremely important to evaluate each adolescent's degree of tolerance of pain—the level of depressive pain that he is able to tolerate in relation to confusion. In our role as therapists, we must consider that a person who does not suffer enough to be able to ask for help himself, probably does not need our help. Clearly this position is extremely satisfactory: this way we have patients who give us marvellous results and with whom we can establish excellent relationships. I believe that the most enjoyable sessions in the life of a therapist are precisely those with adolescents who ask for treatment, and the least enjoyable are those with the adolescents who are referred by other people—the school, family etc. Naturally, as I pointed out previously, we all have different ways of seeing things which depend on how we have been brought up, on the restraints which have been placed on us, and on our own experiences. In order for my approach to be useful to you, it is necessary to integrate it with your own approach. Probably it will not differ significantly, except for the fact that I have laid emphasis on confusion and on knowledge.

Discussion

[*Question not recorded*]

Dr Meltzer: It is a long time since I lost the illusion of being able to make predictions. What I have tried to do here is not to lay down the bases for making predictions, but merely to try to understand our way of acting and reacting to the world of the adolescent—in other words the reasons why we feel hopelessly scared and antagonistic towards an adolescent, or the reasons why we might take on rather than refuse a patient. If you find yourselves in the same desperate state that I find myself in, the only policy to adopt is to give counselling therapy to all those who request it.

[*Question not recorded*]

Dr Meltzer: the function of the homosexual group in puberty is to contain, to hold together, since puberty marks the beginning of a situation of enormous disintegration and paranoid anxiety linked to the pre-genital period. It could be said that from a psycho-analytical viewpoint, puberty is the moment of greatest madness in a person's development. In my opinion, the period spent in the homosexual group is essential for the individual's development, in order to avoid either taking a step backwards towards isolation, or clinging to the family, or diving into a tunnel, feeling obliged to get to the end.

[*Question not recorded*]

Mrs Harris: if "knowledge" is linked to a desire to become strong and important, it can inhibit learning, as we saw in the case presented yesterday.

[Participant]: Does this inhibition also mean the therapist should not make interpretions, in case the patient might project this inhibition onto the therapist?

Mrs Harris: I don't think so; it is necessary to interpret the patient's inihibition, not "take it with him" as the inhibition of the psychotherapist.

Dr Meltzer: When the adolescent, through transference, begins to develop an intense curiosity in the analyst's life or in particular about the sexual life of the analyst, I believe the consulting room becomes so highly charged with these erotic implications that it may have an extremely inhibiting effect on the psychotherapist.

Mrs Harris: I don't believe this was the case for my patient I discussed yesterday. When there is intense curiosity, an interest in knowing what is going on in the analyst's mind, this intense curiosity mixed with envy—"you understand these things and I don't"—is perceived by the patient as dangerous for the analyst.

Dr Meltzer: The last dream of Mrs Harris's patient is the typical dream that might alienate the patient undergoing analysis, because it is fundamentally the dream of entering into the life of the analyst and destroying all his or her relationships.

Mrs Harris: This might well be exemplified by the dream in which the girl wanted to be like her mother, even better than her mother, and wanted her father to notice.

Dr Meltzer: Mrs Harris has spoken of the thirst for knowledge that comes from ambition. One type of ambition is the desire to become superior, another type is to feel that other people are inferior. When curiosity about the analyst begins to operate— looking for defects, elements of hypocrisy, weaknesses—this is in my opinion the point of the most destructive intrusions into the mind of the analyst. Such an intrusion may take the form of an accurate and brutal investigation of the analytical method and the life of the analyst.

[*Question not recorded*]

Dr Meltzer: It seems that the heterosexual adolescent group has two functions: the first is to create a space in the adult world in which the adolescent can be free, the second is that in this space he has the chance of experimenting with human relations. We can imagine this space being bounded by a perimeter, a sort of armour, which becomes stronger the greater the aggression directed against it by the outside world. This heterosexual group is a bit like Noah's Ark: once the flood is over the animals come out of the ark in pairs. During this process the adolescent has identified very little with the group as a group. It is essentially a negative identification: the group is a place where adolescents do not need to find an object to identify with, but where they can have experiences which are necessary for attaining an identity of their own. In this image of Noah's Ark there is a maternal identification—in other words an extremely strong unconscious identification with the inside of the mother's body and with all the children contained within it, and there is also pain caused by claustrophobic anxiety. It is very important for the adolescent that this space has a concrete existence in the world and that adults are kept outside it. For example, it is extremely important that in the family home parents keep "outside" their child's room.

Dr Guaraldi: Are there some adolescents who pass directly into the heterosexual group without having spent their time in the homosexual pubertal group: that is to say who form couples without having had a homosexual phase?

Dr Meltzer: There are two different types: on the one hand there are those who enter adult life directly through the tunnel —who therefore "throw" themselves straight into a heterosexual relationship and who have been looking for a partner to marry ever since puberty. On the other hand, there are those who resist sexual experience until they have arrived at the end of the tunnel, in other words until they obtain success; only then do they feel worthy of choosing the partner they prefer. The risk of disappoint-ment in these two types of choice clearly differs: the adolescent who immediately throws himself into heterosexual relationships convinced each time that it is the right one and that it will last for ever, encounters one disappointment after another, often has sexual relations with much older partners and ends up in a sort of "migratory promiscuity", whereas the adolescent who goes into the tunnel without having had any sexual activity, finds that once he had reached the other end and achieved the social status he aspired to, he has largely lost the real and essential capacity of a sexual response towards others and never finds anyone "who is right for him". From the psychopathological point of view, there is a strong likelihood of there being fairly serious consequences in both cases.

Dr Guaraldi: Dr Meltzer said that in the pubescent group there is always someone who, being last, tries to hold back the others who want to move on, and in the heterosexual group there is an isolated person who cannot manage to find a sexual partner but who serves as a gooseberry who supports the others: what future and what psychopathological risk is in store for these individuals?

Dr Meltzer: One of my favourite ideas with regard to the depressive anxieties of these adolescents is that they also participate a lot in the pain and suffering of others. So in a certain sense they are forced to assume a therapeutic role with regard to the others' depressive anxieties, just as they do with regard to their own. In doing this it seems that they are playing the part of the buffoon or the fool, but these people actually possess a great capacity to love and continue with their life and their development extremely well. One of my ideas, as regards adolescents and their ability to love, is that they experience it as a very vulnerable position—vulnerable in as much as it involves humiliation and they consider someone in love to be stupid. The adolescent who is capable of tolerating this feeling of stupidity caused by being in love is at the beginning of adult life. It is very interesting to note that the people in this group very frequently make more effort to promote relations between their peers, rather than entering directly into the battlefield.

Mrs Harris: One wonders whether the adolescent struggle to try to forget one's own interests in order to serve the loved person or object—with all the pain this implies—is the nucleus of the depressive position? It involves the abandonment of omnipotence and omniscience and the acceptance of no longer being able to control the object.

Dr Meltzer: The ethic of this group of adolescents is to worry about those who suffer, who are not successful, who do not succeed, since the depressive position is in contact with the tragic element of life.

[*Question not recorded*]

Dr Meltzer: If we look at the political shape of these adolescent groups we can see there are two types: a homosexual one and a heterosexual one. The political objectives of these two groups are diametrically opposed: one is to conquer the world while the other is to save it. The first corresponds to a paranoid-schizoid position, while the second corresponds to a depressive position.

[*Question not recorded*]

Dr Meltzer: My experience is slightly different: this group, which we might term "fascist", is a group that sets out to conquer and it has enormous homosexual and paranoid-schizoid implications. Nothing is more natural, for those who belong to this group, once success has been attained, than to become bourgeois and return to the latency period. The militant heterosexual group— the one that wants to save the world—after achieving success and gaining bourgeois status, tends to return to characteristics of a paranoid-schizoid nature. This can also be seen in psychoanalysis, because ever since psychoanalysis has begun to be successful and respected, it could be said that psychoanalysts have begun to form a paranoid-schizoid group.

Mrs Harris: Something that comes to mind is that in university groups, when there is tremendous anxiety over exams, at the end when the exams are successfully passed there is a moment of stasis, a sort of looking around, followed by a state of depression.

Dr Meltzer: This is also my experience. Once they have taken their exams, groups of heterosexual students who already have depressive traits enter into a phase of terrible depression.

Mrs Harris: When the external enemy—which had been identified as the exams—is no longer there, then the enemy becomes internal.

Dr Meltzer: In this way they discover what Mrs Harris was referring to earlier: they cannot protect their objects and they will not be able to save the world.

[*Question not recorded*]

Dr Meltzer: I believe that in the homosexual group there is a group opposition towards each member that leaves. When there is a powerful leader who keeps them together, these groups can operate in such a way as to impede the development of the individual and the leaving of the group. In this group the appearance of homosexual activities is extremely dangerous. The atmosphere in such a group is defensive, superior, condescending, arrogant— features which characterize homosexual tendencies.

[*Question not recorded*]

Dr Meltzer: It seems to me that the homosexual group that aggressively wants to conquer the world very easily turns into a delinquent group: the group becomes delinquent but not the individual. It seems to me that there is a degree of confusion surrounding the meaning of persecution and persecutory anxiety. When we use these terms in psychoanalysis we mean "fear". When we use them to describe social phenomena, we mean "feeling that we are being treated unjustly". I think the adolescents in the heterosexual group feel persecuted by the malignancy of those who hold power. They do not have persecutory anxieties about the latter but they feel that they are being unfairly treated.

[*Question not recorded*]

Dr Meltzer: Rosamund's mental anorexia emerged when she tried to leave the homosexual group in which she had a prominent role, and tried to immediately enter the adult group through sexual experiences which left her feeling severely disappointed.

Mrs Harris: It appears that anorexia emerges at times of disappointment and abandonment, also bearing in mind the story of Virginia, whose anorexia began at the age of sixteen, when she felt abandoned in the homosexual group by Rosamund who was trying to leave for the heterosexual group. Being unable to show her disappointment and anger openly, she turned these feelings on herself.

Dr Meltzer: An extremely important thing about the homosexual group concerns those individuals who are unable either to continue or to find their way back when they are left alone. They do not encounter depressive anxieties but a full-scale depressive illness which manifests itself when their best friend begins to find a sexual partner.

[*Question not recorded*]

Dr Meltzer: In my experience, when adolescents come together in a group which sets itself against adults, this happens because they experience adults as people who want to destroy the world, whereas they want to save it. I am referring to the adolescent from the point of view of the structure of his personality and social structure. Age does not count. This group can be called a basic assumption group—to use Bion's terminology. The assumption is that only "together" can the world be saved. When the adolescent tries to leave the adolescent group that has this grandiose basic assumption, he is faced with an extremely serious depressive disappointment. This disappointment corresponds structurally to the disappointment of the child who not only cannot save his mother or the breast, but he cannot even save himself from the destructive forces within him. He depends on his objects to be saved.

Mrs Harris: The processing of the disappointment which the adolescent group that wants to save the world has to face, leads it to overcome the residual infantile omnipotence: saving the world identifies some limitations in the adolescents' abilities and in the grandiosity of the task which they had set themselves. The adolescent who finds himself facing this enormous task of saving the world is forced to reconcile himself with reality, with the little he can do and with the small contribution he can make in this direction.

Dr Meltzer: In this sense he is like the small child who has to discover that not only can he not save the breast, but that he is constantly endangering and damaging it. The first thing he has to learn is what he must do in order not to damage himself or his objects.

Dr Nissim: In these movements of transition from the homosexual to the heterosexual group, is the more pathological individual the way he is because the group has made him this way—because it gives him this role of a sick person—or is the individual sick in himself?

Dr Meltzer: The important criterion for assessing an individual in this phase of life is his mobility or lack of it. The individual who lacks the mobility which allows him to pass from one community to another and who is fixed in a position that can no longer be developed becomes ill. Therapy must help him to discover his mobility.

[*Question not recorded*]

Dr Meltzer: I have tried to describe the heterosexual group not so much as a group, but as a position. It seems to me—in agreement with Bion—that there are two different types of group: the work group and the group dominated by a basic assumption. I think the groups dominated by a basic assumption are linked to individual pathology only at the level of extremely serious mental illness, which involves processes of splitting and extremely narcissistic forms of identification. In my opinion this kind of group does not have any element that can facilitate the development of an individual. I believe that the homosexual group can be seen as a group dominated by the basic assumption which is formed after the explosion of these splitting processes during puberty. The only utilitarian function of this group for the development of the individual is represented by holding him together; in this way the individual can find his way towards the adolescent position. This is a very personal point of view. Everyone should speak according to their own experience. In my experience, work-groups are very rare, perhaps because I do not know much about working in groups. Mrs Harris is much better at this than I am.

Mrs Harris: I don't agree with Dr Meltzer. In my opinion work-groups play an important role in the development of the adolescent. For example, one can get adolescents to do theatre: they have a task in common which is useful because it keeps them together and because it represents a parameter to which they can refer. In this way they have the chance of getting to know each other and of beginning to understand to what extent their personal disagreements can disrupt the work. If they want to succeed in putting on the show, they must try to resolve their personal disagreements. If they succeed, they will have the sensation of having achieved something. They must learn to overcome both their internal difficulties and those regarding relationships with others in order to complete the task they set out to do. This is a very simple example of a work-group.

Dr Meltzer: I think that they will not be able to complete the task because they will not succeed in putting on the kind of show they wanted, since it is for them "just like" saving the world.

Mrs Harris: They won't have saved the world, but they will have achieved something; this is extremely important.

CHAPTER SIX

Adolescent sexuality[1]
(1969)

Martha Harris

W e have made the point that a child's current relationships and his physical and emotional growth continue
to be affected, if not determined, by his earlier experiences. This is especially true of the sexual development of the
teenager, of his feelings about himself and his body, of his capacity to anticipate and finally enjoy sexual experience reciprocally
with the partner of his choice.

His capacity to enjoy his body and to be able finally to integrate
sexual feelings with tenderness is rooted in the early physical and
emotional relationship he had as a baby with his mother. This goes
for the girl, of course, as well as for the boy. Her very first physical
closeness is also with her mother, in whose arms she first begins to
feel some fleeting physical identity and sense of what belongs to
her body and what it looks like.

As we have already mentioned, a number of things can interfere
with the mother's capacity to accept the baby in a physical and
emotional way, and there are differing factors in each baby
which may inhibit its capacity to utilize and to respond to what

---

1 Extracts from *Your Teenager* (1969); new edition Harris Meltzer Trust, 2007.

he is offered. These half-formulated secret shames about being unattractive, unlovable and lacking in love weigh very heavily on the teenager. Sometimes they lead him to rush prematurely into sexual experience and promiscuity; sometime they inhibit him from seeking it at all.

The capacity to wait until he is really ready, and the capacity to enjoy sexual experience attended with love, depend very much on the kind of picture the teenager has internalized over the years of his parents' relationship, and on the nature of his identification with them. This will not correspond entirely with the real nature of his parents; although this, of course, must have played an important part in determining his views of them and of their marriage.

As he has grown older he will as a rule have come to take consciously a more objective view of his parents. He will want to repudiate or to identify with certain qualities of their characters; and this more conscious process is intensified in adolescence. The healthier his relationship with his parents, the more he will be able to question it, and to question them and their relationship in order to form his own opinions.

But the teenager isn't entirely a reasonable being. If he is really having an adolescent experience which includes revival of the past as well as hope for the future, he finds that he has complicated and far from dispassionate feelings that both distort and enrich his relationships. These derive from infantile unresolved jealousies and idealizations about his parents and their relationship. From the qualities of the idealized parents comes the dream of the perfect partner. From the envy and jealousy come fears of hostile parents, the archaic nebulous forces that lurk in the phobias and night terror of the small child.

These are often left behind in the course of getting more experience of managing the external world. They are, as it were, forgotten in the middle years of childhood, which are so concerned with acquiring skills and facts to manage oneself and one's environment. They are revived in the upheaval and yet potentially integrating experience of adolescence. The only way whereby such fear can be modified, rather than avoided, is by a confrontation with, and a greater acceptance of, the terrors and guilts perpetuated by the destructiveness in one's own nature. Some teenagers do struggle to face this, though they will also project it into the larger scene of social violence and destruction, and into their more personal social circle of parents and authority figures.

Some of the young child's most violently destructive feelings are evoked by feeling excluded and frustrated at not sharing in some treat which he feels is going on. He believe that something is being enjoyed which is denied to him. The parental relationship in its very nature has elements that exclude him. If he has an appropriate close and happy relationship with each of his parents, and is included by them both in a framework that is within his compass, he is not so likely to go on bearing a grudge about the experiences from which he has been excluded.

But some children—probably most children to a certain extent—put aside the grudge rather than relinquish it, and wait until they are adolescent to get even as soon as possible. An over-authoritarian upbringing can lead them to nurse and to justify this grudge. A too permissive upbringing gives them no help in recognising the priorities and the need to make choices: it fails to teach them that you can spoil some things if you try to grab them too much too quickly.

The child needs not only parents who give, who gratify needs and accept with love, but who can say `stop', and help him to stop going on to spoil things for himself. If we have been able to say no firmly enough at the right time to our children, perhaps we won't have to say it so often to them in their adolescence, when it is not so easy to enforce prohibitions.

Premature sexual experience and promiscuity among teenagers is probably in most cases motivated much more strongly by unresolved childish greeds and unconscious competition with the parents of childhood than by love or even irresistible sexuality. The promiscuity obviously implies inability to be satisfied and to develop one adequate relationship.

The boy's diffuse sexual feelings of early childhood become increasingly focused in adolescence upon the penis. At puberty sexual feelings can be experienced as a violent and exciting possession by urges outside conscious control, and the penis can be felt to be the instrument of their discharge. The urge to masturbate can sometimes become compulsive, and attended by fantasies exciting at the time but producing flatness and depression afterwards, with fear of damaging oneself, one's penis and one's mind. Hence so many "old wives' tales"about blindness and madness have taken strong hold and are still heard today.

In later adolescence sexual relationships with a girl or with girls are sought sometimes as a defence against this kind of self-defeating masturbatory experience, and sometimes the girl is just `too easy' sexually, despised as a victim conspiring with an aspect of the boy's sexuality that gets the better of him, as it were. Such a sexuality has no tenderness or appreciation of the object towards which it is directed.

A relationship that is sought mainly in order to discharge sexual frustration is little more than the enactment of masturbation fantasies with another person, and will result in as little real satisfaction. It may be a temporary reassurance, or a triumph, another scalp to add to the collection. If it is seen as a triumph, then the teenager is surely not only competing with and triumphing over his peers, but is acting out deep-seated childish rivalries and sexual grudges against his parents. And this goes for the girl as well as for the boy.

Like the adolescent boy, the girl is preoccupied with anxieties about her sexual capacities. The boy's anxiety about his potency is paralleled by her fear of being frigid. These matters are so much more openly discussed these days when youth and sexuality are equated, idealized and flaunted. The fears of frigidity and impotence express and conceal a more deep-seated anxiety about not being fully alive, of being uncreative, of having death within. This derives from a sense of undeveloped, disregarded aspects of the self, and also from the accumulation of relationships with parents who were internalized in anger and in hatred.

The adolescent girl is most conscious of the resentment and struggle against her mother. Sometimes she may still feel the rivalry as a current and conscious continuation of ancient childish grievances. More often, perhaps, as she grows up, she is aware that it is "her turn". "Oh mummy", sighed a young girl in exasperation as her mother lamented the discovery of a grey hair, "I don't see what you're grumbling about. I mean to say, you've had a jolly good innings." She was clearly feeling that her mother's intimation of ageing was an accusation against herself.

This is quite unreasonable, as any rational teenager would readily agree, judging by standards of external reality. But it is understandable if one recognises that in each teenage girl there is a little girl who at last sees herself within reach of realizing her childish dream of marrying—not maybe her actual father anymore—but that Prince Charming whom daddy appeared to be in her eyes long ago. Thus she displaces her mother and occupies the enviable central position which her mother used to have.

Her touchiness and guilty feelings about this are in proportion to the strength of her continuing unconscious wish to triumph, on the strength of the unworked-through infantile grudges. She can quite easily bring to mind a shadowy picture of a displaced mother, who emerges as a mean and grudging person, but at whose expense she has profited. Remember that the wicked fairy, who was at first left out of the invitations to the christening of the Sleeping Beauty and who then appeared late, predicted that she would be killed by pricking herself with a bodkin when she was sixteen years old. This is a mythical expression of the fate that many a young girl unconsciously fears will snatch away from her the promise of fulfilment just within her grasp in adolescence.

The danger from outside, from fate or ill luck, has to be avoided and guarded against. But it is sometimes easier to bear than the depression about damage within. (pp. 205-209)

[…]

Society has a great deal to answer for in the shameless exploitation of teenagers for commercial ends: the seductive advertising, sexual titillation on screen and in print. But the danger to the teenager is probably not so much even from undue inflammation of his sexual desires as from the continually implied or stated propaganda that unless he is sexually "with it" he isn't really alive —that he is left out, left behind in the race to grab something out of life. To have a boyfriend or girlfriend, and a bank balance—those are the two keys to life!

As parents and educators we, too, are part of that society, and therefore cannot dissociate ourselves entirely from responsibility for what is happening to our teenagers, or from what they are doing Yet it may be equally untrue to assume that we are entirely responsible for their predicaments any more than for their achievements (p. 212).

CHAPTER SEVEN

Infantile elements and adult strivings in adolescent sexuality[1]
(1976)

Martha Harris

Whaen I first came to write this paper I soon realized that its focus would have to be a much narrower one than the title allows. I also found that I was returning over and over again to analytic material from a fairly wide range of gifted adolescents who, as the world goes, were more than usually fortunate in their external circumstances: young people who from any external point of view might seem to have everything in their favour but who nevertheless seemed quite unable to enjoy their good fortune.

In all of them there existed a deep sense of unworthiness together with the quite opposite conviction of being special. There was evidence to suggest that they were regarded by one or both of their parents as special, and that they expected this treatment from the rest of the world although when it was forthcoming they could not use it to assuage their discontent. One could think of them as young people who were in the painful position of having to learn that their appearance, intelligence, emotional endowment,

---

[1] First published in the *Journal of Child Psychotherapy* (1976), vol. 4 (2), pp. 29-44.

and social position were not evidence of innate superiority but gifts which had to be earned by carrying them and treating them as a responsibility. Difficulty in learning this showed itself clearly in their sexual attitudes and behaviour.

Defensive structures that had served them well in latency and had allowed them to have a successful and fairly untroubled development at that time, made them particularly vulnerable to the intense sexual drives and frustrations of adolescence. They tended to have difficulty in being one of the adolescent group and in using it to share experiences with peers, thereby working their way towards more adult relationships; they were impatient to leap right into the world of the grown-ups and to that "happy ever after" which is the young child's idea of marriage.

Theoretical background

It is not possible or useful to try to present anything like a comprehensive summary of the many publications about adolescent sexuality. I shall confine myself to brief references to those which have helped me in my thinking about these cases and in particular to the two to whom I shall then refer.

Freud, as I understand him, saw sexuality in general as dominated by the pleasure principle—the ego seeking a homeostatic solution through gratification and the avoidance of pain (1911). His differentiation between adult and infantile was basically a zonal one, i.e. progression from oral through anal and phallic to genital primacy with eventually the pregenital elements confined to foreplay (1905). This was later amplified by Abraham to include the progress through ambivalence and part-object relations to a non-ambivalent whole object love.

Stemming from her work with children, Melanie Klein was able to amplify the economic concepts of pleasure and reality principle to include the shift in values in the progression from narcissism to object relations (from the paranoid-schizoid to the depressive position). This gave body to the concept of the resolution of ambivalence when consideration for the welfare of the beloved object enables the child to struggle with its greed and self-interest in order to spare that object (1939). She regarded development as greatly influenced by the epistemophilic instinct and saw the infant as growing through a process of projection and introjection, through interaction with the object, in the first place the body and personality of the mother. She saw the foundation of the capacity for pleasure as being laid in that first relationship with the world; the origin of satisfactory sexuality in an enjoyable relationship with the breast; the capacity for pleasure between penis and vagina as rooted in prototype pleasure between nipple and mouth.

This led on to Bion's theories of the "container and contained" (1962 and 1979), of the integral part which maternal reverie plays in the development of the infant and of growth proceeding through mind to mind as well as body to body contact.

Melanie Klein's delineation of splitting processes (1946) gave firmness to Freud's structural theory—of ego, id and superego—and has led to developments such as Esther Bick's investigation of ego strength (of skin and second skin as function of the personality; 1968) and to Meltzer's delineation of the adult and infantile structures of the personality (1972).

These concepts seem to me to be central to understanding the nodal position of adolescence in the transition from life in the family to life in the world. Adolescence may be seen as a period during which the containing function of the family disappears and has to be replaced externally and eventually internally in the personality, when the young person has to proceed through a disintegration to a new integration as an independent adult. During the transition the adolescent group may be seen as a performing a second skin holding function. It is a period when all the old infantile conflicts have to be worked over again in the light of new intense genital drives which test the quality of the internalization of previous object-relations and identifications.

These concepts imply that the development of sexuality is inextricably bound up with character formation and identification processes and that the adult character is different from the infantile structures of the personality. The latter tend to retreat under stress to the paranoid-schizoid position, dominated by self-interest and the impulse to avoid pain. The sexuality of those structures is propelled by jealousy, envy, greed and competition for the pleasures which the child believes the parents enjoy and which are denied to him. It tends to be accompanied by a sense of grievance based on lack of recognition of limited capacity.

These infantile elements are markedly obvious in adolescence but do of course persist into grown-up life and are to a greater or lesser degree operative in us all. They are characteristic of what Melanie Klein termed the paranoid-schizoid position: a state of mind in which self-preservation, egocentricity and narcissism take precedence over love and gratitude to good objects. The adult strivings in the personality begin already in infancy, to varying degrees; when the child begins to be able to attain, however fleetingly, the depressive position; a state of mind in which he is able to introject and identify himself with the parental capacity for concern based upon his gratitude for care that he has received. This implies an attempt to assume some degree of psychic responsibility for his own emotions and attitudes to his objects and to limit the demands that he makes upon them.

In *Sexual States of Mind* (1972) Meltzer spells out the implications of Melanie Klein's theory of the depressive position for understanding the difference between adult and infantile sexuality. He describes how the development of adult sexual attitudes is linked with character development. Infantile sexuality is essentially concerned with getting pleasure and gratification in omnipotent ways, by bodily manipulation or phantasy. It is characterized by the child projecting himself into the phantasied secret relationship of the parents (the primal scene), in various ways, and with varying degrees of illwill and non-acceptance of the fact that he has to wait to be grown-up, and that being grown-up means carrying responsibilities, notably babies, as well as enjoying power and privilege.

He delineates the elements of perversity present to a greater or lesser extent in most infantile sexuality, which derive from a fundamentally narcissistic organization of parts of the self that are set up against the creative union of the parental couple. This organization has its inception when the combination of nipple and breast which produce milk for the baby's mouth, and at a later level is set up against the union of penis and vagina which make the baby in parental intercourse. So according to him the core of this perversity is anal negativism.

A central problem in the analysis of adolescents is the teasing out of infantile and perverse elements which hamper the striving towards more adult responsible relationships and which tend to divert development into some cul-de-sac or another. These are usually at the heart of the matter in the case of those gifted adolescents who are not fulfilling their promise or who are unable to enjoy their success.

I shall now present some material from the analyses of two young people in this category.

Case 1: Rosamund[2]

Rosamund, aged eighteen and a half, came to London to have analysis with me during the year between leaving school and taking up her university place in a town at a distance which would have precluded the possibility of travel. In her last summer holiday from school, when travelling abroad with a group of young people, she had fallen in love with a young musician a few years older than herself. Not until she had become thoroughly involved with him did she find that he was engaged and had no intention of breaking off his engagement. This did not prevent them from having a somewhat idyllic relationship with each other for the rest of the summer.

On her return to school, however, she had drifted away from her former close friends and from her work and had gradually given up eating. She had become imperceptibly thinner until the gravity of the situation became apparent when she returned home for the holidays. Some consultations with an analyst over a period of time enabled her to work again, to pass her university entrance and to resume eating to a degree that allowed her to keep body and soul together. Anorexia remained an ever-present threat and it was arranged that she have this period of analysis before proceeding to university.

2 This is a later and more concise account of the case presented in the seminar transcribed in Chapter 4, "Emotional problems in adolescence".

When I first saw Rosamund I was struck by her beauty and an elegance that transformed the usual adolescent uniform of jeans and cotton top into the garb of a young lady of quality. Although extremely thin she did not look emaciated, and her facial expression though basically rather depressed in a gentle way, could change rapidly and light up responsively. She became eagerly and quickly involved in the analysis propelled by her awareness of the shortness of the time available. Problems of eating occupied here initially, their link with her wonderful summer holiday and her puzzlement at intimations of areas of her personality that were a closed book to her.

By the time she started analysis it was no longer a question of not wanting food or friends but of overcoming something which forbade her to eat and which hindered her in her social approaches. Once she began to eat she was afraid that she might have difficulty in stopping if she did not supervise herself carefully. She would be visited by longing for sweet things like cream buns and stodgy foods and was fascinated by recipes which she would read in the bathroom. She would pick at tempting food in the refrigerator although she could resist it when offered it at table in company.

She was puzzled that with her anorexia had arisen an unfamiliar problem of jealousy of the brother rather less than eighteen months younger than herself. She could not remember this as a feature of her childhood at all, and could only recall many occasions in which she was enjoying helping her mother to look after him.

In short what she seemed to be indicating in these first sessions was that her love affair had evoked in her an upsurge of baby feelings of greed and possessiveness from which disappointment and wounded pride had made her drastically cut herself off. The analytic consultations she had had, and the eagerness to have more of the same kind of talking when she started work with me were threatening her with a greed that she was now more aware of, but struggling to resist. Interpretations linking her enthusiasm for knowledge and for sexual experience with a fundamentally baby greed for the source of food and knowledge—the breast—were accepted by her instantly. She said she was just beginning to realize how possessive she was; when she baked a cake for the whole family it was still her cake. She wanted them to have it but not until she said so.

This was some indication of how she was controlling her internal family: of how, in apparently supervising her own eating, she was supervising her internal objects, her internal family. The cake, the breast, was hers and so she would say who should have it, when, and how much. She had retreated from the adolescent world of competition and struggling relationships to the position of a young matron. That this position of elegant young mistress of the household was achieved by projection into the breast by way of the anus was indicated by the addiction to recipes in the bathroom and the picking of bits of food in the refrigerator.

This became clearer to her when she started to have dreams some three weeks after beginning her analysis. I shall now discuss a few of these dreams, using them to indicate the focus of the work upon which we were engaged during the relatively short period of her analysis.

Following her first weekend back home, she came with two dreams. The first was as follows: *There was a white cat in her back garden. It said "hello" to her which did not surprise her in the slightest, but her family and friends were around exclaiming in admiration and saying how clever it was of little Rosie to teach it to talk. They had never heard the like of that before.* This dream was followed by another on the same night: *Rosamund was piloting an aeroplane which was flying to the top of some very high buildings. It was terribly exciting going up and up but she was afraid that it might fall on its tail.*

In the talking cat dream, we have the adolescent's craving for admiration, but as in this dream she apparently was also sometimes a little girl and moreover the cat was a pet of early childhood, this dream seems to be about the baby who goes to her own back-garden (her bottom) and fills the pussy cat breast with her clever noises. The intense involvement in this talking analysis reactivates at depth—as a defence against separation and its attendant emotions—an omnipotent anal projective identification into a breast that then becomes her pupil, her baby, while she is the clever one who is teaching it. One could easily see how

Rosamund's beauty and quick intelligence were likely in infancy and later to evoke the kind of admiration that would lend credence to this phantasy.

In the second dream, the identification seems to be more with father's penis (he had been a pilot during the war), but a precarious identification with a faecal penis. She may flop on to her tail and find that she is just the baby who has been messing its nappy.

Following this dream there emerged further material about her identifications with her father and her brother and the history of the importance of talking to her. Both her father and her brother were apparently talkative, entertaining, outgoing people. When Rosamund went to boarding school at the age of eleven and felt homesick, she managed to hide this from her companions and then eventually from herself by becoming very chatty and entertaining—a role which she has maintained with great success until in adolescence it had begun to wear a little thin. So this had seemed to be a way of avoiding emotional conflict by slipping into projective identification with her rival object, by becoming it: a way of evading the unresolved infantile conflict about giving up mother and allowing her to be with father or brother, by becoming them.

I shall now report a dream which she had a little later, which is somewhat of a corrective to these two although still a little manic and elated: Rosamund was going back to school with her two best friends. *The younger children were whispering and admiring them while some man was presenting the prizes to those who had left and who had done well. When it was her turn he stopped to make a speech and to give her a specially bound volume of poetry which she had apparently written herself, something like Wordsworth. She then became terribly distressed and tried to say that it was all a mistake and she was not the author. Then when she looked inside the book she recognized some of her words, so the poetry did bear some relation to what she said, had in fact been created out of her statements. She then accepted the prize, trying to persuade herself that she was not a total fraud.*

So here we have the adolescent going back to school hungry for admiration from the younger children, to receive the prize from daddy, praise for her own products, her analytic cookery as it were. There is however some truth in it, some recognition of the nature of the analytic work (the "words' worth"), the fashioning of some harmony or rhythm, something positive in a relationship that is not merely her own production—an advance on the talking cat. Hidden in this dream, however, I suspect is the infant's omnipotent phantasy that the beauty and poetry of the breast are created through being filled with its faeces. Hence the lingering doubt that she does not deserve this prize, that she is really a fake, and the fear of being unmasked and humiliated.

So in the talking cat dream, she is the bottom that is the breast; in the Wordsworth dream she is just the bottom that fills it. A little later comes a dream in which she is nearer to accepting herself as the greedy baby who empties the breast.

This dream followed upon her moving into a bedsitting room of her own. She prefaced it by saying that she had introduced an electric fire of her own which had too strong a current so that it blew all the fuses in the house. She then had a dream about being burned alive. In this dream, *Rosamund was with her godmother and her godmother's two little girls, waiting to be burned alive, taking it all very calmly but thinking it was really rather careless of her godmother to allow the children to see such an unsuitable event. Then it seemed that she had been burned and was reappearing as a ghost to tell the godmother that it was not so bad after all and did not really hurt.* "My old omnipotence", she interposed—"indestructible me". Later on she recalled that all she seemed to know about being burned was the flesh flying away from her face.

She was sure that this dream was connected with her anorexia in some very particular way but could not say how. Then I said that I thought that once again we were dealing with some confusion between top and bottom and that her description of the flesh flying from the face could be referring to something like diarrhoea. She responded immediately, saying that she knew that she had had enteritis very badly as a baby, could not remember whether it followed upon weaning or her brother's birth some nine months later. So this seems to be the connection.

One could then see the electric fire that was too powerful for the system as the passion and greed of the baby for the warmth and life of the breast which it fears it has finally shattered at weaning. Later in the dream as the little ghost that she was after the enteritis, and again became with the anorexia, she is identified with the burnt-out breast, but quite all right and reassuring (god/ good) mother with her little children who represent the breast at a part-object level.

This would indicate that she had felt the weaning and the birth of her little brother as a humiliation, the consequence of being too greedy and destructive a baby. To escape from that humili- ation she had then slipped into being one of the breasts, into a kind of twin sister relationship with a mother whom she reassured and with whom she then combined to be another little mummy for the next baby. This dream heralded a period in the analysis of increasingly greedy infantile demands which expressed themselves in longing for food and little girl hunger for attention. Cream buns for instance appeared in her dreams as infinitely desirable, but unsafe to eat lest she could not get to the toilet in time. At weekends she tried whenever she could to make the long journey home, and was tiresomely exacting as never before in her life. Then, worryingly, compulsive eating was followed by compulsive vomiting for a period of two or three months: a period when she also consistently forgot her dreams. Her ladylike aplomb wore very thin. She appeared more like an infant alternately gobbling and then spitefully rejecting the food as vomit or diarrhoea. Gradually however, she began to want to remember her dreams as well as to try to eat more sensibly and to recognize her more envious spiteful impulses in grudging the breast the satisfaction of feeding her if she could not feel that it was totally in her possession. For instance, she would remember a snatch of a dream about going back to school where she was starting to enjoy herself but then at once had to hide this in case the teachers should see and feel pleased. Then followed two dreams that marked the beginning of a period when she started to build up again both physically and in her social relationships. In the first one, she simply dreamt about *the forscythia branches in my consulting room but could not remember whether they had bloomed or were dead.* The dream following this was of *a plump orphan with a cross face like Bernadette Devlin whom her father went to fetch back from a cemetery. He was bringing her back from the dead to go to school, and rescuing her from her unfortunate habit of going off to heaven every nine days on her own.*

This Bernadette Devlin seems to represent the rebellious anti-government, anti-parent explosive diarrhoea-making part of herself which repeatedly says no ("nein"). It idealizes being alone in the cemetery as heaven, is confused about death and life and needs in analysis a father to bring her back to learn about it. Interpretations of this dream that were roughly on these lines she did not like at the time. She came back however the next day with another dream which she had not been able to forget, although she had tried in her sleep to do so because it had apparently wiped out another very nice dream which she had wanted to continue. The dream she could not forget was as follows: *She was in my family although I was not there, and moreover she seemed to be an intimate friend. My husband was there, tall and fair (like her father) with a lovely cuddly baby. He told her that his wife was not a good wife at all but that she, Rosamund, was wonderful with children—the baby was really happy with her. "Not at all", said Rosamund modestly, "anyone would love this child"; and she thought to herself that the wife must be a hard person not to love a child who was so nice and cuddly.*

Before I was able to say anything at all about this dream she hastily interposed that she knew there was no point in eating because she was just going to vomit it all up again.

In this dream she has come more openly into contact with her competitiveness with the mother/analyst for the baby/patient, as well as with her desire to spoil the parental relationship. The important thing at this point is that she has remembered the dream and brought it even though she does not like it. From then onwards she began gradually to hold down her food as well as to stomach better these more unpalatable parts of herself. Very gradually she began to resume eating, to return to a more social life, and was able to go to university and enjoy her time there.

Case 2: Gerald[3]

I shall now give some material from the much longer analysis of an adolescent boy, Gerald, who first started with me when he was twelve years old at a time when he was still encased in strongly obsessional latency defences. He had been referred for depression and flatness of affect and a tendency to severe bronchial conditions. He was appreciated by his teachers; in short a "good" boy of whom any family or school would be proud, but unable to enjoy the appreciation he received.

In the early stages of his analysis he communicated mainly through drawings and paintings that were extremely colourful and beautiful and into them seemed to go all the life and emotion that was missing in his relationship with me, although he helpfully co-operated in my attempt to understand what he was expressing by answering questions and producing associations. We came to realize that his preoccupation with these elaborate productions was holding up the analytic work, that he would withhold thoughts that occurred to him until he had finished the particular part of the picture upon which he was engaged at the time. He then agreed to try the couch and began to speak much more freely, bringing increasing numbers of dreams with many associations.

He continued with the same meticulous cooperation, politely listening and responding to what I said, yet I was often left after a session with the baffled feeling that it had been much less interesting than it should have been. Dreams and associations that were fascinating and rich in content, full of eminently analysable material somehow failed to lead to development in the sessions. We came to realize that his responses were being carefully edited and were much less spontaneous than they seemed, and were being regarded by him as much more important than anything which I said to him. His productions and most especially his dreams were being regarded as his painting had been: as works of art to satisfy and to keep me happy. The interpretations which I made were not allowed to affect him at the time, although he noted them and could make

---

3 This patient is discussed in more detail (as Malcolm) in Chapter 9.

use of them to understand his material in later sessions without remembering where they came from. Gradually he became more aware that he was missing something that he could get from his sessions as from his life generally; that his parents were willing and able to offer more than he was able to accept; and said of himself (quoting Edith Sitwell) that "I was always a little outside life".

As in the analysis, the latency defences which kept him outside life—i.e. somewhat cut off from his emotions and his internal objects—were loosened; he began to come into contact with a violent ruthless part of himself which formerly had been split off and projected into his younger brother. A hitherto more distant attitude to this brother became one of head-on collision. Then he began to realize in his analysis how this violence was directed towards transference aspects of the father who interrupted his sole possession of mother, and that they were experienced more and more strikingly in relation to weekends and holidays. Also around this time, before his fifteenth birthday, he began to take a closer interest in girls himself instead of being content to watch from a distance with passive voyeurism the vicissitudes of his friends in the sexual field.

The following dream indicated the violent way in which he burst into puberty. He brought it on a Friday following a day on which, quite unusually, he had had to wait for a few minutes in the waiting room for his session. He had not admitted to feeling annoyed at having to wait, but the session was characterized by a subliminal irritation and frustration. On the Friday he arrived preoccupied and filled with foreboding about a party he was giving that weekend—the first to be held at his house. He was wondering how he could deal with possible gatecrashers, recalling the experience of friends who had had their parties invaded, their parents' furniture smashed, crockery broken and carpets stained. In response to interpretations about intrusions into the analytic weekend (the parental intercourse) of destructive unwanted fragments of himself, he said that he had realized the day before on leaving the session that he had been irritable and unhelpful and bent on stopping anything taking place. Following the session he had had a terrible dream as follows: *He was at a party in a drawing room sitting on a sofa talking to a pretty fair-haired girl, having a civilized conversation until an older man came up to join them. Immediately he was seized with an ungovernable urge to have sexual intercourse with the girl and rushed out of the room to find a contraceptive. When he returned the scene had changed utterly. There was no-one left in the room; it was bare of furnishing and the walls were a dirty cream colour, plaster and paper peeling. He found himself strutting up and down the ruined empty place in jack-boots like a Nazi, but the worst thing of all was that he didn't care a bit.* When he woke up he felt shaken to the core.

In the course of working on this dream he gave a wealth of associations which connected it with my consulting room, the session of the day before, and his parents' bedroom in the home of his early childhood. The drawing room of the dream had started off looking like the consulting room but had ended up like the parental bedroom in a dilapidated state with its rose-patterned cream wallpaper hanging down in ribbons. As he left my room the day before he had noticed some paint falling off by the radiator, and had thought that expressed perfectly the bittiness of the session he had just had. The man who interrupted him with the pretty girl was connected with someone he had seen coming to my house when he had been looking out of the waiting room window—my husband, he presumed. In response to query he confirmed that he had had a nocturnal emission the night of the dream, expressed in the rushing out of the room. Also rummaging in his parents' chest of drawers for a handkerchief he had come across a packet of contraceptives, which brought home to him that they still did have intercourse and were not yet past it as he, in his adolescent arrogance, was inclined to assume.

So it seemed that the idealized civilized conversation which he had been having with a girlfriend-mother in his analytic sessions had been rudely interrupted when he had had to wait the day before, by the thought of the husband-father. This had resulted in an explosive expulsion of destructive sexual feeling which he could not admit (or possible even be aware of) during the Thursday session, but which was enacted in the nocturnal emission and communicated in the dream which he remembered and brought to his Friday session.

This violent part of himself is something essentially put down below, as yet unintegrated, awakened by his sexuality and feared as unknown. It has been expressed only occasionally during the latency period: on the rugger field, or in occasional fights with his brother. During the analytic sessions it has been discernible only in very subtle ways: in a certain arrogance in his demeanour, in slightly biting sarcastic remarks. It now began to appear more frequently in dreams, and then burst out in an intensely possessive way a little later in his first steady relationship with a girl, which literally devoured most of his time and seriously endangered his studies.

This first relationship with a girlfriend had a passive clinging leech-like quality, infantile in origin, the continuation of the very special exclusive relationship to his mother which was used to protect himself from the violent sexual jealousy that erupted in the Nazi dream. It was a parasitic quality which contributed to his feeling disposed to remain indefinitely in analysis, although from another point of view he did work well and made considerable progress in the work, as in his life outside.

I shall now discuss some dreams which he had had when he was nearly eighteen and preparing to stop analysis and go to university—looking forward to this, but clinging tenaciously to avoid change. Gerald said that in a dream *I was telling him that at last some particular interpretation had got through to him.* The implication was that other kinds did not. He then said that as he was retelling this dream to me he had the impression that he was making me responsible for interpretations working, rather than taking that responsibility himself. The interpretation which had affected him was about the way in which he was using his mouth as an anus, and it threw some light on another dream which he had had earlier that same night. *This was a science fiction type of dream in which there was a crisis like the end of the world. The whole family was gathered by the sea watching something that looked like a huge rubber bladder getting bigger and bigger till it exploded. Everyone tried to escape from the dreadful substance that came from it and kept spreading. He felt that this was some negation of his responsibility for a mad faecal breast, but in the dream his father appeared to be organizing an escape for everyone.*

The dream reminded him of long ago when as a small child with his father before his younger brother was born, he was fishing for tadpoles and found something in a black shiny shell, which on smashing was soft as a mollusc. He never found out what it was, and had often wondered what it was doing there in the pond, just hanging around waiting for something to happen. As he told me about this he said it was making him think uncomfortably of the way in which he still continued to place the onus on me to get through to him, without making a great effort to understand. He would notice himself just silently waiting, and the very silence was being converted into something faecal. It hid an attempt to worm his way in to get benefit from the sessions without being fully committed or feeling at all dependent.

This is a preparation-for-weaning dream, a dream about an incipient younger brother whose birth is confused with his own and with his anticipated but resisted birth from the analysis. It is a representation of that aspect of himself that feels it has wormed its way into the mother, into analysis, and hangs on waiting for something to happen. One can see how the end of the analysis, birth, weaning, birth of the younger brother, are catastrophic events from which he now looks for help from his father.

In the next dream both parents come to his help. He came to his session saying that he was feeling annoyed with himself for feeling obliged to struggle to think about what he was doing and feeling over the weekend, instead of just indulging himself and forgetting all about the analysis: he dreamt about a girl who was reading Shakespeare and was overcome with a desire to have intercourse with her, but thought that this was a bad thing and so looked over her shoulder at the play she was reading. It was *A Midsummer Night's Dream*. He recognized the words but they didn't make sense. He wanted to tear it from her, and just at the point where he felt he could not control himself any longer his parents came in. He jumped out of bed immensely relieved.

He associated the impulse to tear the book out of her hands with a phantasy of pulling my electric light switch out of its plug at the end of the Friday session to leave me in darkness. He was aware of a strong and childish desire in his school work to point out to me how clever he was. He knew that he was envious of anyone who might produce better work than he, and was aware of being curious about my daughter's prowess which he had heard about through the adolescent grapevine. He had noticed that people were influenced by their family background, and the implication was that hers was a fairly privileged one like his own and he was wondering how well she managed to use it, by comparison with the use he was making of his.

The dream and its associations indicate the progress he has made towards a more consistent awareness and a greater degree of responsibility for himself than he had a year ago, resentful though he may be about the need to go on struggling. The girl whom he associates with my daughter may be seen as representing the mother, as a sister at a diminished part-object level, and the book at this level as father's penis which is feeding her with information, drama, poetry, thereby evoking his curiosity, greed and desire. He tries to get into this from behind, projecting himself into the intercourse through anal masturbation. But significantly, in this way he gets the form of the words only, not the meaning: the equivalent of faeces, not babies; i.e. the masturbatory intrusion does not help him to understand the nature of the parental relationship. He knows theoretically, but he cannot experience it as poetry and life. In his frustration and envy that such a relationship should be taking place, whose meaning is denied to him, he tried to pull this Shakespeare penis out as he was tempted to pull the light plug out to leave me in darkness. The appearance of the two parents rescues him from committing rape (the significance of his masturbation).

When we were working on this dream he asked me irritably why two parents—as if he were especially infantile or especially dangerous in needing them both. He knew very well by this time that the fundamental struggle in his growing up was about allowing the parents to be together internally, was about appreciating them as whole and separate people. That they have been internalized more as whole objects allowed to be together and therefore to come to his aid to rescue him from his perverse criminal impulses, is evidenced by their appearance in the dream. At that time he was relieved; on his way to the session and in the session he grudged or was humiliated by his dependence on them. It was as if confronted by me externally after the weekend as a parental couple he was thrown back briefly to more primitive part-object relationships again: to the paranoid-schizoid position driven by impulses to plug in and be carried as the leech-like baby, to give up the struggle towards separateness and responsibility although he now has more established internal objects to help him towards this.

I shall give one more selection of material from this final phase of Gerald's analysis in which he was having to continue to struggle with this primitive violence and possessiveness towards his primary object, following the progressive and thorough de-idealization of his infantile omnipotence.

He began a session by saying that he was feeling bad about his lack of interest in the new car his father was about to buy. He imagined that his father would probably prefer to have a smaller racing car, but as he had to consider the needs of the family he would have to compromise on speed in order to get one with a body that would accommodate all the children and their friends. His father's consideration for the family made him feel depressed when he considered his own egocentricity. In some part of himself he remained absolutely convinced that as his analyst I functioned only when he was there. As we elaborated upon this on familiar lines that he still clung to the idea of a mother who had no room for father's penis or for other babies, he burst out that he felt more depressed than ever about plugging in and letting me do all the work. It spoiled the sessions. While I was talking he had been looking around the room, thinking that my flowers annoyed him, reminding him of the painting of a child, very simple, very bright. They reminded him of hospitals, and his thoughts went to visiting his mother in hospital when she was ill or perhaps after the birth of a baby. All he could remember was his annoyance when he had realized at that time that she was more interested in seeing father than seeing him. It had been a real blow to his feelings of importance and his eagerness to see her.

When we returned to his pity for father at not having mother as a vehicle all to himself, he broke in to the effect that he did realize this was a projection, that he didn't need me to go over it all again, and apologized for talking in such a boring way, saying "If I don't grumble a little it'll go bad inside me." He said he had had a dream, thought that he knew what it meant and that he should not have to tell me, but perhaps should do so, repetitious though it might be. It was about *the Germans bombing the island of Crete*. He supposed Crete did mean "excrete" and that this was another defaecating dream. He followed this with an outburst of heartfelt appreciation: "You can't think how grateful I am to you for listening to this rubbish. No-one else would bother to do so and nobody would realize how important it is to me."

So what was being worked on in this session was his awareness of his infantile possessiveness and the violence of his attempt to project this into father's penis, crediting him with an adolescent/infantile sexuality which would use the woman's body as an exclusive high-speed vehicle to "get there first". For some time he had been valuing his dreams more as keys to helping him to understand his internal situation than as works of art to divert or impress. Those simple red tulips which irritated him so, carried undertones of his former childish use of paintings, idealized products at which Mummy's eyes were meant to brighten and her lips to praise the prowess of her little boy—a cherished illusion vanishing.

There is also now a much more genuine spontaneous appreciation of the analyst in the receptive role of the mother, of the maternal reverie (Bion, 1962) that receives the projections but is not choked by the rubbish (as he still sometimes feels choked by his "inarticulate" rage), and that helps him to articulate, sort out and think about it; that tries to gather together and hold all the pieces he excretes until they can be evaluated.

Discussion

In the case of Rosamund the disappointment after her first serious love affair plunged her back to conflicts about weaning and the birth of her younger brother, evaded at the time. Analysis revealed the central role of projective identification in her pseudo-maturity: a projection via the anus into the breast (Meltzer, 1965) with resultant confusion between breasts and buttocks. This was an attempt to maintain a mutually idealizing relationshp and to avoid experiencing envy towards a breast with a nipple. At another level this was a defence against envy of the relationship between father's penis and mother's vagina: the creative link between the parental couple.

She had dealt with the mother/father/baby triad by projecting herself into each one, creating a kind of "holy family". Later on when she went to school she had dealt with her baby homesick-ness for mother by identifying with the talkative father or brother and entertaining the family of girls—she became her rival objects. Her charm and genuine kindness and goodness of temperament undoubtedly evoked responses that helped her to maintain the idealization of herself and to continue to evade grappling with the emotions which she split off by omnipotently taking possession of her objects.

Thus she deeply suspected that she was a fake. The severity of her reaction to disappointment in love was not only due to betrayal of trust (she had a trusting nature and had had every reason to feel trust in her world) but to the evocation of unpleasant unfamil-iar feelings of greed and possessiveness with which she had little practice in grappling. Defences that had served her well in infancy due to her parents' love, and at school because of the friends she won by her beauty, intelligence and kindness, were inadequate in adolescence.

The relatively short period of analysis seems to give her the opportunity—which in one sense she deeply welcomed even though it came as a shock—to examine the false grounds on which her self-idealization was based, and to establish a little better the primary relationship from which her good qualities could be exercised with a stronger belief in their authenticity.

Gerald also illustrates the explosive reactivation of pregenital conflicts by the emergence at puberty of strong sexual desires. As with Rosamund, defences that enabled him to be a success in latency—in his case prolonged latency—crumbled in adolescence. He was a boy of more complicated envious disposition than Rosamund. In latency this had produced a flattening of affect which took some of the life out of his personality. Behind his ambition was a weighty and penetrating intellect which he could use to talk about himself in his analysis with considerable subtlety, and a dexterity that would often enable him to pre-empt being taken by surprise and experiencing the feelings he was describing. His analysis proceeded more slowly and less dramatically than Rosamund's because in him the idealization of his own products was more deeply rooted, and linked with a more tenacious negativism and resistance to being helped. He was less easily taken by surprise by his nastiness, less easily repentant, but more deeply introspective and persistent.

So here in brief are some aspects of the analysis of two adolescents who were prevented from enjoying the richness of their endowment owing to an element of spuriousness, springing from a self-idealization which had very likely been colluded in to some extent by parents who were naturally delighted to have children of such quality. The mutual idealization was used as a bulwark against infantile violence and destructiveness which, uncontained and split off, yet gave intimations of their presence and did not allow the young people to feel that they deserved to enjoy the opportunities and gifts which they had. Not until the analytic work effected some shift from the idealization of their own easy products (basically faecal) to some truer recognition of life received from the breast and from the parents in infancy (who could then be allowed internally the freedom to be together and separate) could they proceed more hopefully in the adolescent world towards a more adult attitude to sexuality.

CHAPTER EIGHT

The paranoid-schizoid and depressive positions[1]
(1974)

Donald Meltzer

T he subject I have been asked to talk about today is for many the most central of the psychoanalytic developments linked with the name of Melanie Klein. As with all psychoanalytic concepts it seems to me that, to understand their significance, we have to put them in the context of their history. And studying the history of Mrs Klein's ideas is different from studying that of Freud, owing to the fact that Freud is both a clinician and a theoretician, whilst Mrs Klein is almost exclusively a clinician who describes far more than she theorizes.

The evolution of Freud's thought is like a country that underwent two revolutions: the first being the fall of the theory of hysteria, and the second being the overthrow of the theory of the libido in the 1920's and its substitution by the structural theory. The work of Melanie Klein on the other hand has grown in a way more analogous to the peaceful transformation that is characteristic of English political institutions. It seems to me that Melanie Klein,

---

[1] A talk given in Novara in 1974, published in *Quaderni di Psicoterapia Infantile* (1975), edited by C. Brutti and F. Scotti, pp. 125-41. Translated by Adrian Williams.

not having a particularly theoretical mentality, did not particularly take account of the changes that were taking place in her use of terminology, and the theoretical implications that she was putting forward.

First I shall describe a way of viewing the conceptual changes that lay behind the formulation of the paranoid-schizoid and depressive positions, and then I shall link these to the problem of how to deal with adolescence as a period marked by specific points of change: first the transition from latency to puberty, then the transition from puberty to adolescence, and finally the transition from adolescence to adulthood. Let me underline some theoretical elements that help us to understand these transitions, and then describe the clinical implications of a move from the paranoid-schizoid to the depressive position, after which we can discuss technical problems occurring in your clinical work.

Melanie Klein entered psychoanalytic practice in 1919-1920 just at the time when Freud was starting to change the libido theory into what would later become the structural theory of psychoanalysis. It is important to try to see how the work of these two people links up and also how it is different. The fundamental difference is that Freud's approach was essentially a way of understanding psychopathology, and reconstructed infancy in retrospect; whilst Melanie Klein's approach originated in her interest in the development of babies, and then investigated the connection between this and the psychopathology of adult life. The reconstruction of infancy made by Freud lacks something which actual babies in their relation to the world could demonstrate in flesh and blood. The work of Melanie Klein on the other hand makes too little distinction between evolutionary conflicts and pathological processes.

When Mrs Klein started work in the 1920's, as we know, she began by observing the development of babies and then gradually adapted the psychoanalytic method to the treatment of children. At that time, in terms of theory, she was working primarily with Freud's ideas as modified by Abraham. These included the progression of the erogenous zones, and the pregenital organization and then genital organization of the libido; and at this time pregenital also meant pre-oedipal. At this time Freud or more particularly Abraham retained the idea that the oedipus complex only started in the genital phase of the evolution of the libido. Thus the first contribution of Melanie Klein to analysis falls into two categories: the first (for many the most important) was her discovery that babies are much preoccupied with internal spaces of the body, particularly of the mother and of themselves. Freud never conceptualized this. The second (as a result of babies' interest in these spaces) was the new concreteness given to the concepts of introjection and projection that Freud had already described. Melanie Klein was thus able to delineate the phenomena that she called the "early Oedipus complex". This was different from Freud's view not only in its description of a stage earlier than the development of partial objects, but also because it gave a greater psychic reality to internal objects than either Freud or Abraham had been able to fully conceptualize.

In the course of this Mrs Klein noted the sadism of babies, which gave her the impression that these phenomena began in the earliest stages of infancy, and she started to use the term "position" for the first time. At first she used it in a variety of ways. She mentions a depressive position, an obsessive position, a maniacal position, a paranoid position. By the last she seems to refer to the anxieties connected with sadism and specifically organization of defences against these anxieties. At this stage in her thinking the term "position" is used almost exclusively in a descriptive sense, and is applied to almost any type of anxiety and defence related to the two periods of intense sadism of early infancy: oral-sadistic and anal-sadistic. In 1930, writing on manic-depressive states, Klein started to use the term in a more specific way, and in the two papers on manic and depressive states (Klein 1935, 1940), she used the term "position" in a way that linked with Freud's theory of fixation points, to describe certain states as points of fixation peculiar to schizophrenia and manic depression.

In this period (the 1930's) she was talking of three positions: paranoid, depressive, and manic; and I think that at this time she maintained explicitly that in these respects the mental state of babies is fundamentally the same as that of adults. This one can say is the psychopathological phase of the use of the term "position". Klein talked of babies who "overcome" the position in a way analogous to the way Freud talks of "working through". She tended to talk as though babies suffer from illness equivalent to schizophrenia, mania and depression, and was criticized for having concluded that babies suffer from mental illness. By the time she wrote "Notes on some schizoid mechanisms" in 1946, her use of the term "position" was becoming restricted to "paranoid position" and "depressive position". Gradually she started to join paranoid with schizoid, differentiating it thereby from Fairbairn's concepts. Refining her picture of the emotional qualities of these positions, she became less exclusively preoccupied with sadism and its consequences and came instead to refer to love for the primary object in order to distinguish the states of mind which are preoccupied with the good health and survival of the object, not only of the baby.

So she began to describe the central nucleus of the depressive position in terms of "pining"—a feeling of loneliness, mourning, regret, and awareness of separation. This seems to me to be a very important turning point in her thinking: added to the idea of love in the depressive position as centring on the object rather than the self. Such a change brought to psychoanalysis a vision of love which has no place in Freud's theories, which were from the beginning based on the idea of gratification of the libido.

Later Klein hypothesized that love might triumph over the narcissistic impoverished libido, consequently benefiting the ego. So while the first use of "position" was an evolutionary one linked to the idea of defence, and the second use was linked essentially to psychopathology and the concept of fixation, the use of the term in the1940's and thereafter placed such concepts in the a field that one might call "economic".

But this also changes completely the meaning of the economic concept in metapsychology. For Freud, an economic concept was about quantitative aspects of the distribution of the libido and its vicissitudes. Its roots lay in his neurophysiological model of the mind and in the idea of quantities of excitement. One of the revolutionary elements one finds in Freud is his determination to establish a mental science free from moralistic prejudgements; and in his efforts to avoid assigning a particular weltanschauung to psychoanalysis one might say he proceeded in a manner that was non-moralistic to the point of being cynical. This is not to say that in his clinical work he was cynical or amoral; in studying his clinical cases, in particular the Rat Man, it is evident that his work is completely free from cynicism. Notwithstanding this, right to the end of his life—even after the new theory of the life and death instincts—he tended to try to integrate psychoanalytic thinking with biology in a way that might eliminate any philosophical standpoint or almost any idea of values.

It seems to me that the initial work of Melanie Klein faithfully follows this pattern: in her description of sadism in babies there is not the slightest trace of moral preoccupation. The baby's pain is seen as deriving exclusively from the feeling of persecution; the conflict between love and hate is related almost exclusively to the wellbeing and happiness of the baby; and the child that is exercising his sadistic impulses (in reality or in imagination) suffers from persecutory anxieties. In Klein's original idea of the depressive position, he seeks to escape these feelings of persecution by making "restitution" as she called it. This meant essentially to give back what he had stolen and put together what he had broken. Gradually "restitution" turned into "reparation"; and reparation meant repairing the damage in order to avoid persecutory anxiety.

In the second phase of her use of the term "position"—the psychopathology phase—Klein uses "reparation" in a way which makes it indistinguishable from that which she afterwards called "manic reparation". She specified that this manic reparation is motivated essentially by omnipotence.

In the third phase of the use of the "positions", beginning with writings on mourning and continuing with those on schizoid mechanisms, there is a slow and gradual change. By the time of *Envy and Gratitude* (1957) and "On loneliness" (1963) the entire approach has changed. The paranoid-schizoid and depressive positions start to lose their evolutionary specificity. She no longer describes them as something which occurs at the third month of life and resolves around the time of weaning, but starts to consider them as a type of mental conflict which has its origin around the third month but continues for the entire life of the individual.

The depressive position therefore is no longer described as something which is to be overcome, but something which is entered into. The movement between paranoid-schizoid and depressive positions begins to be seen as a continuous oscillation in the sense later delineated sharply by Dr Bion as Ps<->D. The concept of love is modified to mean that concern for the wellbeing of the object, predominates over concern for the comfort of the self.

I have said this is an economic concept, but a qualitative one. This does not in my view replace the quantitative economic concepts described by Freud, but is in addition to them. If one takes the economic concepts and tries to put them in meaningful order, one would put it like this: the most primitive economic concept is the repetition compulsion; this is the main economic principle of the Id, that knows nothing other than the repetition of previous experience and past activity, directly connected with physiological processes. The pleasure principle modified by the reality principle is the main economic principle used by the ego in its attempt to govern relations with the Id, as distinct from the external world. This is, one could say, purely narcissistic, in the sense of Freud's "primary narcissism".

But the paranoid-schizoid and the depressive position are the main economic principles of relations with the object. The paranoid-schizoid position is a value system in which the health, security and pleasure of the self dominate, whilst the depressive position is a value system in which the health, security and happiness of the object prevail. So in the later work of Mrs Klein the paranoid-schizoid and depressive positions have no special tie to evolutionary phases of development, nor any specific tie to pathological configurations; they are of general economic reference to all developmental phases and all psychopathological configurations. The concept of reparation also takes on a new significance, not as something that the baby is able to do actively, but as something which he permits to happen by restraining his destructive impulses. Reparation comes to be the precise opposite of destructive impulses and is connected very directly with the concept of integration.

In her paper of 1946 on schizoid mechanisms, Melanie Klein describes the two principal techniques by means of which disintegration comes about—through splitting processes, and through projective identification. These are truly named "schizoid" mechanisms, and are the means by which the paranoid-schizoid position comes to be built. Reparation may be considered the principal depressive mechanism and in many ways the neutralization of schizoid mechanisms. Thus that which has been split in schizoid mechanisms is reunited, and that which has been projected through projective identification is taken back inside.

These are the active components of the depressive position and are accompanied by depressive pains of various types: they form a spectrum that extends from feelings of regret, remorse, guilt at one end, to feelings of loneliness, depression, and pain at separation, at the other. She came to hypothesize that the self, when it becomes capable of playing its part in reparation, puts back together that which has been split inside itself, and recovers parts that had been projected outside, suffering feelings of depression because of the damage it had done; whilst at the same time, owing to the feeling of loneliness, it now experiences the objects as separate from the self and this triggers a reciprocal reparation. This situation in which the self reunites split parts and suffers depressive pain, while the parental figures are separate from the self and united in a reparative sexual rapport, is opposed to the paranoid-schizoid conception of the primal scene in which the self intrudes into the parents' sexual union and stimulates a state of excitement, envy and jealousy in which schizoid mechanisms are operative.

With this conception of the paranoid-schizoid and depressive positions as the main economic principles that regulate and one might say direct the developmental processes, one can from the clinical point of view examine almost any developmental crisis in terms of transitions and oscillations between paranoid-schizoid and depressive positions. This is the meaning of Bion's little diagram Ps<->D with the double arrows. And it is from this point of view that we wish to examine the processes of transition that they illuminate between puberty, adolescence and adult life.

Before going on I will highlight some points of delicate equilibrium between the paranoid-schizoid and the depressive positions. One concerns the use of the term "guilt". Guilt as it appears in depressive anxiety is rather more serious than regret or remorse, and probably involves the fear of having caused irreparable damage to the object. Guilt brought to light clinically in the analytic situation tends to be seen as persecutory guilt, and links with Freud's concept of the cruelty of the superego that results from quantities of aggressive impulse generated by the self. Klein has described this in more detail from the structural point of view. The cruel superego that produces persecutory guilt may derive from three sources: the first being splitting and idealization of the object into idealized object and persecutory object.

The second source of persecutory guilt is projective identification of the bad parts of the self into the object, maybe then recombining the bad part of the object with the bad part of the self. The third source derives from the damaged object: the object seen as damaged in an irreparable way by the sado-masturbatory attack. Gradually the work of Melanie Klein was developing, and reached its most evolved form in the *Narrative of a Child Analysis* (1961) and in *Envy and Gratitude* (1957). This last category of persecutory guilt, felt as having caused irreparable damage of the object, seems in her clinical descriptions to centre itself ever more closely on the killing of the babies inside the mother [*see Chapter 14*].

The other point of delicate balance in the relation between the paranoid-schizoid and the depressive positions concerns the concept of reparation. Of the four types of reparation, two seem to lend themselves to the description "false". One type is described very clearly by Melanie Klein as "manic reparation" in which omnipotence is used to try to reverse the damage done to the objects. The second is another type of false reparation, connected with what Mrs Klein initially called "restitution"; it is insincere, like stealing a bottle of wine, drinking it and handing back the empty bottle.[2]

---

2 Tape missing here. Meltzer's view of other types of reparation, and how they specifically relate to the transitions of adolescence, can only be deduced.

Discussion

Dr Nissim: In the depressive position one finds heroic qualities. While Kant asks us to consider man as an end not as a means, and the Gospel asks us to consider others as ourselves, Mrs Klein asks us to consider others as more than ourselves.

Dr Meltzer: It may be very interesting to trace the origins of the concept of love as we have come to mean it today and which has so much importance in adolescence. The modern concept of heterosexual love seems to derive from the 12th Century concept of courtly love, a heroic concept of love which comes close to masochistic submission. The "romantic agony" of the Romantic period is also masochistic. But emerging from it later is a conception of love between adults that is impregnated with parental responsibility. This found expression in Melanie Klein's theory of the combined object, of which she gives a lovely description in *Narrative of a Child Analysis*. In this, the parents' sexual relations come to be considered as something directly linked with reparation of the mother's babies—both those inside the mother, not yet born, and those already born. In my book *Sexual States of Mind* I was advancing the hypothesis that the foundation of adult sexuality consists in the introjective identification with the combined object. A new concept of adult sexuality emerges that directly correlates with the concept of work: work to repair the damage, and work to nourish the mother's babies. We always forget this but it seems evident to me that work is something very pleasurable. One of Mrs Klein's primary discoveries is very relevant here: the discovery that for the baby the body of the mother is equivalent to the world for the adult, whose view of the world is derived from this infantile rapport with the mother's body.

Dr Di Chiara: I should like to make two observations. The first is the movement between the paranoid-schizoid and depressive positions seems very important for all aspects of human culture where processes of projective identification are involved, and I should like to know the mechanism that oversees this movement from Ps to D. In one of his books Dr Meltzer has said we are dealing with a miracle. So I should like to ask Dr Meltzer if he still believes that Freud remains a catalyst in a period of history in which, with two world wars at the beginning of the century, humanity seems to have renounced its parental responsibilities.

Dr Meltzer: We are dealing with a very important question here. Firstly, in every analysis our best chance of studying this oscillation between Ps and D is the place that I have called the "threshold of the depressive position". This is the most difficult moment in any analysis, when there is a crisis in the quality of the collaboration of which the patient is capable. This crisis helps us to better define a concept that Freud cites from time to time but which has not found a proper place in psychoanalytic thought: namely, the concept of introspection. A person has fully entered the depressive position only when he is able to recognize by means of introspection how much this process has cost his objects—not how much it would appear, but how much he actually feels to be the cost. This recognition implies that egocentricity has been overcome and converted into introspection. Different tensions are involved: the person becomes preoccupied not with sensations but with phantasies and motivation. When one has succeeded in bringing a patient to this threshold, where he can be handed over responsibility for his own feelings, motivation and phantasies, then he is ready to start the work of self-analysis.

Replying to the second part of the question, I should say the two most important facts resulting from the two world wars are: the concentration camps in Germany and Russia, and the dropping of the atomic bomb. These crazy events become more comprehensible if we think of the Kleinian theory of the inside of the mother full of babies. The essence of the depressive position consists in being able to worry about envious attacks on the babies.

I should like now to talk about the clinical application of these concepts. I have described the paranoid-schizoid and depressive positions as "economic" concepts, which determine the developmental process and the transition of the individual from one stage to another. Freud and Abraham, especially in "The libido theory" (Abraham, 1924), gave us a theory of development based on the different phases of the libido in relation to the erogenous zones.

This developmental pattern has proved itself very useful in study-ing the formation of psychopathology, permitting psychoanalysts to draw up a scale of primitive disturbances from schizophrenia to hysteria. This psychiatric approach does not however help us to deal with the phenomena that we meet in our work with psy-choanalytic patients as described in my book *The Psychoanalytical Process*. Here I consider the psychoanalytic process itself from a different point of view: that is, as a sequence of developmental problems whose complexity correlates with the growing complex-ity of the organization of the mental apparatus. The moments of crisis and the crucial points of development become manifest here in confusions of every type, and the economic principles of the paranoid-schizoid and depressive positions regulate the quantita-tive and qualitative elements that are occurring at the time.

These confusions possess their own internal logic, which is specifically linked to the development of complex structures start-ing from more simple structures. The order of development is something like this: in the beginning is Klein's observation of the splitting and idealization that permits a differentiation (perhaps somewhat exaggerated) between good and bad. After this comes a confusion between self and object—and in my book I hold that the major intereference in the process of development is the mechanism of projective identification. Next there comes what I call "zonal confusion" between the different areas of the body, the different parts of the body of the object, and the functional rapport between them. This point of crisis corresponds in fact to the oedipus complex described by Freud, and it is the problem of the combined object: it derives from the primitive relationship of breast and nipple when understood as a "combined object". And then, there is the problem of differentiating the infantile from the adult part, and the problem of introjective identification with the combined object.

In the light of this sequence of confusions I would like now to examine the development from latency to adulthood, bearing in mind above all these problems of differentiation between good and bad, between self and object, between the zones; the prob-lems of the Oedipus complex and the formation of the combined object; and finally the problem of the differentiation of the adult part from the infantile part of the personality.

As I have described in *The Psychoanalytical Process*, the development of analysis—like that of the individual in normal life—is not linear. It is more like a spiral in which the entire spectrum from good to bad, from adult to infantile, repeats continually and cyclically the gradual evolution of the mental apparatus. I should like to return for a moment to the nature of latency. According to Freud latency followed the Oedipus complex as a result of the internalization of the imagined parents and the definitive formation of the superego. According to Klein on the other hand the formation of the superego happens in a much more gradual way at a part-object level. The period of latency is thus not something that completes a phase of development; it is more like a defence constellation that produces a developmental arrest, a period of waiting that allows the child to relax its intense oedipal interest in the parents, and to go out into the external world and start to socialize and learn scholastically.

According to Klein there are particular defences in latency that silence the oedipus complex for some while, without actually resolving its obsessional mechanisms. Reading her first works it is not always easy to understand what she meant by "obsessional mechanisms". It became clearer from around 1930 especially with the paper on manic-depressive states (Klein, 1935). Obsessional mechanisms are founded essentially on two operations: omnipotent control of the objects, and the separation of the parental objects in order to prevent the sexual union responsible for the violent feelings and conflicts of the Oedipus complex. The latency period enables psychic reality to be neglected in favour of interest in the external world. In consequence one sees a slowing up or reduction of emotionality and also therefore of imagination. It follows that the concept of good and bad—produced after the primitive splitting and idealization of self and object—takes on a certain rigidity, with a moralistic and legalistic flavouring. The latency organization of the personality presumably permits the child to be away from home without feeling overwhelmed by loneliness, jealous suspicion, and the sense of persecution. It permits him to interest himself in the world in a sufficiently obsessive way, manifest in the hunger for information and the desire to acquire skills of various types.

Whether or not this has biological roots in Freud's sense of repeating the glacial era in the development of the individual, or whether it is perhaps derived from cultural pressures via the influence of the parents who wish to prepare the child for school, is a problem we will leave for anthropological research. I believe the second theory and think that latency may be encouraged by parental pressure. Whatever the origin of latency, there is no doubt that its destruction by puberty is a biological process, directly linked with the emergence of sexual forces and desires. If we have the opportunity to observe clinically a child making the transition from latency to puberty we see how the burst of excitement in the transference absolutely breaks to pieces these obsessional mechanisms.

In puberty it seems the organization of the personality that had been built up during the first ten or eleven years of life suddenly reveals itself to be very fragile, falls to pieces and has to be newly constructed, intensifying the obsessional mechanisms. Thus in the transition from latency to puberty we can see a continuous oscillation in behaviour between that of a turbulent child and of a self-contained adult, in close sequence.

When this disintegration occurs, at puberty, it reactivates infantile confusions in an atmosphere very different of that from early infancy. First of all there is the difference caused by rapid growth, and the changes happening in the body. Secondly there is the change in the child's environment in which new space and liberty opens up to him. Thirdly there starts to emerge a community of children marked out from that of small children and of parents. The community of adolescents starts to emerge. It is in this context of the pubertal community, and even more of the adolescent community, that teenagers start to experience the major part of their emotional lives. One has the impression that in this phase of development processes of intense disintegration are repeated, typical of the paranoid-schizoid position, which from the point of view of dynamics link to the time just after weaning. Entry into the pubertal or adolescent community, the withdrawal of emotional ties from the community of parents and young children, may be directly linked to a phase of development in which the baby at the breast becomes simply one of the babies in the family.

This is the context then in which we can view the case that Mrs Harris will now present [*Chapter 9*]. It illustrates the first area of confusion, that occurs with the destruction of the differentiation between good and bad in self and objects.

CHAPTER NINE

Depression and the depressive position in an adolescent boy[1]
(1965; 1974)

Martha Harris

The clinical material in this paper will be centred around a dream, reported by a boy of fifteen and a half years after some three and a half years of analysis. In its context the dream, which was an important and vivid experience for him, typically conveys, I think, the picture of a patient struggling against those aspects of himself that perpetuate depression and inanition. He struggles to be able to face the conflict of ambivalence and the guilt it entails, and to maintain the depressive position—i.e. a state of integration, of responsibility for the conflicting emotions and parts of himself in relation to valued objects.

I am assuming that pathological depression ensues from an inability to face pain and to work through the depressive anxiety occasioned by some experience of loss or disappointment. This inability then leads to failure to rehabilitate the lost object or the object which has betrayed one, within the personality. In the

---

1 First published in the *Journal of Child Psychotherapy* (1965), vol. 1(3), pp. 33-40; part of a paper jointly written with Dora Lush. The second part of this chapter is a discussion of the same case as it was presented at a seminar in Novara in 1974. The patient (Malcolm) is the same as Gerald in Chapter 7.

course of treatment, early anxieties about loss and defences against experiencing these, come to be relived in the transference relationship at every break, and in the case of patients who are seen four or five times a week, at every weekend. The material which I would like to discuss in detail was stimulated by a forthcoming holiday.

[*Some of Malcolm's background history is omitted here since it has been given in Chapter 7—the case of Gerald—and there are further details in the seminar section below, pp. 128-29*].

Malcolm became more aware of his own subliminal depression as it began to thaw, as the world outside his narcissistic preoccupations seemed a warmer and more exciting place. As in the analysis I became more of a person and less of a repository, he began to feel badly about his boringness, his lack of generosity in giving himself. He said he now realized what a help analysis could be if he could only learn how to keep contact with me. When a more enjoyable working/feeding relationship with me had been established, it was soon again attacked and destroyed in order to avoid oedipal jealousy, which was stimulated by any signs of my private life or other professional commitments, and recurrently by breaks in the analysis. In earlier stages, his adolescent self had usually managed to split off any experience of infantile jealousy of the parental intercourse by maintaining that his parents, like myself, were now passé and dull, whereas all the glamour of life was before him. As he became more aware of—and therefore more able to contain—his infantile jealousy and attacks upon me as the parental couple, his psychosomatic symptoms resulting from the intrusion of objects attacked and damaged by his projections diminished. He became worried at realizing his dependence on the analysis. As he was learning more, he became afraid that if he had to stop, all the benefit he had received would disappear. At weekends he became depressed and resentful about this reluctant dependence (as he once put it), feeling that he was so small and I was so important. His infantile resentment which, when projected, created paranoid fear of me as a self-important father who kept mother and her breasts for himself, recurrently interfered with a learning/feeding relationship with me as the mother in the sessions.

After some months of working on this, he became much more confident that he was able to keep inside himself as a permanent possession what he had learned about himself from analysis. He thought he should stop shortly. He felt badly about being such an expense to his parents; also, no doubt, I had other patients waiting for me.

A little investigation revealed the unconscious hypocrisy in this apparently reparative urge, deflected as it was from the object to which it should primarily have been directed—from myself as the analyst, the breast that had fed him, to whom gratitude and reparation were due. His improvement was seized upon by an omnipotent part of himself which wanted to make off with it to enjoy it on its own.

The dream gives us some information about this part of himself. He dreamed it shortly before a holiday which he was facing with mixed feelings. He was depressed about the break from analysis, but he also wanted to use it as an occasion to test out his progress, to see whether he could engage upon some fruitful enterprise with his friends. He said he was aware that his parents were allowing him freedom. They were not insisting that he should go with them and do what they did, but inwardly he did not feel free to choose.

He came to the Thursday session saying that he had had a vivid dream the night before. It remained as a bad taste in his mouth but he hesitated to tell me in case he was just trying to get rid of it all. It was a long dream: *He was going to a farm with Rhoda to buy a barn or a building. The farm belonged to a man who was terribly hard-up; and rather horrible, perhaps a madman. This man told them about a scheme he had for getting more money to make his fortune. This was to do with injecting stuff into girls to give them bigger busts, and he was anxious to know how he could advertise this. He asked Malcolm if any of the girls he went out with would be interested in the idea. Malcolm was going to say that all the girls he knew were well-developed. He thought that the idea was disgusting and unsafe, and he told the man that the hormone pills which were used for this were unsafe, so his idea must be even more dangerous. Rhoda was very taken aback by the man and withdrew. Malcolm went with her to protect her. The man suddenly became wild and rushed down his little hill shouting "Everything I can see is mine!". Malcolm thought this was terribly pathetic—he had so little, just a measly few fields and a small hill. He went away with Rhoda leaving him to his poverty. Later on however, the man followed them to town with a cartload of old coats to sell.*

Rhoda is a young married friend of his mother's and of the family in general. She had frequently appeared in the analysis as a somewhat idealized version of his mother and myself, but a really good person, the kind of girl whom he would like to marry.

Malcolm's first association to this dream was that the crazy man was distinct and familiar; he could not say exactly who he was like. As he elaborated his descriptions, it was clearly that of Malcolm himself, but with a sallow jaundiced complexion. He described the few fields in the dream as somewhat sickly looking too, muddy and waterlogged. The little hill on which the man was sitting was muddy too.

I suggested to him that his initial hesitation in telling me the dream was due to anxiety lest it came from the crazy man—the mad part of himself which maintained that by injecting me with its flatus it was thereby filling my breasts. By blowing it all into me he would get rid of the bad taste in his mouth caused by awareness of this crazy part and the food it poisoned. He said that in the dream he had enormously resented this man's implication that girls needed to have their breasts made bigger; they were all right as they were. Agreeing to my interpretation that this man was a part of himself, Malcolm said that he seemed to be timeless, to have no regard for time, as if this were some aspect of himself that had been with him always and would never change.

Malcolm himself in the dream had felt that the things this man was satisfied with—that he called "all mine"—were so basically bad because they were puffed up to be more than they were. It seemed absurd that he was not repairing his barn and cultivating his fields which were really a potential source of wealth, instead of indulging in this crazy scheme of expanding breasts. There was such a distinct division between the crazy man and himself with his friend that he felt it was no wonder the man was so furious and susceptible to being got rid of, because he must feel so isolated, although when he ran down the hill he seemed to be going to a wife in the valley. She was not an active person or helpful but someone just like himself and content to do as he did. Malcolm himself—the "I" in the dream as he said—knew the difference between good and bad but he was too weak to do anything about it; he did not know how to talk to the crazy man who did have the power and the ability to improve his poverty if he could only see it for what it was. There was no-one to tell him; his wife was as blind as he was.

This madman is the most complete delineation we have had in the analysis so far of a homosexual part of himself that attempts to acquire power and wealth by omnipotently entering and controlling the breasts with his own flatus and using them as sexually enticing objects. It operates in his relations with girls, where the girls are sometimes evaluated as desirable in so far as they increase his status with other boys. Similarly in his analysis, he has in the past often collected sessions and interpretations to puff up secretly into works of his own designing in order to enlarge his self-importance. Malcolm indicates that it is madness to use the breasts thus, as masturbatory objects into which to enter to void his sexual envy and jealousy, thereby making them unpalatable to a saner baby part of himself which needs to feed from them and to develop: to really learn from his analysis. This baby part is represented in the dream by the pregnancy of Rhoda, the mother whom he protects from the dangerous seducer. It is his omnipotent infantile masturbatory self which has a wife in the bottom of the valley, which seeks comfort from its own bottom when frustrated. Thus in his analysis he has often sat upon my interpretations, made them his own, playing with them and cogitating on them privately, while withholding from me his spontaneous reactions, which could have enabled me to feed him with subtler understanding.

This masturbatory part is without insight and difficult to talk to because it is cut off from the Malcolm who knows the difference between good and bad. It becomes wild when it feels rejected and isolated but he cannot finally get rid of it. It follows him with a cartload of old coats—the worn-out objects that have been used to clothe its projections, the recipients of its masturbation, and with which it persists in trying to eke out a living for itself. It is nevertheless a part of him which has strength and potential real wealth if the strength can be employed in reparation—in rebuilding the barns and planting the fields. Malcolm said that he knew in the dream that the barn and buildings had to be restored first before the fields could be dug and planted: that is, that the internal containing breast-mother who has been damaged by masturbation must be restored before he has a secure basis for genital potency. But the problem is to bring the Malcolm with insight into contact with the real strength which is obscured by the omnipotence. In his analysis, reparation can be consolidated and omnipotence diminished by acknowledgement of what he does learn from me and by recognition that it is harmful and unnecessary to blow it up into something bigger than life.

When the dream had been interpreted in these terms, Malcolm said that on further thought, when the madman said "All that I can see is mine", he was really implying that his possessions were restricted by his vision. If he could only see more he could have more. This reminded him of the previous weekend, when at a party he had a long talk with a friend's father who is a great opponent of psychoanalysis. Malcolm had been telling this man how much he himself had benefited from analysis. He thought he was making quite an impression on him, but later he was terribly hurt to over hear him passing derogatory remarks about both himself and psychoanalysis. He now realized that he must have been behaving in a smugly superior way, like the man on his little hill, smug about himself and his possessions, without realizing how much he was antagonizing his friend's father. He thought it must be this disguised superiority, rather than shyness, that prevents him at times from getting on too easily with people. He agreed to my suggestion that this was a way of evoking envy in others, by flaunting his possession of esoteric knowledge, or symbolically, the idealized analytic breast which he had appropriated in order to avoid experiencing envy in himself at having to leave it behind with me at the weekend, for me to share with my party—my husband and children.

Some time later in the session he said that the ramshackle buildings on the farm had not in fact been sordid—that they were lighter and warmer inside than outside. He had noticed this when he stood inside them at one point. I took this as yet another indication (we had had many others before this) that he felt there were reserves of warmth and understanding inside himself, a lifegiving breast at the core of his being, which could not yet be fully utilized because his omnipotent self-importance was impeding the work of reparation.

Discussion

This brief but richly condensed material of Malcolm's throws some light on the forces that cause and perpetuate his depression. He had said he knew his mother was a good mother, but something came between them, i.e. he realized he had a good object although he could not always reach it. He saw that his young brother could appreciate his mother. He knew from the occasions when the appreciative baby part of himself was able to accept the understanding I could offer him that there was a good analytic breast available when it could be approached in the right way. The madman in the dream is the destructive part of himself which threatens his good object (Rhoda representing the mother), depriving the baby part of himself that needs to be fed from an uncontaminated breast.

This madman can also be seen as a father who holds domain over mother, who spoils the breast for Malcolm by injecting poisonous sexuality, and who is a threat to the maturer protecting relationship which he tries to have with women. The madman is not the real father whom Malcolm currently experiences as encouraging him to enjoy his friends and to have a life of his own, and whom he now visualizes as having an interesting and worthwhile relationship with his mother. It is a lofty archaic superego figure, formed from his own projections, in alliance with his id (the wife in the valley) and equally out of touch with his ego.

Malcolm himself, his ego, is in between. He tries in the dream to recover something from this possessive crushing superego, but is defeated. [The feeling of superiority which, together with that of inferiority, Abraham noted as characteristic of melancholics, is clearly illustrated in Malcolm's dream.][2] On former occasions when for instance I seemed so big to him and he so small, this superego had been projected into me in the transference—had made him feel persecuted by me so that he had to go away, to retreat from contact. In this session he was however, able to ally himself with me as a support to his ego and to acknowledge the crazy superego as part of himself. He was also able to link it with his superior behaviour, an idealizing and possessive way of using the analysis, which does disservice both to himself and to his good object, apparently puffing it up to be so marvellous, but in fact sitting on it as the man does on his muddy little hill—the pot full of faeces. [The narcissistic over-valuation of his own products exists alongside a more normal object-oriented self (Rosenfeld, 1964).]

On the other hand, we have seen that this superego controls potentially valuable objects—Malcolm goes to the farmer to buy a barn, and this barn though ramshackle has light and warmth inside. He needs the co-operation of the farmer, this controlling paternal superego, to recover good life-giving parts of himself which through projection remain unavailable to him, in order to have a rehabilitated internal object as a basis for developing, making a happy marriage and a home for himself and his future family. (Rhoda, if you remember, was looking for a house). His ego needs to recover the power of the aggression which is encapsulated in the superego, reintrojected there after it has been split off and projected into the father's penis. Without that power he remains relatively impotent though not entirely, because he does protect Rhoda. His superego, deprived of insight, is grandiose, restrictive, and liable to degenerate into a blind expression of id impulses—the rushing downhill. (The games field had hitherto provided for him one of the few constructive channels for the expression of this violent instinctual force. This was however to a large extent an expression of a split-off part of himself, rather than an insightful experience of this part of his nature. The fear of this force caused inhibition in other spheres, as for example in his relationship with girls.)

---

[2] Phrases in square brackets are extracts from the original conclusion to the paper, which is omittted here since it relates also to Dora Lush's case study.

I would suggest that it is the crushing weight of this blind omnipotent superior superego which is causing the weakening, the depressing, and the general impoverishment of his personality [the severe superego mentioned by so many analysts from Freud onwards]. Formed by the projection into the father's penis of an envious omnipotent part of himself which is felt to be threatening to his primary good object, the breast mother, it thereby creates for him an internal mother who is constantly menaced by a bad intercourse. In identification with the oppressed and denigrated internal mother, the passive wife in the valley, he is depressed and impotent; he is also depressed about his inability to make full use of himself, of his potential strength which becomes unavailable through projection and encapsulation within this superior paternal part of himself. In the dream, however, and in the working-through of the dream, Malcolm is making an effort to integrate this destructive and powerful figure as a part of himself, although he does not like to swallow it—it leaves a bad taste in his mouth. In trying to take responsibility for it and for the harm it has caused and to use it in the service of repairing his good objects, to further the analysis, he is attempting to use depressive anxieties in a creative way. He attempts to maintain and work through the depressive position as fully as possible. That this must be a gradual process one can see from Malcolm's statement that this mad part is timeless, has always been with him, and from his fear that it will never change.

There were in his earlier history certain situations of actual deprivation and loss which were, however, well within the ordinary range of children's experiences [see below, p. 128]. His family circumstances and relationships are more than averagely good, and to a great extent he has been able to benefit from them and to develop on favourable lines, as he has always been able to benefit from his analysis to a certain degree. He cannot, however, fully realize the richness of his personality and of his creative capacity until he is able to consolidate insight into this mad and destructive part of himself, and the devious ways in which it expresses itself— how it interferes with good relationships with people outside and with his internal objects. By this interference it recurrently brings about experiences of loss.

Malcolm may be right that there is an unalterable core to this aspect of himself. If, however, he can accept this as belonging to himself—remember that the man in the dream became so wild because he was so isolated—if his saner self can learn how to talk to his mad part, to direct it better, to limit its distortion of good objects, then he will have a lesser load of unconscious guilt to carry, be less identified with destroyed objects, and therefore less incapacitated by depression.

Seminar discussion: the transition from latency[3]

Mrs Harris: Malcolm is a boy who had a rather long latency period. He was the second of four children—the oldest boy, with a sister four years older, and two brothers two and four years younger than him. His father worked in the field of medical research and his mother was an amateur painter of some talent. He was breastfed for a very long time and apparently went through the various typical stages of infancy with no particular problelms. However, a short time after the birth of his youngest brother, Malcolm's mother became ill and remained in precarious health for a number of years. From this point Malcolm developed chronic bronchial problems. His parents noticed he became easily tearful and tended to give up easily when confronted with the slightest difficulty. This initially was the reason for his being sent to a psychotherapist. This therapy was broken off during its first year as his psychotherapist left the country. Malcolm's mother was then taken into hospital where she remained for six months during which he saw her on only a few occasions. After this his parents noticed a definite flattening of affects in him and believed he was suffering from depression. He was extremely accident prone, and was a sickly child, and though he did well at school, his parents felt that his development had a very fragile basis and it was at the expense of true emotionality.

---

3 The remainder of this chapter is translated from *Quaderni di Psicoterapia Infantile* (1975) no. 1, edited by Carlo Brutti and Francesco Scotti, pp. 142-52. Parts of the history are omitted for purposes of this book as they have already been given in this chapter or in Chapter 7. Translated by Consuelo Hackney.

This was why, at the age of eleven, he began the analysis which was then suddenly interrupted by the death of the analyst.

Although when he came to me Malcolm was twelve and a half years old—an age when a boy is generally expected to enter puberty—and although he was physically well developed, so that his appearance was that of an adolescent, his behaviour during sessions was that of a child who was still frozen behind the obsessive defences of the latency period. [...] I found it very difficult to determine to what degree his depression and emotional indifference were related to the death of his previous analyst. When he first came to me he said in a few words that his first psychotherapist had left, his previous analyst had died, and that if something were to happen to me he might just as well give up analysis. My impression was that his prolonged latency and the protraction of his obsessive defences were connected with the losses he had suffered. [...] His formal co-operation was good. But as time went on I began to have the feeling that he was acquiring knowledge *about* the analysis, rather than becoming involved in a real emotional process. Although he rarely seemed to be emotionally affected by my interpretations—in fact he kept them at a distance—he would use them in later sessions to understand himself, often without remembering the provenance of these ideas. [...]

As an awareness of certain heartless aspects of his nature began to surface—split off into his younger brother—the up to then distant relationship with this brother turned into one of violent collision. This became somewhat less violent when he began to become aware, during the analysis, that his violence was directed against me—and also feared in as much as it came from aspects of me, who in the transference seemed to represent his father. Such feelings of violence were always experienced more strongly at weekends or during the holidays, and he began to realize that he greatly feared his father—to his considerable surprise as his adult judgment could not explain this fact.

At around the time when Malcolm was becoming aware of these things he began to show the first signs of interest in girls. I then felt that I had a pubertal adolescent in analysis rather than a polite and intelligent latency child.

Dr Meltzer: I wanted to say a few words on what we have heard so far. What I wanted to point out in this boy is not only the obsessive defences by means of which everything was kept constant and unchanging, but the omnipotence and megalomania concealed in his artistic activity, which had the significance of a manic reparation, intended not only to cure his ill mother but also to recreate the dead analyst and the one who had gone away, in order to recreate some primitive period idealized as having been happy, which fundamentally must have been the period prior to the birth of his younger brother.

Mrs Harris: This is certainly true. I can tell you about a dream from the following period in his analysis which gives an indication of the violence of the feelings which exploded in him at the time of his brother's birth.

[*Omitted here is an account of the "Nazi" dream which occurred after the patient had had to wait a few minutes before his session; see above, pp. 95-96.*]

I felt that this dream showed very clearly how the omnipotent masturbatory sexuality led to a sort of catastrophic deterioration of his inner world, formed through identification with the body of his mother and represented by the living room which was transformed into a deserted, ruined room. Everything deteriorates as a result of the attack on the mother, on the father inside the mother and on the children inside the mother; he is outside the parental couple. He is dominated and at the same time identified with an omnipotent and destructive part of himself

Dr Meltzer: I would first like to draw attention to the period of a few minutes spent waiting which can be connected to latency as a waiting period which had been prolonged, in this boy, by the rigidity of his obsessive defences. We have also clearly pointed out the explosive way in which his sexuality then burst through. This is also displayed in his fear that uninvited guests might gatecrash his party, destroying the property, stealing things and so on.

I would also like to underline the pre-genital impotence attributed to micturition and defaecation which is discernible in his paintings and in his recollection of himself sitting on the lavatory in the act of feeding children and young animals, and how this contrasts with the destructive attacks that make the room turn entirely brown, dirty and yellow. This may also have some connection with external events such as the mother's kidney disease and fact that the previous analyst had drowned.

Now, the central feature in his development at this point is the destruction of his splitting and idealization, which had been very serious. What can be seen in this dream is the collapse of a very serious split between an idealized good boy and this evil Nazi part, so that in a flash his sense of identity can pass from one to the other, precisely as a result of this collapse of the splitting.

Mrs Harris: I think it is appropriate to tell you about some material from the analysis of this young lad from about two years later, when he was beginning to be more advanced in his depressive position and began to be interested in girls. When telling me about his sexual relations with his current girlfriend he said he had had the impression that he had been "about to eat her". These were his exact words, which gave me the feeling that he was reliving a total, infantile and very primitive, possession of the breast. But at the same time I think that, while he devoured her it was also clear that he was manically curing her of her illness. In fact, as emerged gradually during the analysis, she was a seriously disturbed young woman. So I think this situation of his was a kind of further acting-out, with this girl, regarding an illness which he still projected onto me in analysis. and his mother's illness for which he felt omnipotently responsible. After this and one or two more dreams he made efforts to detach himself from this girl without hurting her too much, as he had begun to become aware of how far he was from being able to engage in a responsible adult sexual relationship. He then began to have a bit more understanding and respect for the part his father had played in holding the family together.

[*Omitted here is an account of the "Germans bombing Crete" dream and its association with his father's new car; see above, p. 101.*]

Dr Marzani: In dealing with adolescents I have increasing difficulty in working out when it should be possible to terminate the analysis. That is to say, in understanding when these beginnings of the process of repair and reintegration are sufficiently consolidated in the child to allow the treatment to be stopped or interrupted in the event of the family, or the child himself, requesting this for genuine motives. I think that it is generally easier to understand when to terminate the treatment of an adult. In Mrs Harris's case, for example, I would like to know if she is still treating this boy and what stage she has reached with his treatment.

Dr Meltzer: I think that, with adolescents, the problem of stopping analysis is one which is often solved for us by the adolescents themselves, in the sense that he or she makes the decision of when they want to stop. Sometimes this can come about for incidental reasons such as the adolescent leaving university or because the family is moving away. However, I think it is typical of a successful analysis of adolescents, that when they manage to establish an intimate loving and sexual relationship, it protects them from interferences. I think this is partly due to a form of respect for the sexual partner, because often the other person in a loving relationship tends to consider the presence of the analyst in the background as something intrusive and therefore resents it. Mrs Harris's patient stopped treatment when he left to go to university. He had also fallen in love for the first time then I believe. ("No, that was a little later", corrects Mrs Harris.) On the other hand I have noted that when an adolescent in analysis does not want to interrupt the treatment, he or she manages to choose a university that does not oblige him to do so. This is in fact what happened in the case that I shortly want to discuss [*Chapter 10*].

CHAPTER TEN

From puberty to adolescence[1]
(1974)

Donald Meltzer

T his afternoon I would like to move on to the second phase: the transition from puberty to adolescence, which is usually characterized by the beginning of sexual relations. The external manifestation of the passage to puberty is a social one; it is accompanied by an emotional separation from the family. One is no longer a child living in the family but a member of the pubertal group. Going back to the loss of distinction between good and bad, described in Mrs Harris's material, we can say that the pubertal group is really of a tribal type. The two tribes are principally the boys' tribe and the girls' tribe, engaged in a battle of the sexes, making incursions of a tribal nature against each other and returning with trophies which are the pride of the tribe. The dream presented by Mrs Harris in which Malcolm found himself in the ruins of his room while he walked up and down like a Nazi [*pp. 95-96*] clearly describes the spirit of this tribe. Its sexual aspect is an

---

[1] Presented at a seminar in Novara (following material in the last chapter). Published in *Quaderni di Psicoterapia Infantile* (1975) no. 1, edited by C. Brutti and F. Scotti, pp. 152-65. Translated by Consuelo Hackney.

essentially sadomasochistic process and it is essentially homosexual in spirit.

But, outside this tribal life, couples begin to emerge; boys and girls who begin to be attracted to each other in an authentically heterosexual way. Then the pubescent group's tribal life begins to disintegrate into groups of adolescents forming couples amongst whom there is a continuous exchange of partners. It seems to me that it is precisely in this gathering together of sexuality, which is tribal in the first instance and social in the second, that the defence against depression resides. At this time of life we witness a massive denial of psychic reality in favour of an interest in external relations in the adolescent world. It is in this context, where there are groups of adolescent couples, exchanges of partners and a certain amount of going round in circles, that confusion of zones and identities and the development of the Oedipus complex can occur. Part of the denial of psychic reality which accompanies this sexuality is a denial that sexuality should have anything to do with having babies. This is due to masturbation being directly replaced by sexual activities which have the significance of mutual masturbation. Malcolm's dream, which was accompanied by a nocturnal emission, was interpreted as the destruction of his internal object, represented by the room. This is fairly typical of the depressive low that follows an adolescent's masturbation and nocturnal emission. However, the adolescent learns that, if he socializes his sexuality in the company of other adolescents, the depression somehow evaporates through group activities. In a way the depression is felt as something that appertains to the adult world.

The adolescent has a view of the world which goes something like this: there is an adolescent world which is full of life, sexuality and pleasure, and it is surrounded by an adult world which is old, destroyed, envious and de-sexualized, and that observes their sexual activities and wants to stop them. This is an important aspect of the disdain that adolescents feel for everything old and that in their minds equates with depression.

This is how sexuality emerges in the adolescent world—as something surrounded by the depressed and destroyed adult world. And it is only when the zonal and identity confusions begin to be overcome, and the problems of jealousy and the Oedipus complex appear, that the adolescent begins to feel loving feelings towards his partner and to feel the weight of depression. The weight of depression is felt once again when sexuality begins to be reconnected with children, and there is a renewed recognition of psychic reality.

So this afternoon I would like to focus specifically on the formation of the adolescent community and the quality of the sexuality and states of mind that this involves. For this I will describe the story of a patient of mine who came to me for analysis as a child and then again during adolescence. This case demonstrates particularly clearly how the conflicts of the adolescent period represent a renewed version of the conflicts of the preceding period.

An adolescent girl

Dr Meltzer: This patient first came to me for analysis at the age of three and a half. Her behaviour, in collusion with her brother who was about eighteen months older, had become uncontrollable during her mother's third pregnancy. The siblings had begun an exuberant sexual relationship with each other in a manic atmosphere of total disobedience towards their parents. They would constantly be found in bed together or in the bath together. They wandered around naked and refused to eat or sleep. The brother was quite an aggressive, disturbed child and the parents tended to think that my little patient was something of a slave to him. However, she was a very intelligent and sensitive little girl of strong character and it seemed more likely that the two children were acting as equals or even possibly that the little girl might have held the upper hand.

At the start of the analysis the little girl was in a demonstrably manic phase, running around the room, taking her clothes off, laughing, constantly chattering and throwing objects around everywhere. Then she would collapse into depression, would fall asleep, and it would be hard to rouse her. When I interpreted this behaviour with reference to her brother, her mother's pregnancy and the worry that the baby might die, the manic behaviour gradually disappeared, at home the little girl began to detach herself from her brother and little by little the general situation changed. By the time the baby brother was born the little girl had begun to accept him quite well and the analytical situation seemed to have stabilized. The analysis continued for another two and a half years. Initially a fairly extreme transference situation had formed: the child seemed totally convinced that she was my wife, while I was a bad husband because I would not given her any babies. She did everything she could to take me to bed, to make babies with her playthings, seeking baby seeds hidden in every corner of the room, without success. Then she seemed to treat me as a father, calling me "Daddy snow man", a father who was sexually cold towards her. Joking, she would refer to "snowballs" (ie. to "Daddy-snowman-without testicles"), and her transference towards me and towards the room became very maternal in nature. She began to concern herself with searching for children and stealing them from her mother. When she failed in this she began to be very concerned about the penises inside her mother and tried to steal these internal penises so she could make her own babies. It was at this point that there was a frank explosion of sadism towards her mother, accompanied by the most cruel fantasies, serious persecutory anxieties and nightmares. Gradually this calmed down and there was a return of loving feelings towards me as a father. The analysis stopped and was followed by latency. She was seven years old and her development seemed to be proceeding satisfactorily: she was doing quite well at school and was well behaved at home, perhaps a little too quiet and depressed, and fairly detached from her brother. I decided, with no qualms, that it was possible to stop her analysis.

I did not see her again until she was sixteen. During the latency period she had been a good child, docile, obedient and helpful and usually quite attached to her mother—who in the meantime had had a fourth child—while she was rather detached from her father. Although she got on quite well at school, she was not considered particularly clever and she seemed to be growing up to be a pretty and kind, but not particularly happy, girl. She was easily hurt by criticism. She was not very keen to go out to see friends and seemed to have a kind of aversion towards modern things, preferring those that were out of fashion. However this attitude of hers had not been noticed very much as her family was going through a difficult time. Her parents were living like strangers in the same house and her mother had suffered some periods of quite serious depression. Her older brother continued to cause considerable concern, and in general the family lived a disturbed existence. When she was sixteen my patient began to have panic attacks at exam time; she was unable to study and came back to me for further analysis. She was still like a latency child. She did have friends but at school did not seem to really be part of any well defined pubertal group. Her interests were almost exclusively focused on past centuries or oriental countries. She could not bear money being spent on her, and tended to dress in a shabby and outdated style which made her look like a little nineteenth century orphan.

I was astonished to find that she remembered every detail of our previous analysis from when she was a child. During the first month of analysis it was possible to free her fairly quickly from her identification with her depressed mother. The girl bloomed again, her exam anxiety disappeared and she started to take on the aspect of a pubescent girl. She began to apply herself a lot to her studies, her social relationships at school changed and she joined a group called "the bad girls" at school. In reality, as it was a very strict school, the "bad girls" were not so bad at all: at least their actions were not, whatever they may have been in their fantasies or their dreams. In fact they were the nicest, most talented and cleverest girls.

Now some delinquent elements began to appear in her dreams. In her dreams she smoked hashish, she had become a prostitute, took part in bank robberies and so forth. During the day she was part of this group of girls, who were the naughtiest in the school but also the cleverest, the ones who worked hardest and had the best results. At that time she knew that she still had a year of school to go before she went to university and that, if she wanted to continue the analysis, she would have to go to university either in London or in Oxford where I also work. Although only one year earlier she had been considered a mediocre student who would not have gone to university at all, to everyone's surprise, at the end of the following year, she won a place at Oxford. During the year she spent preparing for the Oxford entrance exam, there was an interesting development in the analytic process. A split in her feelings and in her intentions began to appear not only in her dreams but also gradually in her conscious daily life; on the one hand there was a resurgence of her love for me as a father, connected to the expectation that if she were to succeed in getting into Oxford I would really have married her, we would have lived together and had babies; on the other hand there was an attitude of disdain towards me and towards psychoanalysis due to the money I was making her pay. Psychoanalysis was bourgeois, while she was a member of the emerging revolutionary class; it was at this time that she started to get involved in delinquent activities. Her delinquency consisted mainly in staying out at all hours, smoking hashish, getting drunk, doing the very things that seemed to frighten Malcolm—that is to say gate-crashing parties, stealing, carrying out acts of vandalism, etc. My patient oscillated between these two attitudes which she kept completely isolated from each other in terms of the emotions connected with them.

As soon as she won her place at Oxford—which meant that she had nine months before she went up to the university—her attitude towards me hardened. Now she felt that I was directing her life, that I was controlling her in a tyrannical and possessive way, and therefore she decided to take back her freedom. Until then she had not had any sexual relationships and now she began to feel her virginity increasingly as a burden and a humiliation. She interrupted her analysis for a period of eight months during which she went to the Far East, partly for study reasons but partly in search of sexual relationships. In fact she had a lot of fun and slept with several men with whom, mysteriously, she did not have sex, and when she came back to London and went to Oxford and resumed her analysis with me, she had grown up a lot compared to eight months before.

When we resumed the analysis at Oxford she "limited" me to two sessions a week: this was as much as she would give of herself to me and it was partly a measure to control my craving for possession and partly to prevent my tyranny towards her. At that time she thought I was a bit in love with her, however without suffering unduly from it, so that I would have put up with being restricted to only two weekly sessions with her. It seemed I represented her not yet completely de-sexualized parents, who could still feel some small personal satisfaction and so could allow themselves to grant the adolescent a certain freedom. Having thus placed me in a state of semi-reparation, she could move on to a programme of manic reparation of a series of slightly disturbed boys. She met some at Oxford and made a good number of them happy during the following year and a half. It was interesting to see the type of boys she sought out and took to bed, because there was a progressive decline in quality until finally she fell in love with the most disturbed one that she could find. He was a very clever boy who had won an Oxford scholarship but once he had got to university, began to spend his days in bed. By the end of the first year this had been noticed and he was expelled. My patient continued her relationship with him, going to London every weekend in order to try and restore his mental health. It was then that she began to realize that this was a recreation of the relationship with her brother from the time when she first came for analysis. Although I interpreted it for her several times, she did not really take it on board until she took LSD with her boyfriend. During this experience she had a hallucination in which she and her boyfriend committed a continuous series of murders. This awareness allowed her to change her relationship with him and she fell into a deep depression.

Through this material I have tried to show you how the adult analysis was linked with the analysis of the child, especially during the period when the patient was at Oxford and had had some heterosexual experiences. Now her prevailing fantasy was that she was one of those women who are referred to in India as "temple prostitutes"—a prostitute dedicated to a Hindu temple, who had therapeutic sex with people who suffered from sexual perversions and who would be cured by her good sexuality. During this period—as much in her dreams as during her waking hours—her sexuality became exceedingly polymorphous and was represented by all possible sexual acts, all of which were considered good providing the penis was involved. Even though she paid not the slightest attention to the fact, the analytic material clearly demonstrated that this very good penis was a penis which had been taken from inside her mother by means of oral sadism. Moreover this period of analysis followed a period during which her parents seemed to have temporarily resolved their differences; they were happy to be together and the mother had had another child. So it was fairly clear that this was a period of manic reparation which corresponded to the period of maximum oral sadism of her childhood analysis, when she was always in fantasy stealing penises from inside her mother in every possible representation through her play. This made it possible to clarify the first relationship with her brother, confirming the suspicion that, far from being his slave, my patient had really seduced him and was keeping him under her control by stimulating him sexually.

Dr Nissim: Could the fact that adolescents ask to have few sessions (two in the case presented by Dr Meltzer) not be the main cause of the impossibility of reducing a massive acting-out? In other words, do you think it is possible to "contain" adolescents so as to avoid their having this need for such a frequent and often destructive acting-out?

Dr Meltzer: Firstly, any insistence on my part to have more sessions would have been received as a demonstration of my possessiveness, as an attempt to assert control. But there are two other factors which force the adolescent to act and which represent an important part of the analytical process with these patients. Firstly, they are driven towards acting-out by their confusion; secondly, they are part of an adolescent community where action is required in order to belong to the group. So I think that the analytical work at least limited the more dangerous aspects of her acting-out, the LSD for example.

[Participant]: I am thinking of your patient's tendency not to consider the present and to mainly refer back to things from the past, reliving them in rather an ascetic way, neglecting her appearance, and so on. This behaviour reminds me of an adolescent patient of mine who denies her present reality and continues to hide in the past; for example, at university she studies only ancient the feeling that her beauty, like the temple prostitute, was used in the service of her mother, the temple, is represented by the fact that in this way the brothers' and father's sexual potency is restored for the mother's benefit. Consequently, only when the girl had a hallucination under the influence of LSD, in which she committed a murder together with her boyfriend, was there a collapse of her manic defence and depression.

[**Participant**]: I would like Dr Meltzer to clarify the concept of confusion of the erogenous zones better, especially in the heterosexual behaviour of the adolescent understood as a defence and a denial of depression.

Dr Meltzer: As regards the zonal confusion, two main lines of this appeared during the clinical work. The first goes from the mouth to the vagina and the anus and also includes the problem of the eyes and ears as regards their receptivity. The second line of zonal confusion runs from the tongue to the nipple, the penis and the faeces and includes the eyes in their protective function. In particular, in as much as the nipple and penis are confused with faeces, there is also confusion between good and bad, and it is principally in relation to this confusion between good and bad— obtained by equating faeces with penis and penis with nipple— that it seems possible to construct defences against depression.

The typical sequence is therefore the following: the nipple is sadistically removed from the breast, introduced into the vagina like a penis and it is then transformed into faeces inside the rectum, and so sexuality becomes perverse. This zonal confusion can therefore be used to deny the perverse nature of the sexual relationship. And it is precisely this faecal penis that comes into the perverse fantasy of killing the babies inside the mother and also transforming these into faeces. For example, this was represented in the dream and the fantasy through which Mrs Harris's patient became conscious of the fact that, in reality, his omnipotent and creative urine served to mitigate his perverse Nazi fantasies against his mother, thus offering him a degree of relief. Just as Mrs Harris's patient used his urinary and defaecatory fantasies in a manic way, through his artistic work and his dreams, to repair and restore his ill mother, so my patient, in her temple prostitute fantasy, used her polymorphous sexuality as a manic reparation. So Malcolm's dream of marching up and down like a Nazi in a room which was in ruins, corresponds to my patient's LSD hallucination, in which she and her partner committed a murder.

[*Question about projective identification, unrecorded.*]

Dr Meltzer: This too is a historic problem. When Klein described projective identification for the first time, in 1946, she described it only as a schizoid mechanism. What I mean is that, at that time, she considered it as a mechanism with an exclusively pathological significance. Since then this point of view has changed in two ways: firstly that indicated by the material presented to you by Mrs Harris and which I have described as "toilet-breast": the use of the breast as a receptacle in order to unburden oneself. There is a second, more important, sense, which is the description that Bion gives of the functioning of projective identification in the normal care of a mother for her child. Bion thinks this is the basis of communication and considers that the fundamental action that underlies communication is the projection of a part of the self that is in a state of chaos and desperation and that is given back in a state of order and wellbeing.

Dr Nissim: I would like to ask Mrs Harris to talk to us about the great countertransference tension that follows the adolescent's massive projective identification.

Mrs Harris: I was just thinking about my countertransference with Malcolm. Early on, following a session during which I thought he had said some very interesting things, I had the sensation that it was something flat, stupid, boring, as though the process had been rubbish, something from which it was not possible to progress; and it was only when I felt that, in a certain sense, Malcolm was feeding me with idealized faeces, that I did everything I could to try to make these come alive, but without success.

Dr Meltzer: I too would like to say something about my counter-transference with my patient. During the time when she was at Oxford and had "limited me" to two sessions a week and would not allow me to interfere in her life, I found myself in the same situation as her parents when they had first brought her to me for analysis at the age of three and a half. And what I felt inside was history and cannot pass her exams in modern history. In terms of her participation in the group, she finds herself completely isolated; she refuses to take part in her peer group's community, and as for clothing and all those things that appeal to girls, she demands them from her parents but almost always in order to test their willingness to buy them for her, because as soon as she receives the things she doesn't know what to do with them and puts them away unused.

Dr Meltzer: Your patient's situation seems to be comparable to the case presented by Mrs Harris and in particular to Malcolm's dream in which the room takes on a terrible aspect when he "goes back". Your patient is in fact displaying an introjective identification with her mother in that state of destruction, which is a sign of depression.

Dr Gaburri: I would like to ask Dr Meltzer how he decides that the introjection of the penis occurs on a oral-sadistic rather than an anal-sadistic basis as one might suppose as a result of a number of observations, such as for example the way of dressing and other indications in the analytic material. In this respect, the association with the fantasy of the temple prostitute makes us think more of an introjection of the father's penis following an anal modality: the temple, God, and so on. What are the elements which made you use this type of interpretation in preference to the other?

Dr Meltzer: I refer to the nature of the zonal confusion. For this girl, anal, oral and vaginal relations were perfectly interchangeable at this stage. The point relating to the temple prostitute is that this has a relationship with the material we have just been talking about, that is with the identification with a destroyed mother: in fact it represents a projective fantasy about a repaired mother. In other words, the temple represents the mother who has been repaired and is full of babies again (in fact her mother was expecting another child). The boys with whom she had sex represented all the children inside her mother, all the children and the father's penis which was kept in a state of excitement, for the mother's benefit, by her own beauty and her own sexuality. The manic reparative element, referable in this fantasy to her beauty and to the experience of my impotence, which in my view corresponded to what she had felt when her mother was pregnant and she was distressed at the thought that the baby might die as a result of her envy and sadism. So it was only through my countertransference that I was able to understand that what drove her sexuality to that point was not only her adolescent desire but a terrible sense of impotence, of inability to keep a child alive inside herself. Now that she is in a state of depression she is inundated by this feeling of still being a child and of never being able to become a woman; she cannot imagine that her breasts might be something more than a sexual attraction, she thinks they will never produce milk, etc.

This is what we hope to have been able to say today about the problems that adolescents—who despair of ever becoming adults one day—have in really loving someone and really having children.

CHAPTER ELEVEN

Juan: a constant disappointment[1]
(1998)

Jesús Sánchez de Vega and Donald Meltzer

Therapist: Juan is a fifteen year old boy, strong and well developed for his age but his face has a childish air about it and his clothes and his appearance are rather unkempt. In the last academic year he was doing agricultural studies, which he failed; this year he wants to do mechanics at a different professional vocational training centre. I have been seeing him for the last ten months on Tuesdays and Thursdays, face to face. He refused to use the couch at the very beginning saying that it reminded him of assassinated Roman emperors. He is very fond of drawing so he asked me in the very first session if he could do that. We have pen and paper available but he hardly uses them now.

Tuesday session

As I open the door he has his back to it; he turns round suddenly and pretends to shoot me, as in a Western. He is smiling. He sits

---

[1] A supervision seminar with Donald Meltzer, Jesús Sánchez de Vega (therapist) and the Psychoanalytic Group of Barcelona, first published in Donald Meltzer and Martha Harris, *Adolescentes*, edited by Lucy Jachevasky and Carlos Tabbia (Buenos Aires: Spatia, 1998), pp. 247-67. Translated by Crispina Sanders.

down, gives an enormous yawn and says "It's hot in here". He gets up and opens the window. He starts to drum his fingers. There are more yawns, then he says in a soft voice: "I'm collecting my marks tomorrow". (He is referring to his exam results that will tell him whether he gets a place at the Technical College or not.)

> **Therapist**: First you wanted to get rid of me at the door, you came in shooting and now that you are here you feel uncomfortable, locked in, and opening the window makes you feel better.
> **Patient**: Yes… true, I am hot… (*he drums his fingers*) I was thinking about how I want things instantly and other people have to behave perfectly with me but I can do what I like. Is that being domineering?
> **T.**: What do you think?
> **P.**: Yes… (*he pulls faces, drums his fingers*) Paco is also like that and everything he wants to get … But what happens is that I am lazy, I don't do things.
> **T.**: And that is what makes you feel uncomfortable here, with me—
> **P.**: (*interrupting me*) What does?
> **T.**: That you are expecting me to pass you or fail you, to accept or reject you. Our set up-worries you: I will discover your secrets, you can't escape, and opening the window makes you feel better.
> **P.**: (*still drumming*) Blimey!
> **T.**: Yes?
> **P.**: I am just bored… (*he gets animated*) I was in the Corte Ingles today and I played a twelve-string guitar. (*He says this with pride.*)

> **T.**: This patient usually arrives with some time to spare and he goes to the music section of El Corte Ingles.

> **T.**: And by showing me what you can do you feel less uncomfortable here, showing me that you can play a twelve-string guitar and that it's there that you feel fine.
> **P.**: Yes, but I don't feel fine there either.
> **T.**: (*I make an enquiring gesture.*)
> **P.**: Because I can't do it.
> **T.**: You imagine yourself as a great musician but you are not really.
> **P.**: That's what I normally do when I switch off.

T.: I should explain that he didn't do well at school because he would switch off in class, he would look kind of absent and this created a considerable problem.

T.: When you switch into those fantasies about being able to do anything—
P.: (*interrupting me*) Yes, but it's a lie, castles in the air.
T.: Playing the guitar. Like when you masturbate.
P.: Blimey!
T.: To be able to feel good, not to need anybody, just you and your imagination.
P.: Excuse me! It's not as if I were at it all the time…! (*he laughs*)
T.: I mean that's when you feel triumphant, when you feel powerful.
P.: Yes… (*drumming to a beat; he yawns, lost in his own thoughts*) I have been composing the beginning of a song, but I haven't been able to write it. I like long songs, like the ones from the sixties, like symphonies. I would like to do a long one like Beethoven or Chopin but in rock style (*he hums and hits the table*) and with funny lyrics, changing from a serious subject to having a good time, so that people get in the mood and have a good time.
T.: You would like it to be like that here. Although you like my things, from the sixties probably, you would prefer to get me in the mood, to change me, to shape me in your fashion so we could have a good time, instead of the two of us being here, so serious—
P.: No—(*irritated*) you here and me there. Leave me alone.
T.: Me here, in my world where I take things seriously, and you over there. Does "over there" mean in your fantasies?
P.: In my house.
T.: So long as it is not here. You find it hard to come here and think, and it's a relief to escape, compose music and leave me. Me here and you there.
P.: No, me here and you there (*he laughs*).
T.: Changing places with me.
P.: Yes, I would like to feel all right, to say "I don't have any problems any more"; well, one always has problems but not so bad that you need help with knowing what you are doing and how to do things—with knowing what you want and what people want. (*His voice becomes more and more childish, false.*)

T.: You are acting like a little child now, moaning, making me take pity on you to get me on your side so that I'll love you, soothe you, console you…

P.: (*with determination*) No, not that.

T.: No, you don't need anybody to love you. You are self-sufficient. All you have to do is go into your fantasies…

P.: Into my realm, where I am the king of mambo. Is it bad to be the king of mambo?

T.: You said before that they were all lies, castles in the air.

P.: Yes, it's crap. It doesn't help one to work, to think; it doesn't help at all, it doesn't help to get on.

T.: It helps to avoid pain, to avoid having a bad time inside; but it is not useful in external practical life. And it seems that you want to learn that from me—a few hints that I haven't quite given you, so you are trying to convince me, to make me take pity—

P.: (*truly outraged*) Don't look at me with that air of a lamb to the slaughter.

Participant: Lamb to the slaughter means?

T.: Playing the victim.

T.: (*I felt quite lot of violence here*) You feel like hitting me. (*Juan laughs.*) You are telling me that you have problems, you are making me feel sorry for you; but it's me that you see with the pitiful expression on my face, like a lamb being taken to slaughter and you can't bear that. You won't allow yourself to feel pity about anything, to show that you are needy. You have to seem to be tough.

P.: (*he sighs, drums his fingers*) Yes (*in a childish voice*) but I am a lazy bones, I drag my belly on the ground.

T.: You are being a little child again, scratching your belly. But normally you appear much tougher and you just scratch your balls really. (*Juan laughs.*) And sometimes you come here pretending that you are dragging your belly, because if you are sincere with yourself you can see that you look like a lamb being taken to slaughter, worthy of pity, truly suffering, poor Juan…

P.: (*interrupts me, very annoyed*) Sod you! I don't like the thing about poor Juan. It doesn't sound good.

T.: Now you are being the tough guy. You don't like asking for help and if you do it is by pretending so that I think you are a good boy, but—

P.: I'll point my gun at you at the least provocation (*He laughs.*) Like I do with cats. (*He laughs as he plays conning a cat.*) Come here pussy, come… (*Long silence*).

T.: He kills cats.
D.M.: Really?
T.: Yes.

P.: (*He is drumming a beat and seeing that I'm looking at him, he says suddenly:*) That way I don't think.
T.: Thinking makes you uncomfortable—hitting, drumming your fingers, playing the twelve-string guitar; escaping is easier than thinking.
P.: It's just that sometimes things turn out right without thinking. Pepe used to say to me: "Always wear clean underwear because one day we'll go to see some women". I got fed up one day and I answered him: "You may take me to lots of places but in fact to none". It just came out like that (*he laughs, pleased with himself*) —without thinking. It was a way of saying to him that he was lying. (*Pepe is a man in a bar where Juan used to help out*). **T.:** You could say the same to me as you said to Pepe. It seems that you were expecting to have a good time with me; that I would teach you things about sex but I am disappointing you. And what's even worse I talk to you about thinking!
P.: (*funny gestures of disapproval towards me. Silence.*) have seen a video of American football. They hit one another pretty hard, you can see it. (*He explains with some humour the intricacies of the game and how you have to pass the ball.*)
T.: So you've found something funny to talk about…
P.: Yes, but it is no good either. (*Sad. In silence. Then he gets animated again*): I like playing with my friends on the beach but you have to watch out in the tackles because we are real brutes.
T.: It seems to you that that is happening here: you are trying to escape and you feel that I'm going to tackle you…
P.: (*laughing*) Yes.
T.: You escape so as not to feel some things about you that you don't like, worrying things, hurtful, annoying…
P.: Yes (*drumming his fingers*).Things have changed you know.

When I came here at the beginning I couldn't care less. I came, talked and nothing happened. But then I said: well, you could go there, tell him your problems and maybe you'll find a solution and you'll come out happier. But I just can't wait. (*He hits the table.*) I want things to get sorted now; I'm running out of patience. (*He's moaning, whimpering.*)

T.: Everything instantly, but have you come here to tell your problems?

P.: Well, some. (*Silence*) My secrets are no business of yours (*imitating a serious gesture but ending in a laugh*).

T.: You find it very hard to talk about some things.

P.: Yes, in my family I'm kind of the good boy, they feel sorry for me (*perverse laugh*), ha, ha—(*drumming his fingers*) I don't feel right inside myself either. I sort of look at myself and say: "Jesus, you are so ugly!" (*he laughs*). Sometimes I do like myself—but this hair, really, sometimes... But I'm not the kind of person to go to the barber's and say "Cut it like this and leave a bit more here" (*imitating the tone of voice of a contemptuous spoilt child*).

T.: Is that how you feel with me? You don't like the way you are but you find it hard to ask for help? To do that would be to feel like a spoilt child, like making people feel sorry for you, pity you and you find that ridiculous.

P.: (Silence. His drumming turns into hitting the table) Oh! I want to go into Vocational Training. I can't wait. But what if they don't let me in?

T.: You can't find a way to get into me. You try tricks but they don't work, nor does pretending to be a little boy, or even acting the tough guy. Pretending doesn't work... (Juan is worried and nervous. He hits the table for a good while) I ask him: Where were you now?

P.: Nowhere. Time is up, isn't it?

T.: You can't bear it anymore (*in a kind and sympathetic tone*).

P.: No. (*Silence.*)

(*End of session.*)

P.: (*He jokes as he leaves*): You have stolen two minutes from me. Thief!

Participant: Were there two minutes left?

T.: This is something that went on for quite a while, for several sessions; when he came late he would complain that I was stealing minutes from him because I normally finish the session on time, even if he arrives late.

D.M.: What does he do with the cats? Have you any idea?

T.: I don't think that is happening at the moment. At the beginning of the treatment he told me that he used to go with a friend to an abandoned jam factory where they set traps to catch cats and when they caught them they put them in a huge empty water tank and because the walls were so high the cats couldn't get out. Another thing he used to do was to go with a dog trained to kill cats.

D.M.: The point I want to clarify is: can you believe anything he tells you?

T.: I believe everything he tells me!

D.M.: The second question is: is there any reason to believe everything he says?

T.: In order to make him face his real world.

D.M.: Probably, in general, if a patient says to me: "Don't you believe me?" I answer that I don't either believe or not believe him; that I don't believe him because I don't see the point in believing him, as if he were in possession of the truth and were capable of transmitting it to me. I prefer a position in which we both accept that we are not in possession of the truth but we are looking for it. I prefer to investigate with him rather that believe what he tells me. This puts me in a position where I can distinguish when the patient is communicating something and when he is acting in the transference with the intention of doing something to me, making me feel something, think something, do something. What is implied here is that this boy does not know how to do anything, cannot do anything really. He says that he cannot do anything because he has not got the patience to wait for the results, the marks. The same thing seems to be happening in his relationship with you: he obviously wants something, he doesn't know what he wants, doesn't know how to get it, and cannot wait to get it and so he is going to get it by whatever means necessary. That is what is making him behave with you in a manner that is normally considered quite offensive. On the one hand he tells you that his secrets are none of your business, but on the other hand—as he does at the beginning—he says he is acting, like actors in a film, in a Western. Then he continues with the suspicion that the same thing happens everywhere: he cannot be sincere and therefore he cannot feel that people understand him or react towards him in a sincere way. He is all the time acting, fantasizing, and so never has the feeling that people are responding to him—because they are not. He is acting, and so everything slips between his fingers.

I think your first problem is to try to establish the relationship, which means that you hold the position of working out and communicating when he is making a communication and what he is communicating, or when he is acting and what impact or effect he is trying to have on you. We see that he does not like himself, but he cannot differentiate between that and a feeling that his hair is not quite right. As he cannot distinguish you from the barber, neither can he tell you to do it properly or how he wants you to do it, etc. It is hopeless, he cannot communicate and does not know what he wants to communicate, and if he knew what it was would he know how to go about it? etc.

At the moment he seems totally paralyzed in terms of having any kind of relationship with you. The question is: what are you going to do with him? Let's look at the next session.

Thursday session

Juan arrives ten minutes late. He is very visibly tired, panting with his tongue hanging out, and showing fatigue in his movements as if he had been running. At the door he says: "I am late, are you cross?" And adds jokingly: "Cheat, you are stealing two minutes from me". He is carrying a book and a little parcel. He comes in and sits down.

> **T.:** You want me to notice that you have been running to get here; although you are late, you want me to see how hard you have run to arrive on time.
> **P.:** And now the bad news: I've got a place! (*dramatic gestures of joy*

and victory) I did it! I've had to suffer a lot, I've had to work, I've had to put up with things, but—I've won!

T.: What do you mean by suffering, working and putting up with things?

P.: I've had to put up with my mother's nagging, I've had to work because I had to traipse to all those places to get the forms, I've had to suffer the anxiety that they might not take me in (*he sighs*). And what is more I've got the place for what I want to do and where I want to do it!

T.: You had a terrible time thinking that you might not get the place and you are very surprised to have got it. It's a strong emotion, difficult to bear and you are passing it on to me—you say that you have bad news and then surprise me with the opposite.

P.: Can I go to drink some water? I'm very thirsty—or would that make us waste a lot of time?

D.M.: Stop there a minute. Did you believe him when he said he had got the place?

T.: Yes.

D.M.: I don't believe it. It is a different state of mind: I hear him dramatizing having been accepted; I hear his excitement as he dramatizes the event of having got a place, but I do not know if he has or he hasn't. You are saying that to him more or less when you say: "It's a strong emotion, difficult to bear and you are passing it to me, you say that you have bad news and then surprise me with the opposite." He is using you as a sort of paralyzed, stupefied observer, really. It is assumed that your role is to absorb life's surprises for him; this is your function for him. For Juan good news and bad news are the same, because in any case he is not prepared for anything to happen, he is only prepared for fantasies and acting out tough films, but not for anything true—for the things that truly happen to him. Let's continue.

P.: (*comes back from the toilet looking happy*) It is not a lie, or a joke or a surprise; but it has been a surprise for me because I have been waiting for it all day.

T.: It seems that you have got over the surprise in the toilets; it is not a surprise now, it is normal to have got a place.

P.: No, come on, it is not like that... Also I have met a new friend today, his name is Paco, he is a cool guy.

T.: And that's why you came late.

P.: We went to a music shop; he tried a bass, I tried the drums and I was doing the famous "Triana solo", a song that says: "Open the door baby..." (*singing*)—truly good, Andalucian. I really enjoyed myself. I bought a guitar string. Have you ever seen one? (*He opens the packet, takes out the string and shows it to me.*)

D.M.: A guitar string—does he have a guitar? Do you think so?

P.: Ha, ha! (*imitating a sinister laugh; he handles the string and gives me a grim look as he gestures putting it round my neck.*)

T.: It looked as if you were going to show it to me in a friendly way but suddenly, again, you surprise me with a gesture of wanting to put it round my neck.

P.: It wouldn't be a bad idea (*in a childish tone*).

T.: You surprised me before with the news that you had got the place and now with the string. You enjoy surprising me.

P.: I have given you a surprise, you haven't given me one. Is that bad?

D.M.: That is the point. You have to absorb all life's surprises, all the points of impact.

T.: You like to see that I am the one who is surprised, not you. It amuses you.

P.: I have a good time. Have you seen the Pitufos, those blue little dwarves? One of them is Surprise Pitufo, the joker. Ah! you're not with it... That Pitufo always has a little gift with him; he gives it to people and bang! Surprise! (*He gesticulates and hits the table.*) Today has been a strange day. I got the place, in the train I met an old friend, and in the Corte Ingles I met Paco (*hitting the table*). Today has been a cool day.

T.: A strange day for you, full of surprises, cool, nothing to do with the worry that you were talking to me about before—the worry of not knowing what will happen.

P.: No. I was worried that I might not get the place, but if they have given it to me it must be because I deserve it... (*doubtful*).

Yes, it has been a bit of a surprise (*moaning like a child*) but why do you talk about surprises? I don't understand, it's as if I were doing something bad.

T.: Do you think you are doing something bad?

P.: No... only if... it's like that joke about the two madmen who are playing with a rifle. When one of them is looking through the barrel the other one releases the catch, bang! He blows his head off. And the one who released the catch says: "Hey, don't look at me like that, it scared me too!" (*He laughs and hits the table.*)

T.: So waiting without knowing what is going to happen, and surprises, can hurt, like the rifle. But in here you are the one with your finger on the catch, so you can handle it and make sure it doesn't hurt you.

P.: I was very, very happy! Okay?

T.: But it was not easy to go through the scary moments on your own, and you are tense. (*He hits the chair, the beat is becoming more and more frenetic and he gives me a sideways look.*) You look as if you are trying to frighten me, to make me scared.

P.: Tell me, if I break the chair, do I have to pay for it? (*big laugh*).

T.: Why would you break it?

P.: It seems a bit shaky.

T.: So it is the chair that is shaky, not that you are tense, cross and feeling like breaking it.

P.: I don't know... (*Silence; then, while still drumming his fingers, he says he can save some money on books and will have to find out how—but that they will tell him he is a nuisance, because he has gone there so often.*) The janitor will throw me out. (*He laughs.*)

T.: You are saying that when you want something you have to go about it carefully. You think you tire people and that there is a janitor who doesn't let you in.

P.: It's not that I tire them, it's that the doorman is a pain. He did me a bad turn once and I have to be careful because he'll do it again. The other day they gave us numbers, and he was calling them in groups of ten. Well, he went and skipped the group with my number in. Of course I took no notice, I slipped in, sorted my things out and... and.... I've lost the thread.

T.: You were telling me how you slip in tricking the doorman; that you think he picks on you and you have to be careful.

P.: No, he is like that with everybody. He just controls things; he's like a sergeant major making everybody stand to attention. He's the hardliner there and he does his job well. Being a doorman is a hard job which is not appreciated. Children think that the school is there to be battered about. The doorman is the person who has to mend things and I think they are a bit fed up with that. There used to be a very modern secretary with her walkman and her handbag; really nice—very cool.

T.: You were complaining about the doorman before and something happened inside, you lost your thread. It seems that saying nice things about him, being his friend, pays off; that way you'll be able to get things, such as getting close to the "very cool" secretary. I think that you are talking about your tactics with me. Sometimes you see me as a doorman; you have some reservations about me, you think I'm hard. And being scared that I might throw you out, you try to be friendly with me; that way you'll get more from me.

P.: Yes, I think so (*thoughtful*)... but the important thing is to work. Work—just hearing that word makes me ill. Work, work, effort, perseverance, effort (*slow painful tone*), effort...

T.: What does all that mean for you?

P.: Oh! Tiredness, boredom. (*Silence; then he becomes suddenly animated.*) Do you know what I have just realized? Do you know who Cruyff is? [*a football trainer*]. He says: "Players must be under pressure all the time. That's how they work well." I was under pressure and I did my enrolment form properly—is that true or not?

T.: You are in your world, and on the one hand you don't want me to inconvenience you by making you come out—that would be putting pressure on you; but if I do put pressure it pays off, there are happy moments, like today's one. Effort, perseverance...

P.: It doesn't sound so bad when you say it; it doesn't sound bad anymore. But when I say it—e-ff-ort, perseverance, study, work, and possibilities for the future, wisdom... It's what my mother used to say: "A military academy is what would suit you." (*He laughs then suddenly gives me a baleful look suddenly bangs the pencil on the table as if it were a drum.*)

T.: Let's see if you can say what you think.

P.: I'm annoying you, I'm playing the drums which is not allowed because it makes a lot of noise—it's not like that other thing. (*He imitates a violin.*)

T.: You are annoying me because you think that it's me who imposes on you things you don't like and forbids you to do things that you like but which are bad. I am the doorman who demands effort from you to come here, work, to make a change in yourself; otherwise there is nothing doing. And this makes you cross.

P.: The thing is things pile up because I don't do them straight away and then I have to do it all at once. (*He talks about sprucing up his room where the paint is falling off the walls because they haven't been painted or cleaned for eight years.*)

T.: Whereas with me you are in a clean and welcoming place. But it seems to you that I ask you to be good, calm, behave properly, and play the violin and not the drums. You think you don't know how and that I will throw you out. And that's how we get the bad noisy boy; you are going to break everything for those who come after you, the ones who work.

P.: (*banging the table hard*) They are worthless scum (*he laughs; in a sarcastic tone*): Let's say in all honesty, who kicks up more of a racket? (*silence*). Well, it's not true (*hardly audible*).

T.: What is not true?

P.: That I kick up more of a racket than somebody who knows more. It depends who does it.

T.: If you do, it's through being smarter than the rest.

P.: Yes, that's it, more or less (*moaning*). But why?

T.: Because things are like this in your mind: you have to be smarter than the others, move carefully. They lie to you or you lie to them.

P.: They were talking about politics yesterday, saying that Felipe is left wing [*Felipe Gonzalez, head of the Spanish government*] but his policies are right wing. Is that true?

T.: Well, we were talking about that: about you living in a world where things are not what they seem, where it is good to be bad, and where being a good, hard working student is worthless.

P.: Well, there are advantages and disadvantages. I don't think it is bad but neither do I think it's the norm. Personally I like talking properly as much as talking rough.

T.: But it's better to leave certain words alone: work, effort…

P.: Who on earth invented such a horrible and cruel thing? Don't look at me like that or I won't let you sign here. (*He has started to write on the book he had brought with him, and says in a voice that* *seems to be mocking mine*): You are begging me, come on, a signature please! (*He shows me the time.*)

T.: You would like me to sign your book.

P.: No, I'm writing work, effort, perseverance.

T.: Well, you have tricked me. You were writing that to take it away but without signatures, without being seen.

P.: (*moaning*) I just don't move on, I can't see that I am making any progress.

T.: What is making progress?

P.: It is coming out of here and saying: "Today I managed this".

T.: But you are taking the words away in the book.

P.: Yes, but they are no good for anything.

T.: They have been changed though. At the beginning they sounded horrible.

P.: (*imitating my voice*) Yes, work…

T.: You seem willing to please me, to show me the effort you make to be like me and come into my world, so that I don't throw you out and you can carry on coming here.

Our time is up.

D.M.: The point I would like to bring out about this boy, as I see it, is that the concept of truth has got lost together with the idea of beauty. He is feeling very ugly. Is he ugly or handsome?

T.: He is attractive.

D.M.: He is feeling very ugly. He is very identified with the Pitufos. He fears his penis might be like a Pitufo, a Pitufo penis, a bit ugly. I do not know if he has got a place at that school or not, but what is quite clear is that it is inconceivable for him that any beautiful woman would let in or give his penis a place. He feels he is in constant comparison with you; as if you were both sitting in front of a mirror, looking. He feels very attracted towards you and close to you but he cannot find any function whatsoever for you, he does not know what you can do for him that would change him. And so the only thing he has found for you to do is to absorb the shock of news, of pain, which he can evacuate into you. And the pain seems to be fundamentally the pain of feeling constantly disappointed; he disappoints himself constantly. What saddens him most is the feeling that he has been lied to somewhere; he has been lied to about something. He feels that in some way as a child he was led to believe that he was the "king of mambo" and that everything would come to him without effort. And he has discovered that the only things that come to one without effort are the things that are not worth having. That is very frustrating for an adolescent. The only thing you find in a dump is rubbish. What one finds in a place where people have been throwing things out are things that come without effort.

His mother has been saying something, advising him, but he has not been paying any attention for years. He has not been paying any attention because his mother, for reasons that I am not aware of, has been an object of ridicule and contempt to him. One doesn't know if he is spying on you with the idea that he will become a hero in a Western, shooting his gun, or if he is defaecating in you through his lies, or surprising you in one way or another.

The work you have to do now is to enable him to find some other function for you, so that you are not just his toilet—the place where he goes to urinate, defaecate or tell lies. But for the time being you will have to accept that this is the only thing you can do; this is the only way he can use you for the time being, because life is far too complicated for him. He can't tolerate being with you for a long time, as you indicate to him towards the end of the session.

His incapacity to conceive a different way of using you probably has its base in his not knowing how to tell one pleasure from another: that is to say, how to tell that the pleasure of defaecating and urinating is a different type of pleasure from the pleasure of eating, or of learning, etc.

From the technical point of view you must make it clear to him that for the time being you let him use you as a toilet, you are quite used to it, it is quite normal for people at the beginning of analysis to use the analyst as a toilet. The other thing you have to do is not to allow him to speed up, because he goes into a sort of dialogue of set phrases, one after the other, like throwing a ball backwards and forwards—your turn now, and now it's my turn—and he is setting the speed. You must make it clear to him that you need space to think, that he cannot be constantly hurrying you on to give an answer.

His fundamental difficulty is that he seems incapable of introjecting. He can only evacuate and feel relieved when doing so. He finds a comfortable toilet in you because you do not throw it all back at him. In that sense he is attached to you as one is attached to the toilet because one needs it: that is all he needs you for. What I would try to convey to him is: "I shall not believe anything you say to me because I am assuming that anything that is being evacuated is meant to be rubbish, you consider those evacuations rubbish". It is as if he were throwing his excrement at the wall; nothing could convince me that he is painting a mural. You must tell him that what you are interested in is not the picture he has made, but rather the act of painting or drawing, and that what he is trying to do by that act is to confuse you by throwing it all at you. It's clear to you that he is in a very confused state; he is confused between reality and fantasy, between films and schools, confused about whether he is having a relationship or just acting, etc. He is in a state of confusion. And from your point of view, as his analyst, you can see that is the situation. He is too confused to be able to tolerate it and he needs to evacuate again; what he gets rid of are the states of confusion in his mind, and if they are interesting to you it is because they give you some idea of what is confused.

I would go as far as saying that the confusion comes from some disappointment. Fundamentally he is a boy who in some way has been disappointed: he has been lied to, he was told that things would come to him without effort, and he feels that they lied to him. It has been like being dropped into a container with high walls from which he cannot get out, like the one he said he used to drop cats in; and it is cruel the way they have lied to him. At the same time there is a certain background, an underground of transference where he suspects that perhaps you get some pleasure from seeing him paralysed, that you are having a good time at his expense.

This is the situation we find in puberty. A pubertal child is not like an adolescent who thinks the adolescent community has the monopoly of sex, of vitality, the monopoly of not thinking and of considering that life is elastic. The pubertal child is at a difficult point— in a changing situation where he is neither a child nor an adolescent, and in general he feels as if he were playing the fool and being laughed at. This boy deserves your sympathy but he is hard going, a hard nut to crack. Do you find him entertaining, amusing or is treating him just a duty for you? Do you find him enjoyable or irritating?

T.: I don't find him amusing, rather interesting and entertaining.

D.M.: He is not entertaining, he is too bitter for that—there isn't much joy in him. He is too cynical, too disappointed. All these things have to be said: that he is not entertaining and that his techniques to evacuate his frustration and irritation with life stop him from listening and from internalizing anything. However that's how things are. He is like that and you'll have to put up with it.

The other thing that must be taken into account in a pubertal child is the delinquency, which tends to be frequent. In Juan it seems to take the form of going to music shops and playing instruments and so on—which the shop assistants do not seem to object to, do they? So it would be interesting to know something about the string—where has it come from? It seems to be something quite real. Did he buy it? Why did he buy it? What does he want to do with it? It seems to me that it is probably an indication of his feeling of guilt towards them for some reason; I suspect that it is because he damaged some instrument. I would look into the history of the string—what string is it? Which one has he bought and why? You don't in fact know if he has a guitar or whether he plays it. I would bring out everything related to that. One doesn't get the feeling that he has friends. He seems to be in a state of loneliness and confusion which frightens him. But, above all, he is tied with knots of self-deceit; he is deceiving himself, tied up into knots of both deception and self-deceit.

T.: I've got some drawings by Juan here: he paints musical instruments, guitars a lot… These are guitars, these are drums. He used to paint stage sets.

D.M.: It is a stage set. It is very sardonic, very bitter. He has a sense of humour but at present that sense of humour is not very funny. At his age they don't think that they might be capable of doing something useful and of being paid to do it, so the only thing they imagine is that they'll be artists—they'll belong to the music world, the show business world, and they'll be paid enormous quantities of money to be entertaining. They cannot imagine any further.

[**Participant**]: Bringing to the session this string which, especially if it is a nylon one, could be used to make a trap for cats—would it be seen as material regarding his fantasies about the brothers that he has not had?

D.M.: No, I think that at this point—he is fifteen years old now—it is related to rape. If you were to go into it, I am quite certain that you would find his fantasy-life of surprising a woman, grabbing her. Sado-masochistic fantasies.

You have to be patient with him. At this age, between fourteen and fifteen, boys feel that they are dirty, worthless. In the case of girls, getting a spot on their face is total ugliness. Fourteen, fifteen is a terrible age. They also feel that what they are taught at school is nothing, rubbish, that where people really learn is at university; the older boys are there, but what they themselves are given is just pig swill. They discourage their teachers because, no matter what they teach them, these youngsters feel it is all rubbish—that good things are reserved for others, and nothing will dissuade them from the conviction that they are being made to learn things that are not interesting, that are boring, and they'll never be able to get to the interesting things.

I think you mustn't forget that for him you are a member of that normative class of adults; he is highly suspicious of your holding him down, of being happy about his bad luck, except when he frightens you; and frightening you is the only way he has to get even with you or take his revenge. But it doesn't seem that he is sufficiently able to frighten you. Being able to frighten you is his only revenge, but he doesn't even feel that he really succeeds.

The problem in the transference is his inability to conceive that you might have any desire to give him something good, so the only thing he can do is use you to evacuate, especially this type of shock—surprising you, worrying you, confusing you, etc—evacuating everything into you. And that is the only useful function he can imagine for you; he feels he is very close to you in doing so. He is convinced that if you wanted you could teach him everything to do with sex, but you just don't want to—you are not going to let him into its secrets.

[**Participant**]: How would you deal with your counter transference? In this case the therapist is a man, but a boy like this could frighten a woman.

D.M.: Yes, boys in puberty can frighten a woman and manipulate her. And if he brought a guitar string to a woman therapist, he would be holding it and stretching it in front of her. They are less threatening with men than with women; they only try to make them feel ridiculous and frightened, and sometimes they do frighten you with the threat of suicide, so you worry about the possibility of their killing themselves.

It is surprising to see that boys in puberty still feel like children—unless they are with younger boys, then they feel very big; but as soon as they are with adults they feel small, like children again. They don't see that they are tiring you. It is true that they will frighten a man less than a woman.

The countertransference feeling of a man with a boy like this is rather one of repulsion and disgust, because you think they've got such a dirty mind, and are so worthless, so lazy, etc. You have a terrible negative countertransference, but it is partly due to being used by the patient as a toilet where they don't pull the chain and spread faeces on the wall. This is the kind of countertransference. The disgust in the case of this boy is slightly attenuated by the presence of some humour; there is an element of humour but it is too sardonic to be pleasant. And so you have to be very patient with him. How often do you see him?

T.: Twice a week.

D.M.: I wouldn't see him more than twice a week.

[**Participant**]: When he tells the story of the two mad men and the pistol and one of them is looking down—couldn't that be a reference to an attack on knowledge? Is it not worth investigating that?

D.M.: Black humour is certainly not amusing, but one can see the egocentricity in it and also something repugnant. Of course these things can be acted out: I remember a fifteen year old boy who used to come with a Coca-Cola bottle; he would drink it and then smash it against the wall. I had a cabinet with a glass door and one day when he had arrived in a particularly showy mood he broke the glass and started to demonstrate how he threw daggers, which in this case were pieces of glass. He was throwing them at me but trying to avoid me. I was like the stuntman in the circus and he was throwing these pieces of glass which were supposed to just miss me at the sides. That was, for him, sense of humour.

The joke about the madmen was because of his great desire to frighten you, and the guitar string was also to frighten you, and his looks which you describe as grim.

A boy like this is caught in a series of self-deceptions which he doesn't know how to solve. He is pretending to be mad or pretending that he is pretending to be mad, or he pretends that he is pretending to pretend... and finally he doesn't know what he is feeling or thinking or anything. Pretending is the circular aspect by means of which he is simply trying to have his way. One of the reasons why Hamlet is so fascinating is that he doesn't know if he is mad or not.

Note on the author

Jesús Sánchez de Vega is a medical doctor and psychoanalyst and a founder member of the Psychoanalytic Group of Barcelona

CHAPTER TWELVE

Elsa: Fear of the adolescent community[1]

(1998)

Nouhad Dow and Donald Meltzer

Therapist: Elsa is seventeen years old. She was referred to me by the doctor who has been treating her for weight loss for the last five months. She had also asked to have a surgical operation to reduce her breasts. The doctor described her as a patient who alternates between periods of good response to the treatment and others when, out of uncontrollable voracity, she can put on five kilos in a short time, for example over a weekend. What worried him the most in the patient was her state of mind after those episodes when she expressed a lack of desire to live, she isolated herself and took in large doses of diuretics combined with other tablets. This was a health risk and alarmed those around her.

She came to the initial interview with her mother, a good-looking woman who seemed younger than she said she was. I let them into my office together. My patient had made herself up very carefully and she was wearing the latest fashions. You could

---

[1] A supervision seminar with Donald Meltzer, Nouhad Dow (therapist) and the Psychoanalytic Group of Barcelona, first published in Donald Meltzer and Martha Harris, *Adolescentes*, edited by Lucy Jachevasky and Carlos Tabbia (Buenos Aires: Spatia, 1998), pp. 215-46. Translated by Crispina Sanders.

say that she is striking. Her hands are constantly playing with her hair as she talks. She is neither fat nor extremely thin. During the first half hour, although I was talking to both of them, it was the mother who spoke. I was even struck by her answers in the plural form: "We have decided to come to you because the doctor said we should"... "We are trying to lose weight"... "We trust whatever the doctor says"... "We are very close"... etc. She seemed very anxious and at times it was as if she were asking for help for herself rather than for her daughter. During that time my patient said very little, as if letting her mother do the work of expressing her problems, but once she was alone with me her attitude changed, she became more communicative. She started by saying that as she was feeling upbeat today it was difficult to describe what happens to her when she is feeling the opposite. Her main worries were, she said, having always felt different from other people, her craze for losing weight, and the unpredictable nature of her changes of mood. She does not understand how they come about.

At the age of thirteen she was treated for anorexia nervosa; her weight went down to thirty-two kilos and she looked totally unrecognisable. She is 1.6 metres tall. She had taken a dose of tablets (she does not know which) and she had to be taken to hospital where she received physical and psychological treatment. Two years ago she was in psychotherapy for just over a year. She took the tablets, she says, because she was being forced to eat but she could not. After this interview I saw her parents and we agreed on face to face therapy twice weekly with the possibility of increasing the number of sessions. During the holiday that followed the first visits she had to be treated medically for an imbalance attributed to taking diuretics not prescribed by her doctor.

D.M.: Where did she get them from?
T.: She bought them herself.
D.M.: What kind of imbalance was it?
T.: The doctor said that her kidneys had been affected by the excess of diuretics and he feared there might be a cardiac problem as well. This happened after the first interviews when we had agreed that I would see her after the holidays. I was told about the

incident before the start of that holiday because her doctor got alarmed and asked me if I could see her before the date we had set for the start of treatment. I agreed but the patient did not get in touch with me. I had a fantasy that she would not turn up on the agreed day but she did.

D.M.: This is a common story in adolescent anorexia, but not a lot is being said about it nowadays. Please continue.

T.: The sessions that follow are from the end of the second month of treatment.

Monday session

Patient: I'll pay you first of all, otherwise I'll forget... alright? I've counted it all (*she leaves a wad of notes on the table and carries on arranging things in her handbag as she talks*). This morning my father gave me the money for here, for my English lessons and for everything. My mother says that he hasn't said anything...

T.: She is referring to what she had been thinking, which she had told me about, that her father might create problems about paying for the treatment or even argue about it.

P.: I've had a fabulous weekend because I've been studying. I was taking notes, it was super good. Also I got a 9 in Geography, I couldn't believe it because my first mark was a 5, now I've got a 9 and next... and I've been told I passed the assessment test. I also went to see my Literature teacher and said to him "how come I study more and more and my mark is lower?" He said that I didn't explain things the way he asked, so I said "I see". When he finished he looked at me and said "You are not convinced, are you?" "No" I said.

T.: He didn't convince you?

P.: No. We were with Lola and Paqui at the weekend assing about, then we called Fernando—the one from school— but he was not in Barcelona so he called me late in the evening, he got my number from the telephone book (*she laughs*).

Interpreter: I beg your pardon, is assing about playing truant?

T.: No, it's rather wasting time, hanging out, and chatting.

D.M.: Let's make a pause, because this girl talks like a chatterbox and if we carry on she is going to confuse us. The first thing we notice is that she is keeping you in your place, like one of her servants: the money is for you, for the English teacher and for everything else. And it becomes quite clear when she gets to the end of her speech about her teacher that you have not convinced her either. In this material we see quite an arrogant girl. We notice she is as surprised about getting a high mark in Geography as she is about getting a low one in Literature. The impression she gives is that in her opinion neither teacher knows what they are doing.

T.: She tells me that nobody knows what is wrong with her.

D.M.: From what you said at the beginning I think there is certain complicity between her and her mother against the father. I don't know how the teachers are involved, I don't know if they are male or female, although I think that they might be male. There is an element of *folie-à- deux* between herself and her mother, when for example her mother uses the first person plural form. I suspect it is related to their looks. They are both attractive which is linked with her arrogance. What seems to stand out is that she thinks that something is attacking her beauty; something is forcing her to eat in order to destroy her beauty.

P.: He asked me if we could see each other on Sunday, he would call in the morning he said, but he didn't (she laughs). I then went out with my parents and my uncle and aunt; my brother also came... unusual. He just didn't have enough money to eat so he came to the restaurant with us, he ate and left. I talked with the other Fernando; we hadn't seen each other on Friday so he called me on Saturday just as I was going to the cinema. I said: "Listen Fernando, call me later, I'm just about to go to the cinema." "You hadn't told me" he said. "What do you expect if you call at six?" I said. "I was having a siesta" he said. So I said: "Well, I'm very sorry but it's your fault, I shall come back home after the film and I'm not going out." "I will convince you, I will" he said. When he called at nine I said: "No, I can't, I've got to study" and he said: "It's not fair, I stayed in this weekend and I haven't been able to see you"... So I said: "But you didn't call me until six." So he said: "I'm very sorry but you could have called me too." He was cross, he said: "It doesn't matter." I haven't encouraged him, he just invents a story, he says he has fallen for me... Well, I've had a good laugh, even more at school today; I like it there.

D.M.: Let's make a pause and take the material bit by bit. This is a stream of adolescent chatter. There is a flavour of what I suspect is the nature of her relationship with her mother: that is to say she entertains her mother with her talk of amorous adventures with boys. It's basically a delinquent atmosphere, with the feeling that people smile at her, that they answer with approving smiles, that she has a power over boys. And once more we see the convincing element when the boy says: "I'll convince you, I will". In this context it sounds rather like "I'll convince you to go to bed with me". There seems to be some element of homosexual complicity with the mother in fascinating and attracting boys and tantalizing them which is undistinguishable from what she does with you. That is how you get to do what you please, the same way as mother didn't say anything to father. Mother and daughter have secrets, they hide things from father, they ask him for money, they manipulate him. It's a prostitute atmosphere, not in the ordinary sense but rather what I call "gold diggers" who solicit money and presents particularly from rich old men, and in exchange they give as little sex as possible, so they are the ones who benefit the most. She is not only happy and satisfied with her body and her attractiveness but also with her tongue and her ability to talk. She feels she is very skilful with her tongue, in the way she argues with that boy; it was his fault, etc. As to her relationship with you—although it is true that her chatter is not very different from how she could be talking to her mother, it is not very different either from how she would talk to her servant—that is to say the courtesan has a servant to whom she talks about the men who send her flowers, presents, etc. In that context sexuality is bait for catching something. It does not have a meaning of its own but rather it is part of the game. And the game is want and greed: how to get something for nothing.

T.: Your teacher's explanations do not convince you, nor does what Fernando asks for.

P.: It's true… Anyway I had a great time with my parents. My father was in what I call a jokey mood, explaining jokes and saying strange things. We were all in a strange mood at home, I don't know, all three of us were firing off—my father my mother and me. It was eight o'clock and we were in the kitchen, the table was set and we started eating cakes and drinking champagne, the three of us a little bit silly but having fun, it was great.

D.M.: All three of them were clearly behaving like adolescents. Father was playing the fool, telling jokes, showing off in front of the women.

[**Participant**]: A bit like an orgy.

D.M.: No, but maybe with orgy on the mind. It's the foreplay, when it is fun, because when the orgy makes its appearance then it is serious.

P.: And as far as studying goes I didn't do much but I've done well in the exams, I organized myself better, I got up at eight and studied till two o'clock, and then I spent the afternoon happily watching television.

D.M.: The good marks also seem to come into that category of obtaining something for nothing. She didn't study much but she did well in her exams. She is in fact living in a "fool's paradise"— "nobody knows what she does".

T.: You feel great and on top gear in the family when you are with your parents and without your brother, when everything is for you, including the food.

T.: Her brother is an important character in this family. He left school at fourteen because he didn't want to study any more and went to work with his father.

D.M.: How old is he now?

T.: He is twenty. He is not in education, he spends long periods working with his father and then he goes away for a while. My initial interviews were with the father, then with the mother and then with both of them. Most of my interview with the father, as well as the one with the mother, would have centered on the brother if I had not interrupted to take down notes about my patient. At the present moment he is a drug addict. At fourteen he started smoking hash, then sniffing cocaine, and two weeks ago he was admitted into a clinic in a serious state from injecting himself. Now they are going to send him to a rehabilitation farm. He is an important character who figures a lot in the treatment.

D.M.: It sounds as if in some way he has been expelled from the family. Father, mother and your patient have locked themselves up in this erotic triangle and the brother has been excluded from it. Who are the two Fernandos?

T.: They are two friends. One of them is from her present school and the other one from the place where she goes to on holidays. One is older than her, around twenty seven, and the other one is the same age as her.

D.M.: What is her brother's name?

T.: Pedro.

D.M.: What does her father do?

T.: He's a business man. They are well-off people.

D.M.: So, in some way, you have interpreted to her that her brother has been expelled and everything is going to be for her. Carry on, please.

P.: My brother did not come home to sleep, he said he would but he didn't. If at least he would say that he is not coming my parents wouldn't suffer. He just goes to look for my father in his club and in front of everybody asks him for money, but my father didn't give it to him. He is such an odd person my brother; I'd like to slap him to wake him up because he lives up in the clouds that boy... He's just after money, money, money and only comes home to ask my father for money.

D.M.: This all sounds as if she were repeating like a parrot what her parents say, especially her father.

P.: When I was going home he asked me to lend him some money, but I didn't. Apparently on Sunday when my father said no to him in the club he started following him in his car... it's just crazy. He doesn't do anything; he is not interested in anything. When we were in the restaurant I heard him say that he was interested in being a skiing instructor but you need a qualification for that and he doesn't have anything. After the cinema three of my friends from the summer came to fetch me but I was with other people so we agreed to meet another day. One of them lost her father in the summer. I was very fond of that man, one could talk with him, he was friendly, charming. He was in a coma for three days. It was a big shock for me; I still find it hard to believe it because he was only around fifty. I think I felt it more than his own family. His children don't seem to have been affected by it. My friend Vanessa was the apple of his eye but I haven't seen her crying; she has carried on with her life whilst I felt it deeply... I always carry the keepsake card of his death with me. His wife came to have lunch with us on Friday. I love that family very much; most people can't stand them because they are rather special, quite aloof, but to me they have been marvellous. I was very marked by Luis's death; he had said to me once: "Elsa, don't get bitter because of other people, live your own life, you are as you are, don't let them embitter your life". And also, you see, his children are good friends of mine; he had two girls and one boy. Vanessa is my age, Luis, the boy, is twenty, and the older girl is twenty six. I love this girl as if she were my older sister because once when I was going out with a boy who messed me about a lot I wrote to her telling her how awful I was feeling and she wrote back in the tone of an older sister, even though I don't see her more often than about twice a year. I keep that letter. Vanessa who was her father's favourite, looks as if nothing has happened but she was very fond of her father. It's quite sad to say that on the night of the day their father died they were in the discothèque as if nothing had happened. One day of mourning is not too much, is it? The boy is lovely.

D.M.: It's very striking how her talk moves from her brother to this man. Her brother doesn't have the necessary qualifications or requirements, and then this man appears. Can you say how long the pause was between talking about her brother and the friends who came to fetch her and talking about this man who died?
T.: There was no pause. When she talks she joins everything up.
D.M.: The change from one subject to another, from one

person to another is very similar to the change from one group of friends to another. When one is not there to go to the cinema with you move on to another one and the problem is solved: continuous change. What has been left out here is the subject of her father and brother killing each other: either her father is going to kill her brother or her brother is killing her father, but either way they are aiming at each other.

T.: It is like that actually; in my interview with the father his words were literally: "This boy is killing me". I even remember a comment he made, he said: "I can't even have my own chair; he even takes away my chair". The boy steals money from his father.

D.M.: He would be one of the adolescents I was talking about before. The family cannot contain him. It's very striking how this girl moves from one subject to another. She is about to become aware that her father and brother are on the brink of killing each other so she changes the subject. Very rapid changes happen. Like in a film when the scene changes, or even on television when the advertisements interrupt the film. And then we go back to the story: a father has died, his children do not seem to be affected by it but she is; she feels it deeply. The point I want to highlight is that this comes up like a narrative but it is not the truth, it is only the story she tells to keep at bay the emotion and anxiety aroused in her by the fight, by the problem between her father and her brother. Also, it is a story where she is the star, the main romantic character, the one with feelings and the only one who loves the father. What also comes up is that the substitute father completely approves her selfish attitude, her not thinking about the others. And so we have this fictitious figure, the good father, approving what she does: "cutting herself off", separating herself emotionally, living selfishly. We also hear about people who give her good advice. The opposite of you or her teacher—who have not managed to convince her—she has people who advise and do convince her. It's not difficult to imagine the content of the letter from this "older sister": "Do not worry about other people, only about yourself…" And just as the "good older sister" gives her good advice, this other man, the one who died, also gave her good advice as a "good older brother". They both come into the category of the narcissistic organization. Within this narcissistic organization we find the "older sister" who is better than mother, and the "older brother" who is better than father, and they both stand in the way of her relationships and feelings toward the real parents. In fact her mother behaves like an older sister towards her as well, and her father is equally the good older brother, particularly when they "ass about" together. At this stage of functioning the family has disappeared. It is replaced by an adolescent band of three people who excite one another in the adolescent orgy. And when the family is more intact, when the brother puts in an appearance, as he does in the restaurant or comes to ask for money, one can see that everyone in the family tries to contain him a bit but they show themselves incapable of doing it; they cannot handle this very explosive adolescent. And just as the family lacks sufficient structure to contain the explosive adolescent, it also lacks a mature enough structure to contain this very seductive adolescent. And she is as effective at destroying the family structure with her seduction as her brother is with his explosiveness. Then the question is what has all this got to do with anorexia? True anorexia is that which oscillates with bulimia—throwing up, the obsession about weight, reducing the size of the breasts. It is this that we should really call anorexia nervosa. The structure of the anorexic part of the personality—and I'm referring specifically to the case of women because true anorexia happens more in the female sex— seems to be split off. It is split in two parts: one would correspond to the vain little princess, and the other to the poor little orphan, the Cinderella, basically dilapidated and fragile. It is the princess who is anorexic, and the bulimic feels she is just a tiny little girl. But neither of them has a family: the little orphan does not have parents, or a home, she is in the street... and the princess has either been kidnapped, or has lost her father or her mother and the other parent has remarried, and at the very most she has seven little dwarves who look after her. In this area of the personality, oscillating between bulimia and anorexia—which is evidently not the entire personality—we can observe this double configuration.

In the transference the therapist tends to be treated for a long time like one of the dwarves. An anorexic patient I used to have would say to me: "What small feet you have!" or "Your neck is small and sweet". Your patient will treat you like her maid or like one of the little dwarves.

T.: And her parents too! and her teachers! who are around seven: the ones at school, the English teacher, the dance teacher… and from the surgery of the doctor who treats her we must add the doctor, the first nurse, the second nurse, who all are all marvellous with her.

D.M.: Grumpy, Sleepy… interesting!

T.: You worry about the relationships between children and parents. You said to me on one occasion that you were the apple of your father's eye or that your mother had told you. Are you afraid you might react like Vanessa?

D.M.: She won't pay any attention to that kind of thing.

P.: Her father was a man who was present in his house; he occupied and was the house. He worked in the mornings only. He was the man of the house and everything was for his children. Sometimes I think that if my father died I would die after him. He might have his faults but he is a very important person for me, and I see that other people don't seem to be affected.…My father gets nervous sometimes and I feel it. Perhaps I am too sensitive.

D.M.: This is the little princess talking—"too sensitive"! she!

T.: And you feel that you need your parents a lot?

D.M.: It is clear that the man she was so fond of was one of her little dwarves, her white servant; the children's servant. This doesn't mean that she cannot love and admire a man dedicated to his wife and children, but at the moment he is one of the dwarves; that man is her dwarf father, her white servant who is being compared with her father who is now "the big one". Maybe what we are seeing here is the nature of her link with her father, the big rich man.

P.: Yes, I try not to let it be so. I might say "My parents are so and so"... they are this or that" but in fact they are everything to me, they have helped me immensely. Without them I would have done nothing, I wouldn't be here, wouldn't have been able to follow my diet, to go to the doctor, nothing. My father was asleep this morning and he had to leave me some money for here and for my English lessons, I wrote him a note with how much he had to leave for me and then I added: "Thank you, one day I'll pay you both back what you have done for me." My mother said that he had liked it a lot.

T.: She communicates with her father through the mother.

D.M.: "One day I'll go to bed with you but for the time being I need a new diamond bracelet." She is very superficial; she is showing very little depth here.

P.: That is how I feel it, it is the truth. I have told them a million times: When I am older I know I won't be able to pay back even half of what they have done for me.

T.: Perhaps you can, by being healthy.

P.: I suppose so but I see it more in financial terms.

D.M.: One is struck by how incongruous she is when she says "I wouldn't be here"; it is because she is ill that she is here!

T.: There are two main feelings in me with regard to this patient. Not so much now, but in the first few months of the treatment, I felt that every time she came was going to be the last. And my other feeling is that she does not come to be treated, but to comply with what is required of her, so that she can then go and have her breasts reduced and feel easy about it, without ups and downs in her moods.

D.M.: Like the work permit her brother needs, his requirement to go skiing, she needs to fulfil this requirement in order to get what she wants. The problem lies in being able to join together the little princess and the little orphan so that the patient may become aware of her incongruous situation and her inner conflict: a conflict between starving and eating too much. And this is really linked to the need for true, authentic human relationships. Her egocentricity is tremendous.

P.: I'm very well now; I think I have changed a lot; I can see it very clearly. I know which way I want to go and I am beginning to have a good time with people. As my friends say (*she laughs*) I know Barcelona and a good bit of abroad. They mean that I know a lot of people. I do know lots but I am not in one particular group. I like going out with Pepe one day, and with Juan another day, or Maria, or Antonio; it doesn't matter. Before I didn't use to value that, I always felt I was on my own.

T.: Before?

P.: Before two months ago… or something like that.

T.: Before coming here.

P.: Yes…maybe…yes. When I feel like going out I call my friends, Pepe or Juan, or I even say to my parents: "Do you feel like going for a stroll?"

T.: In the last session you said to me that you weren't sure that your father would want to give you the money for the sessions and that he only talked about money; but today you seem more confident.

P.: They've put their trust in me and I can't even imagine that instead of pulling through I might trip over. It would be very disappointing for them… Maybe it won't happen but that's what I think.

D.M.: She says it is what she thinks but these are not really thoughts, they are just clichés, slogans. The basic assumption of this group is money, which is the root of all goodness. It is not that money is the root of all evil, but the opposite. It's the capitalist basic assumption: money is the root of all goodness.

T.: You fear that you might disappoint your parents the way you disappoint yourself when you trip over… You fear that everything you have done might go to waste.

P.: Yes, yes. I throw out everything I had done before when I trip over and I only think of what I've just done and what might happen; I don't think of all the good things I did before.

D.M.: This is very interesting. This is a true observation. When she is feeling manic, everything is put into the future; it's all looking ahead, expectation and excitement. But when she is bulimic, depressed, it is all looking back to the past—depression, pessimism... Please continue.

T.: Maybe you are afraid of seeing in your parents your own intolerance.

P.: Anyway, my parents have never vetoed anything; they are people who trust me one hundred per cent. When I go out at night and ask them at what time I should come back they just say "Don't come back late". I have their entire confidence.

T.: That seems to be true. When I had my interview with her parents they said that she is responsible to a fault, quite the opposite from her brother.

[Participant]: Yes, but all this trust and affection towards her parents sounds a bit...

T.: Well, that is what is false in her. What I meant is that it is true that they trust her when she goes out at night.

D.M.: The question is how to go into material of this kind. From a certain point of view this material is not a communication but simply acting in the transference. Although what she communicates contains a lot of information about her, none of it is really worth interpreting. What does deserve an interpretation is feeling like Snow White and the Seven Dwarves and you being there to serve her, like her attendants. You are of no interest as somebody who might deserve to know anything about her life; you are just there to serve her. Now, if you put it that way, it will seem as if you are irritated or cross. And so whatever you indicate to her must be accompanied by the interpretation of the infantile significance of it all. This is how babies function, this is the world of the baby: so long as he is well looked after, well fed, clean, and his parents are around he will be satisfied and feel that he is at the centre of the universe. The birth of your patient probably meant the expulsion of her brother from that world. This kind of interpretation must go together with pointing out to her that she feels she is being expelled with the next baby. This is what happens with these babies that are fed every three hours; if for any reason mother is held up and can't get to them they become bulimic, they grab the breast in a rage, they don't let go of it. At that moment they feel that that situation mustn't be allowed to last forever. They have a panic crisis, they are desperate. With that kind of configuration it seems necessary to make an interpretation of this kind in order to establish the analytic situation. You mustn't expect that such an interpretation will have a therapeutic effect but rather that it will cut out this acting in the transference—that is to say it will dismantle this type of pre-formed transference, establishing a true infantile transference. The only way to achieve it is by making an interpretation that will truly surprise the patient. And so it is important not only to go little by little but also to give her a good knock. Then two possibilities will open up: either the analytic situation gets established, or the patient does not come back. But it must be done with good humour, with a true smile in the voice, really feeling the baby in the patient. All of this naturally requires time. When you do experience her like a baby then you will not look irritated but rather as if you had a smile inside. But in any case I think you are achieving something with her because she is very scared that the bulimia might show up again.

T.: On one occasion you told me that they trusted you so much you felt that they didn't look after you.

T.: She said that in the first interview. When I asked her about her relationship with her father she answered that he never denied her anything, and that in a way she was jealous of her school friends, because she always got high marks and her father didn't say anything about that either.

P.: Maybe. When they tell me to come early, I would prefer them to say: come back at two o'clock.
T.: For example; you would prefer a fixed timetable.

T.: She is in fact always extremely punctual.

P: That's it. Partly yes, I would prefer it if they drew a line for me because I can arrive at four, or quarter past four, and they are not going to say anything; but I'd partly prefer to be given a time, to be told: "Come back at four" because then I'd know how far I can go, don't you think? Because, you know, I think: what will happen if I go a little bit too far? If I don't come back on time they will feel bad, won't they?

D.M.: What we see here is that she is a very obedient but very frightened child. She has the example of her brother who has been expelled for being disobedient. This is life in the basic assumption group—ruled by obedience.

T.: And if they don't draw the line, you fear that you might not set a time yourself.
P.: Yes, yes. I'm not sure of myself, I don't trust myself. It's the same with my diet. When doctor G says to me: "Eat one hundred grams of greens", it suits me because I'm afraid of not trusting myself and going too far—in anything, it doesn't matter what.
T.: On the one hand you need to see that you re being paid attention to and on the other that a line is drawn, by doctor G, by dad and by me here. Not having boundaries or losing them makes you afraid?
P.: Because no boundaries are set for me then I've got things organized here inside (*she points to her head*). I know I can do X things in X time and until X time. I can come here from such a time until such a time; I can go to doctor G from such a time till such a time, etc. Even when I'm studying I set out from what time till what time I've got to study this or that, etc. It's a sort of system I've got here inside my head and if that system goes everything goes. I was saying that to my friend Teresa this afternoon: I can't watch the film on the telly because I finish lunch at 3.30 and I have to start studying. From 3.30 to 4.30 I do translations, from 4.30 to 5.30 something else, and so on. And if some day this system I have inside me falls down I will fall down. If it's 8 o'clock one day and I haven't started studying I get truly nervous.
T.: It seems that you need to have everything very much under control.

D.M.: Here we begin to see her difficulties somewhat: she needs to have clear lines of obedience to the hierarchical organization, to authority. If one is not obedient one is expelled and doesn't have any of the good things. There are substantial gains in obeying. But at the same time this big daddy so different from the pleasant small daddy; he requires something of her. Big daddy requires her to be a very exciting and seductive object. It is very difficult to be at the same time an exciting sexual object and an obedient nun. The same problem appears in the relationship with you. We see the conflict about on the one hand you asking her to be there at a certain time, which is easy—to talk, that is easy too—but also to say interesting things; now that is something else. When she is taking an exam at school she is not asked to say interesting things of her own—she is asked to give a second-hand report about interesting things. But you are like a teacher who asks her to write a composition about whatever is going through her mind and she can't. Has she brought you any dreams?

T.: No, she says she doesn't dream. The only thing she remembers from her previous therapist is that whenever she went into the consulting room she was asked to tell a dream.

D.M.: Maybe he was Meltzer!

T.: And when I've asked her about her dreams she's said that she doesn't have any or that if she has she does not remember them.

D.M.: I think that when a patient is stuck like this one is— afraid that you might not find her interesting and that you'll get bored—dreams can come as a relief. It is useful to explain to an adolescent patient the importance and function of the dream. It is important for the adolescent to know that for a long time the dream can be treated as something that has nothing to do with the person, as something that happens to the person while they are asleep, but that it is also something that allows an exploration of psychic reality without abandoning its denial. She is in a difficult situation. Although you can be a little dwarf and a servant, at the same time she needs you to give her a sort of certificate, so in fact you also have some authority. Whether that authority comes from an investment by the parents, or by the doctor who referred her to you, or out of something in her personality, it is difficult to state exactly. But I would suggest that it is the latter—that it has come from her. For some reason she has not been able to relegate you to the category of teachers who don't know what they are doing, and so she fears you, she is afraid of being rejected by you.

P.: Yes, yes when I lose that control it is as if I myself were falling down, as if I failed myself. I hurt myself, I don't go and hit a wall, and I even punish myself consciously or unconsciously.

T.: Perhaps you feel a part of yourself is like a severe and demanding judge.

P.: I don't know; I should accept myself a little bit because everybody gets disorganized at some point, but I don't know how to. There are certain things I can do better now. For example, as far as my diet goes: I know that at the weekend I can eat whatever I please. On Friday and Saturday I ate what I wanted and on Sunday I went back to my usual rule. So, I have been able to do that this week-end, but I'm not sure about other things. I don't know how to explain it; it's as if when I give myself some freedom I grab more and more.

T.: You grab more and more—and a part of yourself would never be satisfied.

D.M.: The patient seems to become very disorganized at this point. The fact of suggesting to her that she is demanding seems to have unsettled her.

P.: The same thing happens with my studies, I have the feeling that I have not revised but I have; what happens is that if I slack just once I feel I have not done anything. I make a plan to do twenty-two things at the weekend and if I don't do them all it's as if I didn't do any. I'm very strict about that. Last weekend I had to read and do an entire exercise book as punishment for making a spelling mistake in an exam: I wrote "beber'" [to drink] with a "b" and a "v". In the other school I wrote mostly in Catalan and just because of that mistake the teacher made me fill out a whole spelling exercise book. So, I just wanted to get the book out of the way once and for all and I did it.

T.: A whole book?

P.: Yes, like those stupid ones for kids, where you have to choose between a "j" and a "g". It was two hundred pages, but it's okay, it's done. I like to get things out of the way; even if it is the first day, I prefer it, because if I leave it for later, things pile up. On Sunday dad asked me if I wanted to go to the club with him and I said no because I had to do an exercise. He said that I was "a conscientious person", that nobody did that. It is true but I can't afford not do it because if I'm asked for it I run the risk of getting a bad mark; or for example I can't go to an exam without having revised, not knowing anything. Lots of people have a crib or they copy from their neighbour, but I prefer not to go and say that I am ill.

T.: You prefer to fail yourself than to be failed.

P.: Very often, when I think that I don't know anything, even if I remember something from the lessons, everything goes out of my mind; and whatever people say or ask me I just don't know anything.

T.: Like, for example, the money you owed me for the sessions.

D.M.: The problem is that this is being presented like something learnt by heart. It's all fraudulent and fictitious—simple obedience. I'm beginning to feel sorry for the patient. What she is really trying to do is to serve two masters. One of them demands servile obedience from her and the other that she be exciting and striking. It worries her to have to say no to her father about going to the club, lest he discover that she serves another master as well. There is a strong obsessive element.

P.: And even after an assessment text, when everybody remembers what they wrote, well, I just forget.

T.: I think you are telling me that perhaps what we say here goes out of your mind.

P.: Oh no, no. Well, some things I do forget, things that you say and that I have thought myself. I don't know if I have told you I used to be somebody with a big memory, and I don't know, I suppose one can rub out things one wants to rub out, things that I have done. (*The door bell rings. Elsa goes quiet.*) I don't know what I was going to say.

D.M.: She is scared of you. She feels she is not doing her homework adequately.

T.: Maybe as you heard the doorbell things went out of your mind.

P.: I forget more things than I used to. For example the other people do remember the thing about Quevedo, I only remember it vaguely. I also wanted to tell you that I often feel as if I were being observed, in class for example. Fernando seemed to be looking at me and I didn't like it.

T.: You don't like it because you feel controlled but you need it in order to feel that people take notice of you.

P.: Perhaps, I agree. For example I walk in the street with my shoulders hunched and my head down because I feel people are looking at me. Even my mother tells me "Have you noticed how you walk? Your shoulders are always bent forward". I think it's because I have a hang-up about my breasts and I feel that when I walk people only see my chest at first; then they see me. I'm going to have an operation on my breasts, I am!

D.M.: Everybody is looking at my breasts! Everybody thinks I have milk in my breasts! But I don't. The teachers think I have knowledge in my head but there is nothing in it, I function like a parrot. They expect from me something that I am incapable of producing!

T.: You are going to have an operation to take away a feminine attribute.

P.: Yes, but this time I *am* going to have the operation.

T.: Our time is up.

P.: I think I gave you two thousands pesetas too much. You can give it me back next time.

T.: If you prefer you can take it all back today and bring the correct amount next time.

P.: No. I don't want to walk in the street with that money. I'm scared of losing it.

T.: You want me to take care of the things that you cannot contain; you want to leave me something of yours to look after. (*She looks in her handbag to see if she can find the right money to pay me but can't. She tells me to keep what she has given me and in fact it is not the full amount.*)

D.M.: The idea is that the money that is in her handbag and the ideas in her head are quite interchangeable. It is something quite concrete; it is the same as bringing what you ask for and what the teachers ask for—it is all the same, everything is quite concrete. The problem related to her anxiety about disobedience is better reflected in the material about her brother. When children come into conflict with their parents there is a danger of killing each other. Does she throw up when she is bulimic?

T.: No, she can't; she tries to throw up but she can't.

D.M.: I ask that because the material has suddenly reflected mental incontinence and incontinence about money. I think it is necessary to formulate this acting in the pre-formed transference in terms of infantile anxieties. I would tend to formulate it in political terms: that she is living under a totalitarian regime where obedience is an indispensable requirement, and part of the obedience consists in being happy. Happiness which is shown by being content, exuberant, imaginative, sexual... And it is very difficult to be like that when you are frightened or dead. That is her pre-formed transference: coming to you like she goes to school and to all her activities. And that is the life of the woman who is one of the lovers of the rich man, or the dictator or the king. The picture is that, like Scheherazade, she has to tell the prince a story each night or he will have her head cut off. It is difficult to do when that threat is hanging over you. She is nicer and one feels more sympathy towards her at the end of the session than at the beginning when she was only making manic chatter, superficial and unpleasant.

Let's see another session.

Thursday session

T.: Before we start I want to say that you paid me one session short.

P.: Ah yes? I didn't realize. I counted eight.

T.: It's nine.

P.: (*in a low voice and muttering between her teeth*) I have spent the entire week studying and eating like a mad woman. I can't bear it, I just don't understand it, the whole week eating; it's like an obsession.

T.: Eating like a mad woman…

P.: Eating the whole day; I just don't stop, I don't know why. Not this last weekend, or on Monday; I came here on Monday. I went home, I studied, I went to the cinema and then I went to the kitchen to carry on eating (*she is whimpering*). I ate whatever was left over; then back to study; five minutes later I would go back for a glass of water and some bread. I can eat three baguettes—it's all the same to me, I stuff it down without even knowing what I'm eating. If at least they were things I enjoy eating, okay, but I go to the freezer and I eat frozen bread.

T.: It's not because you like it or it gives you pleasure.

P.: I don't know if I like it but I do it.

T.: You eat without tasting things, you swallow. It seems that you are filling a void.

P.: When I go to buy pastries I eat them so very quickly; I spend the whole day eating and I don't study. I've had a very bad week; yesterday I didn't go to English, or to jazz and I'm not going to jazz today either. I'm not doing anything. (*Silence*)

T.: You have come here.

P.: On Friday I ate, on Saturday I ate. On Sunday I was better, and on Monday too. I spent Tuesday and Wednesday eating.

T.: You eat when you don't feel well and when you don't come here.

P.: (*Silence*) I don't know… I get dressed in the morning, I see that I can't get into my clothes and I get cross and take it out on everybody.

T.: You take it out on everybody?

P.: At the moment I take it out on myself but it used to be my parents. Now when I get home I'm nice; I change completely so that at least they don't have to see my bad mood but as soon as I go out it comes back.

D.M.: This really started at the end of the previous session, with the operation; she was going to have her breasts operated on and then there was that muddle with the money. The wad of money was part of the manic atmosphere; she gave you two thousand pesetas too much.

[**Participant**]: But it was too little, although the patient thought it was too much.

D.M.: Yes, true. She didn't do her homework well. What was there from the beginning was the anxiety about not being able to satisfy you; you make demands from her like the rest of the people and she cannot fulfil them. It would seem that these demands are structured in a malign or malicious form so that it is impossible to meet them; they are a sort of torture. She feels very persecuted: you are not happy when she gives you too much money, but if she takes it with her she might lose it or get cross; and then it turns out that she forgets to pay for one session. You are asking from her more than she can give. She is out of control in this session, feeling trapped by the demands of the situation, which are mutually contradictory and she cannot meet them. Part of the problem is that filling her head with knowledge, with studying, and filling her tummy with food are indistinguishable. Therefore the inference is that if she pleases her teachers she will get fat and she won't be sexually attractive. However being sexually attractive is a problem because people will look at her breasts to get something from her, so there is a feeling of being horribly trapped.

Then there is the problem of her concreteness and her incapacity to distinguish between giving and receiving. It's an equation to which is added the aspect of incontinence—that is to say, her not being able to keep and bear what has been given to her.

It's very difficult to interpret to this patient, as in the countertransference, you fear that she might not come back after each session, and for her part she is scared of being expelled. In that preformed transference the problem is splitting: to the "little princess" you are the servant, and to the "poor girl" you are the rich woman who has everything she would want herself. The patient is in torment really because she doesn't know how to go on in the analysis. Please continue.

T.: You are not well either in the house or outside although you make an effort not to make everybody pay for it.
P.: I am bitter with myself. (*She stays silent for a moment, then begins to cry.*)
T.: Maybe you are sad on the one hand and furious on the other. Perhaps you felt empty and wanted to fill yourself up but you can only do it furiously.

P.: I think about eating all day long (she is crying as she says it). When I leave here I'll think about what I am going to buy to eat; I'll go into the first shop and buy two or three or four packets of biscuits, whatever I've got enough money for.

T.: Maybe you eat in a rage, against somebody as it were. You are in a rage with me now.

P.: I'm going to do it.

T.: You have said that as soon as you come out of here you are going to buy all the biscuits you can; then eat them, and then you will try to get them out.

P.: The thing is it's all the same to me, I can't stand it, I'm like this so very often.

T.: You are here to see if you can get some help.

P.: I don't know. I'm all right at home; I'm alright with my parents... I don't know what's the matter with me.

T.: Maybe a part of yourself doesn't allow you to feel well. It is when your parents bring you here, manage to get you into treatment and you seem to be happy that you take the diuretics in the way you did.

P.: I'm taking X again to get rid of air.

T.: To go flat: you feel pumped up with rage and maybe you want to make people treat you like somebody they have to look after, like a baby.

P.: I am going to Valencia tomorrow but I don't want to go. I want to go but I don't want people to see me.

T.: You don't want people to see what is happening inside you.

P.: No; it's different when I'm with people; in class I'm different as well; I forget everything. But it's not like that in Valencia; I don't want people who haven't seen me for a long time to see me. I have friends there. My obsession has always been to be superthin and superfine; I have always said that when I am eighteen I will be like them.

T.: Superthin, superfine.

P.: Like my cousin who is superfine, well.... thin (she cries). The only thing that matters to me is to be thin.

T.: You don't want to be seen like a needy and empty person who does nothing but fill herself up and get fat. You think that if you are fat they will discover that and reject you.

P.: At the moment I can't repair anything, I can't do anything good.

T.: Today you have come here, not like another time when you called me to say that you had something important at school that you could not put off. Today you feel more needy, and it makes you angry.

P.: Today I had to go to the doctor about my back, and my mother said I should call you to cancel the session, but I told her I could not miss it, so she got annoyed and said: "I'll call the doctor to change the appointment."

T.: Perhaps you feel that you need to be helped and so you think you can't miss the session. You are able to preserve the session.

P.: (*Silence*) I can't see clearly sometimes… (*Silence*). In my class there is a boy I like—Fernando. I don't know if I like him or not. We are always making jokes. I was sort of half asleep in class yesterday and he asked a friend: "What is the matter with Elsa?" and she said "nothing", so he asked, "is it anything to do with me?" and she said "ask her". He called me, and I told him that my head was in a muddle, I'd called Marta…

T.: The nurse of the doctor who referred her to me, who appears quite a lot in the sessions. The patient has a dependent relationship with her, and when she's thought of leaving home, it is with her that she has thought of going.

P.: …and would be going to see my back doctor tomorrow. He said he also sees a psychologist; we agreed to carry on the conversation later but he didn't call me. I was cross this morning so I asked him what had happened. "I called you but you were engaged"; but then he admitted that he had not called and to make up for it he promised he would send me a note in class. I am going to Valencia this weekend and his note was about something he wants me to bring back for him. "Write me something interesting" I said. "I can't think of anything interesting, I'll think of something interesting later on."

D.M.: That is very important, "something interesting".

P.: He asked me who was going to fetch me and I said: "My other friend called Fernando"; he asked if he was the one with the convertible car and I said he was. He asked: "You are sure you are going to Valencia? Because if you are not we could have dinner together." I had written a note for him in class but I didn't give it to him. In the note I said I'm muddled up and I need to speak to somebody, so I'm going to rant away to you because I need to. What happens is… oh well, I can't explain anything. And then I wrote "I love you", but crossed it out and wrote: "Take no notice of what I've crossed out." But I have not given it to him.

D.M.: One feels more and more sympathetic towards the patient: you can see her terrible loneliness, her need to love somebody, her obsessive paralysis, the problem of her sexuality and the difficulty in being interesting to anyone. And if you can't be interesting at least you must be thin and attractive. If you are not interesting, or thin or attractive, you'll be discarded. And so she has clung to you desperately because she doesn't know what to do. Perhaps it might be necessary to put this obsessive chaos in some order. I think you have interpreted her baby part, her needs. And what she needs is to be contained, to feel that what she brings is interesting, that you are worried, that you find intelligible what she contributes and that you'll provide the setting, you'll contain it all and that way you will think together. That is to say you will change that authoritarian transference, where she feels that demands are being made that she cannot satisfy, for a dependency situation in which you will do the job of thinking for her—because she is not capable of doing it for herself— that is, exchanging the hunger for food for a hunger for being understood which the analysis can provide. And so what is required is to wrap her up a bit, because she is totally uncontrolled, and when you are like that in adolescence you can become very suicidal.

T.: Why didn't you give it to him?
P.: I don't know how he would have taken it, because he is like a child. Still, he might have taken it well. I crossed it out because I wasn't sure that it was true. I wrote it out of habit and next to it I said: I'm not sure but at least I would like to be with you.
T.: You would like somebody to be with you but you don't know how to ask, or if you ask you might be treated like a little girl. Also

perhaps you don't know what you want to ask for; you are not sure of what you need, or of how the other person is going to respond.

D.M.: Perhaps this has been happening in the family for a long time: paradoxical demands are made to be obedient and at the same time to be interesting and lively. But it is very difficult for the child to be interesting and lively when inside she is full of fear.

P.: Fernando came to fetch me the other day. Poor Fernando, we were supposed to go and have something, but I told him that I had to see the emergency doctor at three o'clock and asked him to take me home.

T.: So you didn't go out, and gave the emergency doctor as the excuse?

P.: I didn't want anybody to see me.

T.: You tell Fernando that you need to speak with somebody, and the other Fernando that you don't want to go out because you are going to see the emergency doctor: it is as if you didn't know what you want from each one.

P.: It all revolves around the external fact of being seen because I feel super-heavy today.

T.: You don't want to be seen feeling bad, worthless, so muddled and ill, super-heavy for the other person.

P.: No, I am scared they might tease me; they've done it lots of times.

T.: Who has teased you?

P.: All the boys I've been out with, or at least that's how I feel.

T.: You feel that they tease you and so you do it first. Or perhaps you avoid being invited by somebody to go out to have something together, to relate more closely to you.

P.: Well, my relationships have never been very serious.

T.: Maybe you are afraid of getting closer.

P.: It isn't fear, it's that I get tired quickly and I say "enough", and that's it. My relationships don't finish, they stay open. I can bump into a boy I went out with a year ago and maybe I'll see him again because the relationship stayed open.

T.: Relationships don't finish, they stay open?

P.: I put an end to them when it's time to say enough. But I still call that person and they call me.

T.: It's like your diet: you say enough, you put an end to it, fill yourself or stuff yourself up with tasteless, frozen things as you said at the beginning of the session. You freeze the relationship. You are afraid that you might be teasing yourself and you think it is other people who tease you.

P.: (She nods and there is a silence) I don't know, don't know… perhaps.

T.: Time is up.

D.M.: What you really have to do is bring her into the transference and wrap her in it, given that the patient is out of control and confused. She is not sure of what she thinks or what she doesn't think, or of what she wants. Moreover she is not capable of thinking clearly about anything because she is in a panic. The problem with these anorexic girls is that they fear having to stop being joined to the family and going out into the adolescent community. And in this girl the problem has been made worse because she has the example of her brother who has been expelled. And the problem is that the conflict between the little princess part and the poor girl part becomes sexualised. The little princess makes herself more attractive to the boys, but she doesn't go to bed with them; whereas it is the opposite for the poor girl: she goes to bed with the first one who comes along. At the point at which promiscuity comes to the fore they can be very vulnerable to any woman, i.e. to a homosexual seduction by the first woman to approach them. The poor girl who goes to bed with the first boy who comes along doesn't feel anything in the sexual relationship—it doesn't mean anything to her, it catches her by surprise because all she wants is curl up and be held, and the sexual relationship doesn't mean anything. This can increase her lesbian side and she needs the therapy desperately.

[**Participant**]: I was struck by your mention of suicide. Do you think that there could be a suicidal equivalent in this bulimia? I remember a patient, also bulimic, who had a panic attack when she saw the film *La Grande Bouffe*.

D.M.: The problem is that in the desperation of the bulimia they feed themselves up with drugs, that is to say with tablets, and then they have to be taken to hospital to have their stomach pumped. Neither bulimia nor anorexia carry with them an association of attempts at suicide, but people come to it when their desperation becomes intolerable and they look for means of filling themselves up.

[**Participant**]: It would seem like an addiction.

D.M.: I see it rather as a compulsion than an addiction, because it is not slavery to a bad object, but a desperate need for a good object—it is different from addiction. She is really trying to fill an empty space inside her, as the therapist said. However she mistakes the place and the object to fill it with. The same thing happens with nymphomania, where through a compulsive sexual relationship the person tries to fill a void. It is not useful to look at addiction as a compulsion but rather as a natural extension of sadomasochism: slavery to the bad object, a masochist state.

The patient has an obsessive turbulence that can be very dangerous. What we see in these impulsive suicidal cases is an "I can't bear it any longer, it's the end" and they jump in front of a train or into a river. I think that this girl needs more time than you are giving her.

T.: We have agreed that she can increase the number of sessions.

D.M.: It's essential for you to offer it.

Note on the author

Nouhad Dow is a clinical psychologist and psycotherapist and a founder member of the Psychoanalytic Group of Barcelona; she taught projective techniques at the Universities of Bogota and of Barcelona.

CHAPTER THIRTEEN

An adolescent voyeur[1]
(1997)

Donald Meltzer

A young man came up to Oxford six years ago, sent to analysis by his counsellor mother, saying that he did not intend to stay long but had come only to see what it was like, but sure the place was full of snobs. He was a well-built but rather coarse-looking fellow, speaking in a rather rough way with a heavy working-class accent: not in keeping, he admitted, with his family culture. He had obtained a place to read Human Sciences, to everyone's amazement for he'd never worked at school. He sported a nose ring and looked generally uncouth.

However he did stay, obtained a first-class honours and generally improved in appearance over the next six years, transforming after an abortive attempt at a doctorate, into a medical student. The nose ring disappeared, the accent improved and the clothing became cleaner but the analytical work was a sticky affair. The central problem, silence, relieved only by a good recall of dreams, revealed itself as a consequence of a lack of interest in anything other than sex and boozing. He did very little studying and got a

1 Written for the Psychoanalytic Group of Barcelona, January 1997; published in *Adolescentes*, edited by Lucy Jachevasky and Carlos Tabbia (Buenos Aires: Spatia, 1998), pp. 207-212.

good degree he did not deserve, as his girlfriend told him, by his skill as an exam answering machine. He could soak up information effortlessly and intelligently perceived the answers required, padded out with a gift of the gab which never appeared in the analysis but was a relic of his years as an assistant disc-jockey at a night club.

Being socially inept but hungry for company, Harry took the role of impresario of entertainments at the junior Common Room where he could disk-jockey and ogle the girls with his rather dead eyes. This eventually turned into embezzlement of the funds to master-mind the making of a pop record (himself not a musician), which was a flop. During this period of his first two years at university, Harry's transference was very sticky and developed along the lines of Cyrano de Bergerac to the analyst's Christian, and soon Roxanne appeared and he fell helplessly and shyly in love. He wormed his way into her circle, engineered frequently to encounter her "by accident" but could never invite her or converse, while continually monitoring her window and keeping an eye out for her appearance.

His drinking increased and his sexual life took a bound when he was seduced by a very promiscuous girl at a club. That night he had a dream which was pivotal in the analysis: *He was sprawling on the steps of an Aztec pyramid and a "sex-machine" bird was climbing all over him and he kept pushing it away. The analyst commented on the passivity, related it to the recent seduction and suggested that someone at the top of the pyramid was having his heart cut out.*

And so it was. Emboldened by his sexual experience he became more forthcoming with Roxanne and she seemed to accept him as a little brother to whom she reported her amours. She occasionally came to his bed but would allow no sexual acts whatever. The consequence was a flood of nocturnal emissions and compulsive masturbation and voyeuristic dreams, as he monitored Roxanne's roster of boy friends.

Matters went on in this way through to the end of his course, and his pride in his First was rather squashed by Roxanne's contempt and probably anger because her current boyfriend did not get a first class degree. Around this time Roxanne's mother died and she planned to go to Africa to study some aspects of wild life for a higher degree, and Harry arranged to go with her. In the context of a delayed mourning for her mother, she seems to have launched herself on a rather nymphomaniac course of fellatio, including suddenly sucking Harry.

But the trip together was barren sexually and rather a failure and seemed to tip him into a somewhat paranoid state in the transference, with much silence and probably some suspicion of the analyst as playing Christian and conducting a secret relationship with Roxanne. At times he openly accused the analyst of having fostered his love for Roxanne and felt that he now was driving him crazy. The love turned to a bitter hatred; at no time was he able to concern himself about her mental health and the impact of her mother's death. His attempts to begin to work towards a doctorate foundered and he worked as a secretary for the remaining year. During that time his monitoring of Roxanne continued while some recovery in the transference took place. He became more communicative, acknowledged the problem of masturbation and its relevance to the dreams.

He managed to drop the doctorate and was instead accepted as a medical student in another college of the university. When he started he was unable to take any interest in the medical studies, but a strange transformation in the transference took place, signified by his taking a great interest in the famous American physician William Osler—replacing Cyrano. At the same time he began to lead a healthier life, taking up rowing for the college with an obsessive energy. His participation in the analysis became more open, dreams more frequent and interesting to him. His eyes and voice became more lively and his affections turned to a new girl who was neither so seductive nor tormenting to him as Roxanne, whom he dreaded to meet. Very gradually over the next eighteen months he began to be interested in the medical studies themselves. But then, after eighteen months without sex, a college girl he barely knew seduced him; *he dreamed that he was back at the house, like the one at Alexandra Road where he lived in the front room, but the old landlady's dog was menacing him outside the door, so he went out the window.*

This brief outline of Harry's analysis, which has lasted five years to date and which may be said to be over the hump but far from completed, does not convey, I fear, the great difficulty of patient and analyst. For both, the nebulousness of the transference-countertransference process was severe. He could not experience the emotionality—nor could the therapist, who had to be guided by a vague countertransference of boredom leavened by occasional sparkling dreams, like the Aztec pyramid for instance. He was not secretive nor confabulatory, but rather, unaware and incapable of introspection.

When the transference became more apparent to him it was rather persecutory, later frankly paranoid, and produced sessions of silence. During that period, which was one of compulsive masturbation, he also smelled very bad, which was difficult to talk to him about as it did not stem from carelessness of his hygiene; and thus increased his social unease. At times I thought he was deteriorating and wondered if he was drugging, which I think he was not. When he abandoned academic life for secretarial work I wondered if it was a slippery slope into indigence. At no time did the support of his parents falter, although they were not rich and he was inattentive to them and grossly ungrateful.

All in all the dead eyes, the flat voice, and the poverty of emotion made him unattractive, and the atmosphere of voyeurism was frankly creepy. He was hard to like but even at his worst was not hateful, but rather, pitiful.

Theoretical aspects

I learned a lot from Harry about the workings of voyeurism/exhibitionism and their relation to passivity. Insofar as passivity can be viewed as defensive, it wards off violence, which was restricted to his science fiction dreams. But passivity is essentially an alteration of object relations from having an object of desire to being a subject of desire. This places a person in the position where choice of interests and their implementation is replaced by selection of proffered opportunities: the danger being only the embarrassment of riches, as with the sex-machines of the Aztec pyramid. Later, when a neighbouring girl on the college staircase kept coming into his room for sex, he knew neither how to get rid of her nor— since she was not desirable to him—how to satisfy her except by employing masturbation fantasies.

Consequently the sexual urges of passivity take no pleasure in conquest but are open to being conquered, as in the fellatio episode. This event threw Harry into a turmoil of fantasy and dreams because his obsession with Roxanne had as its aim the voyeuring of her relations; and to be both the object of her desire and the object of his own voyeurism raised his excitement to the second power, fusing all his restraining equipment. The result was a truly paranoid suspicion that Roxanne and the therapist were in some collusion to drive him out of his mind.

In my experience passivity in men combines very easily with voyeur/exhibitionist tendencies to make for an addictive combination with explosive potentialities. Harry is, after all, a kind of Malvolio to Roxanne's Olivia.

Endnote by Kenneth Sanders

These pages allow a glimpse of Dr Meltzer's preparatory ordering of his impressions and thoughts about his experience over six years with the analysis of a gifted but confused young student. He traces a process of development from preoccupation with infantile sexuality and mindlessness to a point where—after many adventures—there is escape by defenestration from a claustrophobic trap. A picaresque novel with this material, if Dr Meltzer's inclination to write had taken him in that direction, would have been a unique contribution to that genre.

CHAPTER FOURTEEN

The Claustrum and adolescence[1]
(1992)

Donald Meltzer

Undoubtedly the tendencies, through masturbatory processes, to enter into intrusive identification with internal objects, have their origin in the earliest weeks and
months of post-natal life. That they have a connection, a reference to memories of life in the womb can be assumed, but the
great difference has been traced. It has also been suggested that
states of mind influenced by intrusive identification may be very
different from those related to a split-off part of the self which
has not been born, left behind, a victim of premature splitting
processes, like the little crippled boy who was left behind when
the Pied Piper led all the children into the mountain:

> Did I say, all? No, one was lame,
> And could not dance the whole of the way;
> And in after years, if you would blame
> His sadness, he was used to say,
> "It's dull in our town since my playmates left!"
> I can't forget that I'm bereft
> Of all the pleasant sights they see,

---

1 Published in Donald Meltzer, *The Claustrum* (1992), pp. 143-48.

Which the Piper also promised me.
For he led us, he said to a joyous land,
Joining the town and just at hand
Where waters gushed and fruit-trees grew,
And flowers put forth a fairer hue,
And everything was strange and new; …"
(Robert Browning, "The Pied Piper of Hamelin")

In considering the role of intrusive identification in the phenomena of adolescence, it seems necessary to consider the adolescent community as a whole, then those who are "over the top" (and in fact into the bottom), and also those who are left behind. Browning's description of what the Piper promised, in its great resemblance to Milton's depiction of the Garden of Eden, is a vibrant picture of the vision pursued by the adolescent community. In its developmental function, this socialization of internal processes can be viewed as experimental: essentially as experiments in departing from the protection, services and regulations, behavioural and ethical, of family life. For it to be safe, ties must not be severed, there must remain a home-base, a room of one's own in the family, even if unoccupied owing to having found a "room of one's own" elsewhere.

But it is just this word "safe" that is anathema to the adolescent, for his new size, bodily development and sexual potency make him feel invulnerable. The dangers of which he has heard his parents preach in the past are seen in the light of devices for control, analogous to hell-fire preaching. The communal quality of the new experiences gives an aura of universality, the joyousness an atmosphere of purity, and the readiness for new relationships a flavour of innocence. Restraints are enslavements, the future is simply the present extrapolated. The plethora of fantasy disguises the poverty of imagination.

Within this communal atmosphere the fluidity of projective identifications is encouraged to allay the confusional states of multiple splitting processes. In the clique, the gang, the group roles shift with the changing light so that like-mindedness seems to replace any awareness of compliance with the leader of the moment. Instability and promiscuity take on the guise of friendliness, shattered only when rivalries break through in unmistakeable fashion. The reality of slavish conformity is hidden by the infinite tolerance of trivial idiosyncrasy.

This apparent safety of the group is necessary for the developmental experiments which must be made: fundamentally a review and reworking of all the evolutionary conflicts of childhood. Since they have moved "out" and "into the world", a view-of-the-world differing from that implicit in parental attitudes towards the ambience outside the family must be constructed. The first casualty of this break-out is the ethical distinction of good and bad, assumed to be behavioural in parental terms. It becomes fluid, relative. Yet it remains behavioural, therefore moral rather than ethical, for the latter requires both penetration and a capacity for abstraction and symbol formation. These qualities are temporarily lost in the heat of the freedom from tradition. In a strange way language becomes very concrete and at the same time flud, so that argumentation tends to lose its anchorage in observation and experience and becomes a duel of verbal facility, of aggressive assertion, and moral blackmail where the implication of cowardice is intimidating above all. "Put up or shut up!" and "Put your money where your mouth is!" closes the debate. Hearsay, facts, statistics are delivered like hammer-blows.

This communal state of obscured confusion seems absolutely necessary for the working over of the developmental confusions which bar the way to individuality and intimate relationships. And for most participants they succeed, at least temporarily, even though the later stresses of earning a living, constructing a family and raising children may knock them back into conformity, conservatism, timidity, and the waning of imagination in favour of denial of psychic reality. The necessity of routine for adaptation so easily turns into ritual and saps the emotionality of grownup life. Thinking is so tiring!

Of those children who are left behind by this communalizing process, some of course are simply clinging to a rather rigid and enthusiastically approved latency period. We are not concerned with them, for they seem to go underground to the adolescent community, hoping to surface in the future when they have established themselves in the community to take up the postponed problems of sexuality. But others are left behind in the sense that their inability to socialize their rebellion leaves them in the lurch, cut off by secrecy from both family life and behavioural participation. Generally speaking they become holed-up, in a masturbation chamber either at home or in digs, largely unable to study, only able to hold down jobs far below their mental ability or education. The sense of being left behind, particularly with regard to sexuality, is usually accompanied by preoccupation with defects in their sexual attractiveness coming close to somatic delusion. This is at its most extreme and most puzzling where the girls are outstandingly beautiful and the boys especially attractive and charming. Their obsession with imagined defects leads directly into compulsive habits of food intake, exercising, health measures, and religious or quasi-religious ruminations. Their orientation to the adolescent community, and particularly to the sexual flamboyance, is highly voyeurist, bitterly envious and despairing.

At the other pole are the youngsters who are left out of the healthy and necessary experimentation, whose pubertal masturbation chamber becomes socialized in a restricted sense to the subgroup of the wildly promiscuous, drug and alcohol addicted, and the thrill of criminality. Their recklessness smacks of despair and suicidal longings. When politicized or turned towards religious cults, they are fanatical. Because this over-the-top aspect does not bring ostracism but often admiration, it finds little to restrain it other than breakdown into physical or mental illness. Due to the lapse of parental influence they are rarely sent for therapy unless frank violence breaks out at home. This is not true of the Oblomovian luxuriators, whose frantic parents do send them, usually to little avail, for therapy. The dangers of venereal disease, of violence or of addiction deter them very little from the compulsive activities. Both groups of the left-behind from the joyous experimentation are riddled with tragedy.

And for both groups the way back from this brink is difficult, starting as it does in puberty with escalating alienation. As in all claustrum problems, the sexuality is so deeply rooted in unresolved pre-genitality and early emotional deprivation that the incapacity for emotional alliance, coupled with a deeply pessimistic view-of-the-world, makes it unlikely for them to have the kind of saving experience of being the object of a passionate love by a more healthy and mature person. Instead they easily fall prey to exploitation by dedicated older perverts, paraded as loving concern, whether homosexual or hetereosexual.

Whether we are therapists, parents, teachers, or other representatives of the adult community, an understanding of the claustrophobic situation and its alienation from family life and the emotionality of human intimacy, may support our efforts to "stand by". In order to be restrained from interference and yet hopeful, it seems necessary for parents not only to remember the child at his best earlier on, but to be able to see the desperation in the left-behind ones despite their bravado, contempt, provocativeness. A claustrum view highlights this shift in sense of identity, making it possible to recognize that they are different from earlier times, not only in their mental qualities, but also in the world they inhabit. One sees similar alterations in the refugee who cannot shake off his nightmare.

CHAPTER FIFTEEN

A theory of sexual perversion[1]
(1974)

Donald Meltzer

Last August, when I was discussing adolescent states of mind, and the linkage with the earlier emotional caesura of the entry of the child into the world, I tried to convey how the relationship of the child with his internal objects prepares him to address the external world and his relationships within it.

Now, turning more particularly to perversions, we need to examine more closely the qualities and intricate details of those internal object relations, and the narcissistic manner in which a young person may attempt to bypass the pains of sexual difference and intimate relationships. While teenagers have to deal with the whole spectrum of confusion, when talking about perversions we need to focus on a particular type of confusion: the confusion, that is, between good and bad. While adolescents struggle intensely with a thirst for knowledge—the desire to understand, and the desire and effort to resolve confusion, we also note an opposing psychological force—the use of deliberate confusion, created as

---

[1] A talk given at a seminar in Novara in 1974 and published in *Quaderni di Psicoterapia Infantile* no. 1, edited by C. Brutti and F. Scotti, pp. 79-100. Translated from the Italian by Neil Maizels and Vicky Nicholls.

a defence, and used as a cynical attack on truth—as a means to consolidate a narcissistic defensive structure.

As always however, when talking about psychoanalysis, I must first of all speak of its history. The reason for this is that some theoretical discoveries have a kind of "illogicality" in their evolution as concepts, because the concepts are not always an explanation, *per se*, but only the tools for more model-making. But new tools allow the researcher to recognize new phenomena, and in turn, new phenomena then push us to develop new theory, and so on. Thus the history of psychoanalysis is a story of growing complexity in its formulations of phenomena, and I suppose that although we may often regret this growing complexity, we cannot avoid it.

Freud began with very simple ideas and many preconceptions, most of which are contained in the *Project* that he wrote of to Fliess in 1897. Then after ten years of psychoanalytic work, he produced his first book on sexual theory, the *Three Essays on Sexuality*, which states that since theory-building is an essential element in any medical practice, it cannot be regarded as a purely psychoanalytical indulgence. The first theoretical description of the Oedipus complex could actually be considered as Freud's first discovery in the psychoanalytic field of sexual development.

Freud is especially determined here to sweep away the cultural bias on sexuality and children. In this sense, it is definitely a revolutionary piece of writing, not just a research document. It could be considered a kind of manifesto about sexual freedom for children. At that time, Freud was mainly absorbed in his study of the operation of repression, which in his mind was not very distinct from the cultural oppression of primitive instinctual behaviour, and was therefore especially concerned with the interaction between instinct and culture. His idea was quite simple: those sexual instincts, which are not allowed to express themselves freely, build up into a form of energy that is curbed, or finds expression through repression in spite of this interference, and this is how symptoms are constructed, psychologically. Later, he formulated the concept of sublimation, whereby the instincts can be deflected into an action that is acceptable to society, and from then on he maintained the view that the sublimation of sexual instincts is the foundation for higher cultural progress.

In 1905, when he described the infantile sexual constitution as "polymorphously perverse", he concluded that the development of sexuality consisted basically of an integrating process in which oral, anal and genital drives become unified, subjugated to the "control" (so to speak) of "mature" genitality. By 1915, the concept of "organization" was extended to childhood sexuality through Abraham's description of the pregenital, which emphasized the phenomenon of ambivalence—love and hatred—inherent in it. Freud did not mean the concept of ambivalence to include primary sadism but rather, the infantile reaction to frustration.

Freud then adopted another "revolutionary" position in relation to religion and morality. He talked about mental life in a way that discouraged making judgements about good and evil impulses, and concerned itself solely with understanding. Later, in *Beyond the Pleasure Principle* (1920) he tried to correct his theory of instinct in the light of this. Only in his latest work were perversions treated as a complex and distinct problem in relation to the structural theory; in his earlier work, the perversions are simply the equivalent of infantile sexuality. When considering them as the negative of neurosis, he was opposed to making moral judgements lest these interfere with the ability to penetrate deeply into problems of mental functioning.

All this provides the framework leading up to the thinking of the twenties and after. In my personal view, the history of psycho-analysis is essentially the story of the intertwining of the thought of Klein and Abraham with the work of Freud, beginning at that time. Freud's approach, working with adult patients, was that of psychopathology through reconstruction; the only exception being the case of Little Hans, which he used primarily as verification of his theory of infantile (Oedipal) neurosis. When you read it, you can see that it is rich in evolutionary implications that Freud was not particularly interested in. The work of Klein, on the other hand—working from the very beginning with small children—is oriented in a mental-evolutionary direction; whilst interest in psychopathology seems secondary and is treated in a schematic way.[2]

I think it would be useful to attempt to unite or reconcile these two approaches into one that looks both backwards and forwards. If we stop to look back to Freud's position in the 1920's we can see the limitations in his conceptual tools. He had at that time described the general phenomenon of narcissism, but it was overburdened by dependence on phenomenological observation. He defined it as a position in the male libidinal development somewhere between autoeroticism and genital relationships. His ideas on bisexuality were limited by his idea of female sexuality which was treated purely as passivity, dominated by unconscious penis envy, ignorant of the existence of the vagina and therefore infantile. Freud's attempt to use the instincts theory as a basis for distinguishing between male and female sexuality led to the model of unconscious phantasy in which the child equates female genitalia with mutilated male genitalia. His view of male sexuality was complicated by castration anxiety and the child's fear of losing a penis. The vagina and testes were considered devoid of significance. This was consistent with Freud's increasingly joyless conclusion that pleasure was more to do with the reduction of anxiety than anything else.

In appearance, Mrs Klein's approach was similar to begin with and she saw herself as an orthodox Freudian. But as she worked with small children and listened carefully to them, her interests took a very different direction. She discovered children were driven by a desire to investigate the truth of things—predominantly, the body of the mother, which was for them not just a surface but an interior full of objects. She also discovered that violence and destructiveness were inherent in the mental life of all children and an important feature of their sexuality.

Yet when she began to describe these findings in the early 1920's she seemed totally unaware that they differed strikingly from Freud's theory of the libido, and that her observations of

---

2   Meltzer reviews psychoanalytic theory of sexuality in *Sexual States of Mind* (1973) and treats psychoanalytic history more fully in *The Kleinian Development* (1978).

the mental life of children sounded quite different from Freud's reconstructions. Her children gave a meaning to the terms "polymorphic" and "perverse" that Little Hans had never given— unless you look very carefully at the places where Hans speaks of riding with his sister in the box, or tells of fantasies of himself and his father violently penetrating enclosed spaces. These revelations were not paid much attention by Freud at that time; yet there is but a short jump from this to the material in Mrs Klein's first writings in *The Psychoanalysis of Children*.

By the time Klein began publishing, Freud had already reformulated the theory of instincts in terms of Life and Death. She immediately embraced the concept unlike Freud himself who considered his *Beyond the Pleasure Principle* to be a "simple biological speculation". But he returned to the nature of perversion only after this newer formulation, addressing the problem of masochism. He was the first to understand that masochism as a phenomenon lay outside the two "principles" of pleasure and reality. This became clear when mental pain seemed indistinguishable from mental pleasure. Freud had already approached this in his consideration of melancholia, where he discovered that the apparent mental pain of the melancholic is different from the real mental pain that affects the person in mourning. The question was raised, who was really suffering? He concluded that it was not the self that suffered, but an internal object that was being attacked, denigrated and abused—a primitive idealized parental object. From his description, the ego and the ideal are bound in a sadomasochistic relationship. So the melancholy can be understood as a kind of perversion. When Freud returned to the problem of masochism he reached a similar conclusion—that perversion and sadomasochism are closely entangled.

We are now around 1927. Klein's *Psychoanalysis of Children* was published in 1932 but had mostly been written by 1926. This seemed to address children's perversity but more in the sense of polymorphously perverse phantasy life. Her descriptions of play do not extend to psychopathology and so do not seem to connect with Freud's work. In the 30's Klein was interested in the early Oedipal complex and with unconscious phantasies about the inside of the mother's body. Much of this early work seems to centre on the intensity of love and hate, primary instinctual impulses, and the way hate and destructiveness are expressed very naturally in sadomasochistic phantasies. The other central preoccupation of her work at this time concerns the interior of the body as an absolute psychic reality—primarily the body of the mother, then the inside of the child's body, being psychic spaces occupied by various objects and the self. The primal scene was somehow implicit in the work of Melanie Klein from the outset, although she was finding it difficult to talk about it in theoretical terms.

Let us now go back ten years to Freud's formulation of the primal scene in the case of the Wolf Man (1918). In a way this had little influence on Freud's thought until he came to use it in *The Ego and the Id* and his work on perversion. Freud never expressed any conviction about the value of primary process phantasy; on the one hand he saw phantasy as universal, promoted by instinctual impulses; on the other he saw it as like an accidental visual or auditory intrusion into the life of the child. Yet with the Wolf Man the ground is laid for his theory to begin to leave the sexual instinctual domain and to journey into the realm of the development of the ego (the structural theory). The primal scene freed Freud from preoccupation with the physical body, enabling sexual theory to change from its neurophysiological basis in excitement and the distribution of libido, to a theory able to encompass the tragedy of human relations. This led for the first time to the need to understand emotions. In libido theory emotion is treated as something accidental and quantitative, with the individual characteristics of emotions being essentially random. Only through the theory of the primal scene does emotionality become the heart of the problem. I therefore believe that the case of the Wolf Man is an early indicator of the new psychoanalysis. I think it was by far the most important clinical experience in Freud's life, and proved to have as great an influence on his later formulations as that previously made by his self-analysis.

If I simplify the history of psychoanalysis (somewhat outrageously) by seeing it as the work of two people, Freud and Klein, then Freud was the one who worked with adult patients, interested in psychopathology and its roots in childhood; while Klein was the one who from the start worked with children and was interested primarily in their development but was not particularly concerned with adults and their psychopathology. In the mid 1920's we can see how their work overlaps but they do not quite fully encounter one another. The difficulty with Freud's work was his view of adult sexuality as a mere continuation of infantile sexuality, with zonal phases under the leadership of the genital. He tended to see bisexuality as of biological origin, but linked this to the instinctual struggle between activity and passivity. Because of this and for other cultural reasons he was naturally inclined to see femininity as an inferior type of sexuality equivalent to passivity or even masochism. Yet masculinity with its genital impetus was disturbed in two ways: by the anxiety of castration, which had it origin in the biology of the genitals, and by the feeling of impotence that arose from children's small size and lack of capacity. His view of homosexuality was based almost entirely on the "case" of Leonardo and was understood basically through the theory of narcissism—the child's erotic impulse taking its own body as the object of its first sexual search. Later Freud reformulated narcissism in terms of withdrawal of libido into the self. On this basis it was natural for Freud to see homosexuality as something aberrant in cultural terms, and to see its "sublimation" as a major source of creative cultural achievement (he did not appear to think the sublimation of female sexuality could lead to very much). Although "introjection" had been described by Ferenczi, it had been given a strongly pathological connotation by both Freud and Abraham, as underpinning melancholia. Love was conceived entirely in terms of response to gratification, and hatred as the frustration of gratification; and even when he formulated the duality of the life and death instincts he seemed reluctant to link hate to the death Instinct.

Klein, however, seemed to have discovered from the beginning the existence of good and bad in the self and in the internal objects, and her work therefore implied a moral theoretical framework, whilst Freud's theories remained anti-moralistic and in a sense a-moral. While Freud never developed the concept of a concrete inner world, Klein saw from the start the child's preoccupation with the complex space that housed its internal objects, both part-objects and whole objects, and how the inside of the mother's body contained essentially three types of object: the penis, the babies, and food. All three of these can be experienced as good or as bad; and the baby experiences his own body to be similarly populated.

Like Freud, Klein seemed to suggest that adult mental life was a continuation of infantile life, but with greater capacity for integration and organization. Like Freud, she was aware of the problem of mental pain in relation to one's identifications, which raised the question of who was really suffering the pain. But she was not interested in the pathological implications of perversions as she seemed to take the perverse aspects of adult life as corresponding to the violent and destructive impulses of children. So when Freud was beginning to think that perversions were complicated structures requiring a uniquely intricate explanation, Klein probably continued to think about them merely in terms of infantile sexuality.

It was Freud's achievement to elevate to the level of interpersonal drama that which had first been explained simply in terms of energy economics and neurophysiology. On the basis of the Wolf Man's dream, he reconstructed a scene that he believed to have happened in the actual life history of the child at the age of six months, or a year and a half, or two years and a half. He dramatically tracked the consequences of this scene, linking it to a series of changes in the development of character and the formation of symptoms. Ten years later in *The Ego and the Id* (1923) he described the Oedipus complex in a new way, with its foundations firmly in the primal scene, thus giving substance to the idea of bisexuality in all people.

There are at least two scenes then, depending on what is experienced by the male or the female child; yet through identification, every Oedipal child has both these psychological aspects. At this time Freud placed more importance on what the child actually sees or hears, than on what was imagined through primary unconscious processes. Of course this had an enormous influence on Klein's thinking. But in her work, the primal scene is taken primarily as a phantasy central to the child's sexual development. She accepts the child's nature as bisexual but her accent is placed on the child's desire to know and understand—which she calls epistemophilia. So she underlines the child's confusion, uncertainty and anxiety about knowledge, while the emphasis in Freud's model is on the child's urge to minimize the frustration of his desires.

A few years after *The Ego and the Id*, in *Inhibitions, Symptoms and Anxiety* (1926) even Freud concluded that mental pain was at the heart of the problem, and that anxiety was not as previously thought the result of frustration, although it did constitute an inhibitory pressure, but was in fact the cause of the inhibitions. He did continue to think that the instincts and the demand for instant gratification were the central phenomenon to be studied. Klein however (without acknowledging or being totally aware how her theories were diverging from Freud) was occupied by the relations of love and hate—towards the mother and secondarily the father—and the ways in which uncertainty about the goodness or badness of these objects generated anxiety. In her writings therefore, anxiety is not connected with frustrated instinct, but with the pains of knowledge. In Freud's theory, pain is linked with what happens to the child in the external world; in Klein it derives from the child's understanding or misunderstanding of the external world.

Castration anxiety remained for Freud the basis for thinking about childhood sexuality, and he saw it as originating in actual threats of punishment for practising masturbation and in the child's "sexual researches" which appeared to demonstrate the theory that the female genital is a mutilated male genital. Klein does not seem to have doubted that the female genital was somehow known to the small child from the beginning, and that owing to the phantasy of the mother's body as containing a penis inside her, there is a very early preconception—essentially creative—in which the mother is enriched and restored internally by sexual intercourse.

Freud's approach was expounded in *A Child is Being Beaten* (1919) and in *Fetishism* (1927). In the former, he made a lot out of the ubiquitous phantasy that children have about existing inside their mother's body, and that mother's sexual intercourse with father is an attack on their own body. In Fetishism, he describes a phantasy that the woman is "punished", but seems to conclude that this is directed at the male genital inside the mother rather than on her own body.

So by around 1930, Klein had described the fear of persecution and the primitive Oedipal complex but did not give much importance to perversions *per se* as a feature of adult life; and Freud was beginning to investigate perversion as based on an identification with the punishment of women, together with his theory of masochism as the death instinct turned against itself; but he was not much interested in this phantasy world of the interior of the mother's body. Two lines of development need to be brought together at this point in order to formulate a new theory of sexual perversity—one that goes back to the roots of psychopathology, and the other following the development of the child. The new theory that emerges from their combination has at its heart the meaning of the primal scene: where one feature concerns the child's uncertainties and anxieties about the goodness or badness of the act of intercourse (Klein's contribution), and the other feature concerns the child's desire to participate (the contribution of Freud). If we put these together we come up with a theory of the perversions that is based on the child's desire to participate in what he believes to be "bad" sexuality. Where good sexuality relates essentially to producing babies, bad sexuality derives from the wish to kill the children. It is of course an entirely different theory from the one which equates perversity with infantile sexuality; and it elevates perversions to structures of great complexity.

I will now talk about the link between sexuality and badness—meaning sado-masochism. In Freud's writings on fetishism he discovered that the central motivation for killing children is punishment—basically the punishment of women for supposedly having done something bad during intercourse, being dirty, stealing a faecal penis. The perversions therefore are fundamentally regressive, a psychotic confusion infused with oral or anal sadism.

This leads on to the question of responsibility and the culpability associated with passivity. It seems to me there is nothing in

Klein to suggest her view about personal responsibility is much different here from Freud's. It is necessary to distinguish between the desire to be the masochistic object of someone else's impulse, and the intrusive sadistic impulse to steal something from an object. It is complicated, because the sensuality involved in the act may have nothing to do with the destructive significance of the phantasy. For an act to be significant there must be a phantasy that relates to the passage of time: it must be conceived as a moment of interaction that has a past and a future. Perversion does not require such a phantasy—it may consist only of the sensual act, without any regard for present or future implications about its meaning. It is therefore a movement towards mindlessness. This of course implies that the evasion of culpability is highly pathological, in displacing the consequences and responsibility for a particular act entirely onto the person who instigates it physically. This seems to be the case in sado-masochism: the person who is in the masochistic position assumes no liability or responsibility for the consequences of the act. So in Freud's structural model, the culpability would have to reside outside the purview of the superego—it would have to be an area free from guilt or conflict. But sado-masochism is not divisible; a person who has any involvement in a sado-masochistic act is psychologically involved in both sides of it.

So to get back to the theories of Freud and Klein: what seems to happen is that in any perverse act of sadistically punishing ("faecally" killing the internal baby), the person who plays the passive role is both the mother and the child who is being killed. What pushes a person into this role may be a crude attempt to avoid culpability, but it also prevents the enjoyment of sensuality. Freud's idea of the primal scene needs to be augmented to take into account the nature of what is happening inside the body of the mother (bisexually), and in the case of masturbatory perversion, the whole web of identifications. All this is extremely complicated.

We need to recognize that there is another important factor in the formation of perversions that is not adequately explained either by Freud's death instinct or by Klein's extension to it of hatred and sadism, nor even by her subsequent concept of envy.

Perverse negativism is probably a form of envy but is also a special condition in its own right. The roots of this concept go back to the wonderful descriptions in Freud's Schreber case (1911), in which he says that Schreber's delusions were formed during the "reconstructive stage" of his illness following his phantasy of the annihilation of the world. He says Schreber rebuilt a world where he could live, not bigger than the one he had destroyed. But here is the core of negativism: it not only rejects the world as it is, but aims to build a better world. It is not only unnatural (as implied by the term "perversion") but in competition with nature and like Satan attempts to build a Hell better than Paradise.[3] This is the key to the basic arrogance of perversion: life in the outside world tends to be put in place with an air of apparent normality and adaptation in which perversion may be exercised without any outside interference. The analyst should not be surprised that the patient does not actually want the perversion itself to be treated, but merely the inconvenience and trouble consequent to the perversion. Such patients want to learn how to create a tranquil apartheid within themselves.

To sum up: I have tried to describe how the work of Freud and Klein overlapped, without actually touching, in the 1930's, and to build some theoretical bridges between the implications of the tracks of their thinking. We see how the projection of destructive impulses into the faecal paternal part-object manages to avoid depressive guilt yet has severe mental consequences, including the loss of the capacity to think. In focusing on perversion however I have not spoken about the good qualities of the primal scene. While the perversions have as their central phantasy the killing of an inside baby by a bad faecal penis, adult sexuality must be based on identification with objects whose function is to create and nurture children by putting life-promoting substances into the mother's body. This role is at least as complex as that of perversion, and absolutely cannot be simply a matter of infantile sexuality ceding authority to genital command.

---

3 The reference is to Milton's Pandemonium in *Paradise Lost*.

Discussion

Dr Mancia: I would like to ask Dr Meltzer to clarify the concept of "faecal punishment" and its relation to perversion.

Dr Meltzer: I may have spoken too strongly in coining the term "faecal punishment"—a poetic term, but also too graphically specific. I chose the term "faecal penis" because it seems to me to closely correspond to what I have seen in children's phantasies and play—a material plasticity par excellence which can give any form and any meaning to any physical object. I used this term in that sense.

Mrs Harris: Is the faecal penis, then, how the child deals with people and things—by omnipotently shaping them as if they were substances such as faeces that can be manipulated into any form?

Dr Meltzer: What you say relates to two aspects of megalomania (about which I have deliberately not spoken thus far). One aspect concerns the way that the megalomaniac tries to imitate anything uttered by the analyst. The other is the attempt to use objects—initially the stool—to control and tyrannize over others. One of the reasons for not having spoken of megalomania here is that it seems to me a concept far too complicated to just touch on briefly.

Dr Mancia: I ask Dr Meltzer if he can clarify the concept of the phantasy of killing the internal child within the body of the mother.

Dr Meltzer: This is what I think is the central phantasy, so I have focused on it today. It is open to infinite variation—varieties of instrumentation, of identification, deep and superficial phantasies etc—which is what induces the perverse patient to believe that he always has something full of interest.

Dr Moretti: I would like to ask Dr Meltzer if the perversion can also be seen as a defence against depression, as can be seen occasionally in adolescents.

Dr Meltzer: I was trying today to deal with the perversions as a mental entity and avoided discussing their relationship to the personality as a whole. I have therefore avoided speaking of depressive and persecutory anxieties, although I mentioned the concept of defence. I placed structural emphasis only on the phantasy of the primal scene. If we want to place the psychopathology of perversion in relation to the entire structure of the personality we would need to consider relationships within the external world also, so my scope has been somewhat restricted in this seminar.

Dr Iacono: I think the central focus of the negativity of perversion is on sexual bad behaviour. Can you connect this to what you said about the confusion between good and evil? Can we think of a centralized phantasy about sexual misconduct?

Dr Meltzer: We shouldn't think of negativity as the child just saying "No, I don't want to do anything good", but as saying "the bad thing is a good thing". It is this stubborn reversal of the good and the bad that is in my view the central feature in the operation of perverse cynicism.

Dr Gaburri: May I ask Dr Meltzer if he considers that castration anxiety does not play a special role in psychic reality, and should just be subsumed under the general heading of persecutory anxieties?

Dr Meltzer: Let me try to respond by reiterating what I think underpins the structure of the perversions, leaving to one side for now the economic problem of their place in the personality as a whole. I want to stress again that many phantasies might fall into the category of sexual misconduct, yet are not perversion, because they differ from the central perverse phantasy of "killing the baby". There are so many types of sexual activity that might seem to be perverse sexuality; but what I have tried to define, taking Freud's and Klein's positions into account, is a psychopathologically complex structure called "sexual perversion" which is totally different from infantile sexuality. Although it has its origins in childhood sexuality, its complicated structure means that it is better understood as placed in opposition to adult sexuality.

Dr Gaburri: I wonder if your ideas relate to what has previously been called "moral masochism"—where in some females there is a phantasy of attacking one's own femininity and fertility, maintaining a resentful attitude to males, behind which there is the phantasy of appropriating the father's faecal penis, which is also an attack on the capacity of the mother to unite sexually with the father.

Dr Meltzer: All the elements of which you speak are to be found in the general category of "destructive sexuality". What I am trying to do is tantamount to describing a particular way of painting, more than just the materials—brushes, canvases, oils and other crucial components. I'm looking at something which is almost impossible to describe yet which draws its materials from normal, everyday psychic activity, which is made up from good and bad aspects of the personality interacting with good and bad internal objects.[4] It has a very close relationship with the delusions. This is how I saw a connection between the Schreber case, sexual perversion and delusional thinking—really the road to madness. Therefore perversion must be taken very seriously as a severe form of mental illness.

Mrs Harris: We could perhaps say that you have described something that in its essence is an attack on the goodness or the beauty or the sincerity of life itself, and which seeks at the same time to omnipotently build a life completely opposing the creative way.

Dr Meltzer: The sexual perversion may involve either a small part of the personality or the entire personality. However, given that perversion is itself a massive attack on everything that is good in life—as you just described—then the principle of nihilism, which basically aims to establish a delusional anti-live system, is the road to madness. What is different from the lesser elements of sexual misconduct (which are often popularly depicted as perverse) is that it becomes an organized system.

Mrs Harris: Could you say that within the total personality, perverse areas can cause great anxiety to the other parts of the personality, but in the perverse areas themselves there is no anxiety owing to the omnipotent sense of absolute righteousness?

Dr Meltzer: Well, I am not sure that's always true. But what is sure is that the central attitude of perversion is one of arrogance—which is worn like a badge of honour amongst thieves. Since the perversion always involves at least two parts of the child self (the masochistic becomes the sadistic partner at another time), these two

---

4 In later works such as *The Claustrum* (1992) Meltzer clarifies that the bad internal object is in fact derived from a projection of the self.

parts despise and hate each other. Although they make a game of it, they are never far from murdering one another; thus the perversion or perverse masturbation can easily become a real suicide. People often are killed in their perverse masturbation rituals, and fellow perverts are never very far from "accidentally" killing one another. So, I think there is anxiety in the perversions; but this anxiety is likely to be camouflaged amongst the more obviously arrogant and contemptuous manifestations of the personality, and hidden by the scornful face shown to the outside world.

CHAPTER SIXTEEN

Narcissism and violence in adolescents[1]
(1989)

Donald Meltzer

The second post-war generation has now reached adolescence, and the present adolescent community is the first to have been raised in the atmosphere of the sexual revolution following the turbulence of 1968. The changes in values and behaviour help us to separate out the cultural from the intrinsic factors in the adolescent state of mind. Gone is the Romantic Agony of the nineteenth century, but also gone is the tendency to fall in love Instead of the expectation that love will lead to sexual intimacy, today's young people expect that the sexual activity will ripen into love. The earlier predatory pubertal gang sexual behaviour, in which the boys boasted to their fellows of the conquests and the girls flaunted their capacity to attract and frustrate the boys, has given way to a more athletic mental-hygiene approach with mutual seduction. The brutality of "fucking" has yielded to the triviality of "bonking". In its openness it has replaced the secrecy of masturbation.

---

1 Published in *Sincerity: Collected Papers of Donald Meltzer,* edited by A. Hahn (1994), pp. 564-566.

Unfortunately, the young people who come to analysis are largely those who stand outside the active adolescent community for reasons of psychopathology. They yield us information about their incapacities but very little insight into the essential nature of the adolescent state of mind. This we have to gather at the other end of the analytic population, the people who cannot emerge from the adolescent community, its values, behaviour, and state of mind. They comprise primarily the upwardly mobile "yuppie" who comes for training, the ambisexual who cannot shake off his perversion, the woman who operated on the basis of negative identification with her mother in her attempt to raise her children. They have an adequately adjusted social carapace and yield themselves to the infantile transference with difficulty. But from them we reap a rich insight into the state of mind beyond which they have been unable to progress, despite evident success in their progress up the social ladder. They have been well adjusted indeed to the adolescent community, and its charms still hold them.

The picture of adolescent life-style that slowly emerges is one in which the concept of family has been replaced by a political structure of benevolent patriarchal or matriarchal quasi-democracy and socialism, in which the ideal of justice through understanding has been replaced by egalitarianism between grownups and children. The essence of this political system is the denial of the development of judgement through experience. As a consequence, systematic self-effacement by the grownups is aimed at dispelling any sense in the children that the parents are in possession of mysterious knowledge and powers, and therefore suitable objects of transference from the figures of psychic reality. Common sense and the capacity to argue for the fulfillment of desires is valued and encouraged in the children, with consequent stifling of imagination and emotionality, tenderness, and dependence.

This political concept of family life, which forms the conceptual background of both their adolescent rebellion and their later attempts to form their own family, has hidden in it a complete confusion between private and secret. This is central to the denial of psychic reality. Having thus cut themselves off from the infantile level of dependence on internal objects, which stand accused of elitism, tyranny, and mystification, they are thrown into a slavish dependence upon the company of their fellows, in which a homogeneity of opinion and attitude provides a snugness that substitutes for an internally generated sense of security—that is, a feeling of readiness to face the consequences of their individual judgement and decisions. The upshot of this dependence upon their fellows is a value system in which success is the ultimate arbiter and values become cynically relative to the culture. This is nowhere clearer than in the loss of aesthetic sense and its replacement by fashion. It must be stressed that this is not only evidenced as a rebellion against or criticism of their original families in particular, but against the culture of which their parents were exemplary. It carries, therefore, the banner of revolution rather than of rebellion. The sanctimony is daunting. Just how this politicizing of family life and values and the blunting of aesthetic sensibilities generates violence requires a considerable exposition.

CHAPTER SEVENTEEN

Adolescence: after the hurricane – a newspaper report[1]
(c. 2002)

Donald Meltzer

As the dazed populace of the village of Puberty emerge from caves and storm cellars, rubbing their sleepless eyes in incredulity, they find themselves staring at one another as strangers, possibly as enemies in a world torn open like blown flowers inviting looting. Who can resist when "everyone" is doing it. A frantic type of excitement replaces the exhaustion of sheltering in the dark, listening to the barrage above.

Frenetic excitement simulates sexuality; needing only the drums in the night of jungle telegraph to spread, as the reinforcement of one element by another, wind by wave, whip the atmosphere into Walpurgisnacht.

Thus puberty has come to an unmistakeable end. Are the parents dead? Or gone on holiday? Or just sleeping in? Certainly no one is fixing breakfast for the children or hurrying them to school. Hurrah, it must be a bank holiday. Even the bank is broken open and inviting the looters. But wait a moment. Are those spots catching? Is it an epidemic? A wave of panic spreads. The plague, like in the fourteenth century. People are falling. Just exhaustion.

---

[1] Unfinished paper, previously unpublished.

The smell in the air is just from the uncollected rubbish, broken open by the dogs or by the scavengers. Where are the police? Or the rubbish collectors? They say they are the police. Call for volunteers. You must be joking. No one works without being paid, all whores and rent boys, suddenly, as the black market has sprung up like the wild oats in the barley. That is where all the money is, and with the drug "companies". The anatomy of chaos. How can it end?

It must end, either in plague or winter. The exhaustion begins to shiver. Open the schools, where are the teachers? We will gladly learn our timetables this time. Sorry or "sowy". Cringe begins to spread. We'll be good. Settle down. Form into rows. Someone take the roll. The teachers are always the first to volunteer.

With this short and epitomized picture of puberty as the background for describing and exploring adolescence, we intend to infer that the pubescent qualities do not evaporate but continue to contaminate the corn crop, partly as a persistent nostalgia for freedom and supposed creativity (partying and holidays and drug-taking). These qualities weaken the fabric of the adolescent community *as* a community through deaths and new plagues such as AIDS. And so the recovery is only partial, for the parental objects never fully recover their former god-like status. Their temporary abandonment is never fully forgiven but is replaced by continued critical scrutiny and by the blossoming of secrecy, in the name of equality and democracy. A serious loss of sincerity is characteristic. "Saying it" is taken to be as the same as "meaning it" (the oath). "Are you calling me a liar?" The slippery, tricky misuse of language. "He started it!" and "It's not fair!" Conceptual failure.

Another important residue of puberty is the sudden growth of the body and functions, particularly the sexual aspects, and with this the vanity, albeit blemished in various ways (freckles, pimples, enlarged pores and misproportion). This vanity is not strictly physical but mental, almost delusional (size of the nose, large hands, size of the genitals, and hips in women). The fluctuations from over-estimation of physical beauty to delusions of ugliness are clearly manifest in character and deportment—mistakenly called "shyness" or self-consciousness. These are features of heightened observation and critical attitudes.

Important as these typological descriptions may be for the individuals concerned, they do not cover the adolescent's overall worldview. They belong to the segmental view of the world with regard to gender, class, ethnic group, language and the body behaviours related to geography such as gait, posture, habits, impediments and facial posture. Viewed "out of focus" they reveal the identification processes operative with parents, with peer groups, with celebrities and mythical figures. These processes also heighten our awareness of the role of confusions in aspects of identification—particularly gender confusion, betrayals of various kinds, and the interplay of activity and passivity, hence of incipient sado-masochism. Such considerations stress the importance for the professional observer of detailed attention to the patient's deportment, and the significance of careful judgement, paying careful attention to the panorama of behaviour, posture, and gestures, and employing intuition for the exact estimation of the impact and impression created. For it is truly an artistic composition with which we are presented. Correspondingly, one does not "listen" to the patient as much as "observe" his speech habits.

It is probably true that the adolescent, as a member of a community of peers, resents being "observed" and cannot behave in a "normal" way which reveals his political position in his community. He is immediately impelled to "put on an act" which is meant to demonstrate his ideas of himself, his ideology. The characteristic ideology of adolescence is to save the world by eliminating materialism, greed, revenge and inequality. It always turns out to be an egalitarian panacea, thoroughly Christian and unheard-of before, Buddhist in fact, with a secret happiness drug thrown in, with flower-children and slogans like "make love" whatever you do to make a living. Abolish wealth and other sources of inequality; abolish the death penalty and the tax on alcohol and tobacco. The last form of slavery to be abolished would be marriage—and childhood, well, child labour and child prostitution—and of course the bomb and fire-arms. A truly abolitionist platform, sure of election. And exams, of course.

Well, we are not to mock our adolescent politicians, for after all the politicians themselves are still adolescents impelled by the ambition to grasp what is beyond their reach or to reach for what is beyond their grasp. The ultimate vanity. Our only hope lies in one man one vote.

This finally brings us to a mystery of the adolescent politicians, namely their success. The secret lies in their complacency, as manifest in voice and demeanour, and in the certainty with which they give their opinions as if they were facts of observation. This irresistibly persuasive complacency is not a matter of vanity, though they are certainly attractive and in that sense celebrities. It is a matter of some other quality, which they clearly think of as aristocratic, modelled in this country on the eighteenth century and its literary characters: the husky voice of the women, the throaty voices of the men, the hesitant humming and ha-ing—above all the irritability, faultlessly polite despite its rudeness and aggressiveness.

Let's put aside this journalistic exploration and get back to the concreteness of the analytical method.

Cooperation by the patient in analysis is a fairly rare phenomenon at the beginning. It has to be learned and developed. Eventually it is compounded of openness, frankness, courage, a readiness to tolerate pain and humiliation, and a growing pleasure in the intimacy with and confidence in the analyst, and the experience of relief from the process. The defects of cooperation are various and may be graded from secrecy to confabulation and deceit. Secrecy is habitual, and variously justified on the grounds of utility and aversion to mental pain. Confabulation is also habitual; it seems to be intended to entertain and to arouse interest, and relies on confusion and on trust in the concreteness of words. Deceit is more malignant: it generates contempt for the auditor and requires collusion, internal or external. It is more coldly exploitative and in a sense criminal.

Obviously the overcoming of the various forms of uncooperative behaviour is a task for the analyst that requires attention, patience and tolerance. The overcoming of irritability and aversion to the patient, and resistance to seduction, are matters of character which his own analysis should have helped; but goodwill is vital, and so is resistance to the urge to cure. Instead the quest for the truth is vital for patient and therapist alike. Seldom is it reinforced by the values of our culture with its wanton materialism. The fee situation is a challenge to both, where greed is not modified by custom nor helped by comparison with the practice of colleagues. The ethics of analyst and patient are both put to the test.

This central picture of a characteristic adolescent demeanour deriving from the delusion of aristocracy—generating belief and inventing knowledge—stands in contrast to processes of discovery, that are characterized by exposition with evidence. And the primary question is "what constitutes evidence?". The first requirement is "observation", which in turn requires "attention". This "attention" entails a minute interest in detail and continuity, with the senses combined and integrated through intuition. And here's the rub: sense experience spills over under the influence of wishes, and the sense data drip into the residue of dreams. But dream life, as is well known, is the spring from which intuition bubbles up. Thus the borderland of intuition is also the borderland of delusion—imagination's territory, in the absence of which the spring dries up.

This "newspaper editorial" can serve as background to an examination of the various systems which have been invented to save the world, such as those of politicians and clergymen. It is all covered by the two fables of "The emperor's new clothes" and "The belling of the cat"—fables of belief and of realism. The quest is imaginative because, based as it is on daily experience, and amplified by reading and other forms of communication such as debate, literature and the graphic arts, it may generate conviction but not belief. Belief is built into a given view of the world and its history, merging with the misleading element of hearsay, which is not very different from gossip. The compounding of belief and hearsay is the invocation of "reason": it must be reasonable. "It stands to reason" rules our statistics, particularly in the general form that "everyone knows" or agrees. But the ultimate criterion of true reasonableness is a labour of love, and it results in the achievement of beauty—in its ultimate form, poetry.

REFERENCES

Abraham, K. (1911). Notes on the psychoanalytic investigation and treatment of manic-depressive insanity and allied conditions. *Selected Papers on Psychoanalysis.* London: Hogarth, 1927, pp. 137-156.

Abraham, K. (1924). A short study of the development of the libido. *Selected Papers on Psychoanalysis.* London: Hogarth, 1927, pp. 418-501.

Bion, W. R. (1962). *Learning from Experience.* London: Heinemann.

Bion, W. R. (1979). Making the best of a bad job. *Bulletin of the British Psychoanalytical Society.* Reprinted in W. R. Bion, *Clinical Seminars and Four Papers,* ed. F. Bion, pp. 247-57. Abingdon: Fleetwood, 1987.

Browning, R. (1994). *Poems.* London: Wordsworth.

Brutti, C. and Scotti, F. (1975). (Eds.). *Quaderni di Psicoterapia Infantile* no. 1. Rome: Borla.

Freud, S. (1895). Project for a scientific psychology. *SE* 1, pp. 283-397.

Freud, S. (1905). Three essays on the theory of sexuality. *SE* 7, pp. 123-34.

Freud, S. (1911). Psychoanalytic notes on an autobiographical account of a case of paranoia [Schreber case]. *SE* 12, pp. 3-82.

Freud, S. (1914). On narcissism. *SE* 14, pp. 67-102.

Freud, S. (1917). Mourning and melancholia. *SE* 14, pp. 239-258.

Freud, S. (1918). From the history of an infantile neurosis. *SE* 17, pp. 1-124.

Freud, S. (1919). A child is being beaten. *SE* 17, pp. 175-204.

Freud, S. (1920). Beyond the pleasure principle. *SE* 18, pp. 1-64.

Freud, S. (1923). The libido theory. *SE* 18, pp. 1-64.

Freud, S. (1923). The ego and the id. *SE* 19, pp. 3-66.

Freud, S. (1926). Inhibitions, symptoms and anxiety. *SE* 20, pp. 77-174.

Freud, S. (1927). Fetishism. *SE* 21, pp. 149-157.

Hahn, A. (1994). (Ed.) *Sincerity: Collected Papers of Donald Meltzer.* London: Karnac.

Harris, M. and Bick, E. (1987) *Collected Papers of Martha Harris and Esther Bick*, ed. M. H. Williams. Perthshire: Clunie Press.

Jachevasky, L. and Tabbia, C. (1998). (Eds.) *Adolescentes: Donald Meltzer y Martha Harris.* Buenos Aires: Spatia.

Klein, M. (1930). The early development of conscience in the child. In *Developments in Psychoanalysis*, ed. M. Klein et al. London: Hogarth, 1952.

Klein, M. (1935). A contribution to the psychogenesis of manic-depressive states. *International Journal of Psychoanalysis*, 16: 145-74.

Klein, M. (1940). Mourning and its relation to manic-depressive states. *International Journal of Psychoanalysis*, 2:125-53.

Klein, M. (1946). Notes on some schizoid mechanisms. *International Journal of* Psychoanalysis, 27: 99-110.

Klein, M. (1957). *Envy and Gratitude.* London: Hogarth.

Klein, M. (1961). *Narrative of a Child Analysis.* London: Hogarth.

Klein, M. (1963). On the sense of loneliness. In *Envy and Gratitude and Other Works 1946-1963)*, ed. B. Joseph et al. pp. 300-313. London: Hogarth Press, 1975.

Meltzer, D. (1967). *The Psychoanalytical Process.* London: Heinemann. Reprinted Harris Meltzer Trust, 2008.

Meltzer, D. (1973). *Sexual States of Mind.* Perthshire: Clunie Press. Reprinted Harris Meltzer Trust, 2008.

Rosenfeld, H. (1959). An investigation into the psychoanalytic theory of depression. *International Journal of Psychoanalysis*, 40:105-129.

Rosenfeld, H. (1964). On the psychopathology of narcissism. *International Journal of Psychoanalysis*, 45: 332-37.

Segal, H. (1964). *Introduction to the Work of Melanie Klein.* London: Heinemann.

INDEX